CONTEMPORARY WEST AFRIC

AFRICAN STUDIES SERIES 65

GENERAL EDITOR
J. M. Lonsdale, *Lecturer in History and Fellow of Trinity College, Cambridge*

ADVISORY EDITORS
J. D. Y. Peel, *Professor of Anthropology and Sociology, with special reference to Africa, School of Oriental and African Studies, University of London*
John Sender, *Lecturer in Economics, School of Oriental and African Studies, University of London*

PUBLISHED IN COLLABORATION WITH
THE AFRICAN STUDIES CENTRE, CAMBRIDGE

For other titles in this series see page 217

CONTEMPORARY WEST AFRICAN STATES

EDITED BY

DONAL B. CRUISE O'BRIEN

Professor in Politics with reference to Africa,
University of London

JOHN DUNN

Fellow of King's College and
Professor of Political Theory in the University of Cambridge

and

RICHARD RATHBONE

Chairman, Centre for African Studies,
University of London

CAMBRIDGE
UNIVERSITY PRESS

Published by the Press Syndicate of the University of Cambridge
The Pitt Building, Trumpington Street, Cambridge CB2 1RP
40 West 20th Street, New York, NY 10011-4211 USA
10 Stamford Road, Oakleigh, Melbourne 3166, Australia

First published 1989
Reprinted 1991, 1995

Printed in Great Britain
by Athenæum Press Ltd, Gateshead, Tyne & Wear

British Library cataloguing in publication data

Contemporary West African states – (African
studies series; 65)
1. West Africa. Social conditions
I. Cruise O'Brien, Donal B. (Donal Brian II.
Dunn, John III. Rathbone, Richard IV. Series – 966)

*Library of Congress cataloguing in publication data
applied for*

ISBN 0 521 36366 7 hardback
ISBN 0 521 36893 6 paperback

UP

Contents

Contributors

Jean-François Bayart, Fondation Nationale des Sciences Politiques, Paris

Robert Buijtenhuijs, Afrika Studiecentrum, Leiden

Christopher Clapham, Department of Politics, University of Lancaster

Christian Coulon, Centre d'Etude d'Afrique Noire, Université de Bordeaux I

Donal B. Cruise O'Brien, Department of Economic and Political Studies, School of Oriental and African Studies, University of London

John Dunn, King's College, Cambridge

Yves A. Fauré, Centre d'Etude d'Afrique Noire, Université de Bordeaux I

Fred M. Hayward, Department of Political Science, University of Wisconsin, Madison

Richard Jeffries, Department of Economic and Political Studies, School of Oriental and African Studies, University of London

René Otayek, Centre d'Etude d'Afrique Noire, Université de Bordeaux I

Shehu Othman, St Anthony's College, Oxford

Richard Rathbone, Centre for African Studies, University of London

Preface

The authors of these studies have wished both to review the significant changes which have taken place in the region in the ten years that have followed the publication of *West African States. Failure and Promise* (John Dunn, ed., Cambridge University Press, 1978) and to assess the shifts that have taken place in the scholarly analysis of these states over the same period. The studies have emerged from a small conference held at the School of Oriental and African Studies in June 1987, where scholars were invited to contribute papers on particular countries of the region. Contributors were asked to use narrative as the foundation of their analysis, so that the volume might be a useful text book as well as a contribution to a review of the nature of the state and political processes in Africa.

A decade's political change in the region is marked in one way by the inclusion of new areas of interest: the chapters on Chad, Burkina Faso and Cameroon are intended to match the changing concerns in the field with data on areas untouched in the previous volume. Both the introduction and the conclusion suggest the salient thematic shifts: these include the remarkable retreat of dependency theory and Marxian analysis and the rise of free-market theorising on the part both of governments and of scholars. The selection of Francophone scholars is a recognition that some of the best new political analysis for the region has been emerging in French, produced by the new scholarly generation which surrounds the journal, *Politique africaine*. The inclusion below of some of this French writing in translation will, we hope, serve to introduce readers to a major body of scholarship which has been far too often ignored on this side of the Channel.

The editors wish to recognise their many debts in the production of this volume. The Nuffield Foundation was generous in its support for the 1987 conference, and we would like to thank both Patricia Thomas and the Nuffield Trustees. We are no less grateful for the financial assistance of the Research Committee of the School of Oriental and African Studies and for the help and guidance of its secretary, Martin Daly. Above all we are grateful to our colleagues for sharing their ideas so openly and amicably. In addition to the authors we would like to thank Patrick Chabal, Naomi Chazan, Stephen Ellis, Mike Hodd, Richard Joseph, Wyatt McGaffey, Sam

Nolutshungu, John Paden, Hillard Pouncey and Kaye Whiteman for major contributions to the conference proceedings. Chris Gray not only helped with the conference organisation but also with the translation work. Marion Swiny, secretary of the London Centre of African Studies, was as always both benign and efficient in overseeing our proceedings. We are also grateful to Maryjayne Hillman for coping with a mountain of re-typing, and to Stephen Schartz for compiling the index. Lastly we were encouraged by Cambridge University Press's Liz Wetton whose contribution to African studies at the Press has been of enormous assistance to the field. And of course we would insist that none of those who have helped us be blamed for our mistakes.

1

Introduction

DONAL B. CRUISE O'BRIEN AND RICHARD
RATHBONE

The imperfections and limitations of West African states have been much
remarked by outside observers over the period of close on three decades since
independence, while another topic, that of the very survival of the state, has
slowly emerged. It should of course be admitted that the critical comments
of journalists or academics on the subjects of official corruption, poor
governmental performance, the prevalence of unregulated social conflict or
institutional decay are in broad terms often justified. But such critical
commentary is properly to be set against the important fact that these states
without exception have maintained themselves in being. The states of West
Africa have, for example, escaped the more drastic forms of political
disintegration apparent in Uganda or Sudan, in Zaire or in Mozambique.

In the process of surviving, the West African states may have more or less
subtly altered in character as their rulers and citizens have modified their
political expectations, discarding the innocent hopes of the early years of
independence, but the state as political unit appears to rest on a significant
measure of popular acceptance. The state has in general scarcely been
challenged with any resolution, in principle a surprising fact in the case of
such an allegedly artificial political entity, the creation of European colonial
rule. The case of Biafra remains the outstanding exception in this regard, for
outside of Nigeria it is the absence of concerted challenge to the state which
is remarkable. We would infer from this absence of challenge a (perhaps
provisional) popular acceptance of the state, latent if you will, but an
acceptance which has its unarticulated logic: this is, that the discernible
future possibilities, in the absence of the state, are very much worse than the
flawed reality of the present.

Looking into the political future in the event of a collapse of the post-
colonial state, the outside observer may consider the consequences of a
possible reconstitution of traditional political entities – the Asante con-
federacy perhaps, or the Sokoto caliphate. Such reconstitutions could only
be achieved at the price of a more or less prolonged period of war. From such
a period of warfare, furthermore, there would be no certain victors: the
short-run certainty would be of institutional fragmentation and social
conflict, haunted by Hobbes' nightmare vision of the war of all against all.

1

The present post-colonial peace has in general rested on the notion of a religiously neutral or secular state, this compromise being increasingly threatened by Islamic militancy in many West African states; and on the ascendancy of European languages as languages of state, this compromise being as yet little challenged by the advocates of African languages (which languages to recognise?). The post-colonial peace may be worth preserving in the form of these communal compromises, at least pending the emergence of viable political alternatives.

The states examined in this volume have a less and less valid claim to the label 'new states'. The symposium which drew our contributors together met over thirty years after Ghana became independent: none of the other states exactly exhibits the bloom of youth. Apologists and analysts sound less and less plausible when they propose inexperience or the malign colonial heritage as excuses for incompetence or failure. These states have, then, reached maturity. Each has an adult generation which grew up in a sunlight unshaded by the *Tricolore* or the Union Jack. Each state is manned by a large, some would say too large, body of professional, expert administrators whose careers have been, with a declining number of exceptions, those of civil servants trained in the management of sovereign states. Each state's armed forces, educational and medical services, industries large and small are directed and manned by Africans whose expertise and experience are considerable. Trial and error over time have allowed them to preserve those elements of colonial practice they admire, to reform or abandon those they deplore, and to innovate where appropriate or necessary. Similarly in the political arena the vast majority of actors have cut their teeth in the post-nationalist era. The choice of methods of operation and strategic decisions are, like managerial decisions anywhere, informed by an international context, but they are ultimately arrived at locally and independently.

This volume differs from its predecessor not least because those who care about and study these states and their inhabitants come to their analysis shorn of the expectations that are inherent in 'newness'. West African states can and must be analysed like any other regional cluster of states. They must then be examined without the essential paternalism that inheres in the terminology of novelty. But, if this 'coming of age' is, as we would argue, a set of discernible and concrete phenomena, it has been accompanied by a remarkable shift in the ideas which inform analysis. In the ten years which separate the initial volume from this, its successor, analysts and politicians alike have experienced not only a rapidly changing world but also rapidly changing ideas about that world.

In those ten years the material basis for many of the apparently established truths about the post-1945 world has changed radically. In the midst of these processes, optimism appears to have died. Liberal democratic thought has been forced to abandon much of its Keynesian underpinning and has adopted at least some of the monetarist reasoning of the Right. Socialist theories have had to be recast in the light of the acknowledged failure of planning which relies on large projects rather than individual endeavour. It is of particular importance for us that a degree of almost bizarre convergence has emerged over the question of the state itself. The state, at its blandest a provider of personal security, public amenities and a resolver of conflicts, must be paid for. In all countries, rich or poor, socialist or liberal–democratic, there has emerged serious questioning about whether the state's activities themselves might in some circumstances make it more and more difficult to afford the state.

The expansion of the colonial state, in the period following the Second World War, now can be seen as having prepared the way for the post-independence programmes of West African regimes. The period of welfare colonialism (from 1945 to 1960), with more ambitious programmes notably in the fields of education and communications, thus reinforced the idea of effective control from the centre – with improved roads, more telephone lines, and more bureaucratic manpower. The greatly expanded government departments of the terminal colonial period were not of course very effective, and in other African circumstances the proliferation of new government services at this time indeed arguably led to a decline in government control.[1]

The formal centralisation of government in the years following West African independence is thus the prolongation of an existing trend, with accelerated civil service expansion in the service of ambitious development objectives – the dream of industrialisation. This is well enough known, as is the fact that concentration of power at the centre has led to the reality of personal rule in the absence of effective government institutions. The theme of centralisation is developed below notably by the French contributors, but also emerges, for example, in relation to mineral resources in Sierra Leone and Nigeria. Diamonds and oil have thus provided the bulk of government revenue in these states, making possible a greater weight of central government.

The unintended consequences of this formal centralisation in West African states can however be remote from the official intent, as in the case of Senegal where President Diouf's programme of bureaucratisation and centralisation, conceived on the Jacobin model, has in effect created 'empty spaces' into which the government's opponents have moved. Thus Muslim funda-mentalists have gained as the government attempts to do without the traditional intermediary services of the *Marabout*, and thus also the independence movement in Casamance has gained as the government again dispenses with the services of that region's political patrons. 'Seeking at all costs to assure its direct social control, the State loses all sense of communication and encourages political adventurism' (C. Coulon and D. B. Cruise O'Brien, chapter 9 below), with repeated riots and the development of a movement for independence in this southern region of Senegal.

This theme, of government losing contact with its social base, recurs in several contributions below, notably in relation to the revolutionary regime of Thomas Sankara in Burkina Faso. The plethora of new institutions created by the Sankara government – People's Defence Councils, Workers' Defence Councils, Revolutionary Defence Committees – thirty new administrative regions, are revealed as being 'without much grip on reality' (René Otayek, chapter 2 below). The Sankara government's anti-corruption drive, applauded by many foreign sympathisers, stirred mass discontent inside Burkina Faso as patronage resources evaporated (similarly with the attack on bureaucratic overmanning: every dismissed civil servant had sustained a clientele of dependants). Worst of all, this government's attack on chieftaincy, stigmatised as 'feudal' and 'reactionary', was generally unpopular (and particularly resented by the Mossi). The chiefs came closer to being a legitimate authority than anything established by the revolution, which helps to explain the apparent indifference of the Burkinabé at the time of Sankara's death.

The tendency to a separation of state from society may have been particularly evident in this case, at least retrospectively, but it lurks in many of the cases reviewed below. It is in this context that one may understand the continuing fascination of popular elections. 'Democracy' under West African conditions may provide a convenient pretext to extend the powers of the head of state, a means for the president to get rid of his unwanted subordinates (Yves Fauré on Côte d'Ivoire, chapter 5 below) or to ensure his supply of foreign aid, but it would be wrong for an outside observer wholly to dismiss the electoral exercise. Ordinary people may make serious personal sacrifices in casting their votes, risking violence and intimidation, as Fred Hayward rightly remarks of Sierra Leone, chapter 10 below. Internal elections within a single (or dominant) party are furthermore often keenly contested, and provide for a considerable turnover in personnel among the political class, with the voters' motivation sharpened by the prospect of access to official patronage.

Elections in West Africa nonetheless are obviously a weak instrument in the constitution of a government, with rigging and official manipulation a prevalent pattern. Accountability under such conditions remains a distant dream, a situation deplored by Flt.-Lt. Jerry Rawlings among others, although it is possible to discern the outlines of a regional variant: thus the notables of the True Whig Party in Liberia were 'accountable not in any effective electoral fashion, but at least in the attenuated sense that local political activity was required in order to gain the party nomination for congressional sects, while local legislators were expected to spend much of their time in their constituencies' (Christopher Clapham, chapter 7 below). The downfall of the True Whig Party, Africa's longest-running single party, with the Doe coup of 1980, thus could imply an actual decline in accountability despite the parade of multi-party elections in 1985.

While mass elections provide no more than a distorted medium for the government to hear the people's voice, contact between government and people may be more effectively provided by the intermediary auspices of chiefs as in Burkina Faso/Upper Volta or Muslim notables as in Senegal.

Such intermediaries, building their economic and political power on the basis of an authentic popular authority, may also be seen as possible providers of government by patrimonialism, in contradistinction to the faltering project of government by the bureaucratic state. These intermediaries may be seen as providing a continuation of the colonial principle of government by indirect rule, although they are also together capable of self-defence when threatened by today's central power – *La revanche des sociétés Africaines*.[2]

The revenge of African societies provides a heading under which one may include not only the instruments whereby chiefs can resist central government, including the politics of the supernatural and the manipulation of kinship as in Burkina Faso, but also the survival strategies whereby the individual seeks to do without the state – *vivre sénégalaisement* – as they say in Dakar. One should also mention ways in which religious organisations can provide a refuge from the state, as for example with both Catholicism and Islam in Burkina.

Representation of popular opinion has its channels even in the authoritarian circumstances of most West African states. A considerable freedom of the press should be mentioned here, notably in the cases of Cameroon, Senegal or Nigeria, thus the possibility of some political influence on the part of those who write for, produce or own this press. Institutional representation is also possible, notably in the case of the trade union movement, even when this is in principle under government control. The political role of the trade union appears to oscillate between that of the tribune of the people, acting as the vanguard of popular protest and on occasion precipitating the *coup d'état*, and the apparently opposed role of protector of the privilege of a civil service elite. Most of the unionised labour force being in some form of government employment, the trade union is inevitably called to the defence of bureaucratic overmanning when the new austerities of the International Monetary Fund are invoked. Some institutions can act effectively enough in the defence of their own interests, as when the bank holds up its paperwork in Sierra Leone to prevent government from imposing a new oil supplier.

Personal rule in West African states, however, does of course involve a general weakening of institutions, a trend well exemplified below in the case of the Stevens regime in Sierra Leone with its sapping of the life of universities, agricultural cooperatives, farmers' associations, business and professional organisations. Linkages between the ruler and society in such circumstances proceed by a series of patron–client ties, amounting to a state-wide network (Siaka Stevens in this case perfecting what Albert Margai had begun). Even in such circumstances, however, one may remark a continuing autonomy of chiefs, professionals, and even ordinary people, with the Backbenchers' Association providing 'the only effective mechanism of criticism in Parliament' (Fred Hayward, chapter 10 below).

The most basic attributes of the state, in the collection of tax and the provision of law and order, can be called seriously into question here. Thus

President Goukouni in Chad frankly announced in 1981 that the government (GUNT) 'does not dispose of any power, or finances, or regional administrative authority over... factions which constitute real states within the state. The GUNT is a government only in name.' As Robert Buijtenhuijs notes, the central government of Chad for three years (1979–82) 'lost control of almost the whole country, with the exception of parts of the capital'. Taxes were not collected, the civil service was not paid in the north of Chad, such trade as continued was by smuggling, such postal services as continued were maintained by the missionaries, with road maintenance by the Coton-Chad company. Chad is, however, the extreme case among West African states, in this period of Frolinat disintegration and warlord rule. But extremes can be revealing: law in West African circumstances is less by state courts than by the informal arbitration of chiefs, religious leaders or other patrons. Tax in West Africa is more by levies on major commercial operators at the customs post and on hapless peasant producers at the marketing board, than it is by any personal income tax – difficult to collect, and resented. The citizen's involvement with the state tends not to be close, and it is not only in Senegal that he or she seeks to avoid contact with the state so far as possible.

Some recent commentary has revelled in this reality, seeing in tax evasion, 'second economies', and in smuggling and banditry a romantic resistance to the state.[3] It is easy to forget that in such circumstances those who enjoy enough autonomy to be able to pose as tropical Robin Hoods tend to be the powerful. For the poor, for the majority, the state alone can provide major medical facilities like mass immunisation, pipe-borne water, pensions, law and order, relief at times of catastrophe and a wide range of other life-sustaining functions. Although each and every one of such vital functions can be subverted and corrupted into exploitation and cruel misuse of vulnerable people, there are widespread civic expectations. These are perhaps most visible in the evident general support for campaigns to curb flagrant abuses of office. One of the explanations for the tenacity of the state at a time when many predicted its disappearance in many parts of Africa, is the widespread understanding of the less predatory and crucial roles of the state. In a situation of a war of all against all, the vast majority of people lose and this is widely understood.

The legitimacy of rulers against such a background can indeed be seen as the 'occupational delusion' of those in power. It is more realistic for an outsider to speak of acceptance than legitimacy, as Christopher Clapham remarks of Liberia below. If Weberian categories are to be drastically adjusted in dealing with West African politics, severe adjustment is again in order when we come to the Marxian categories of social class. West African businessmen have succeeded in differentiating themselves, while 'straddling' between private and public employment.[4] Such private business is of course heavily dependent on the state throughout West Africa – for import licences, price controls, contracts, and extra-legal tolerance – although the successful businessmen do seek to develop their commercial contacts and investment opportunities throughout the industrial world. Jean-François Bayart in his treatment of entrepreneurs in the case of Cameroon, chapter 3 below, finds little of the spirit of capitalism (or, for that matter, of bureaucracy) but an elegantly typified mesh of public and private interests: 'a field of interests intimately mingled by contracts, by credit, by acquisitions, by marriages'. It is absurd in such a context to try to differentiate between a 'national' bourgeoisie and its 'comprador' ugly sister, or between a national and an administrative bourgeoisie. The salient fact is that the businessmen have emerged, that they are largely but not wholly dependent on the state; with a little luck, they can always move themselves and their fortunes elsewhere when times get hard.

Where social class is concerned, it is the peasantry which perhaps provides the greatest challenge to analysis. In most West African states the bulk of state revenue has of course been derived from agricultural production, building on the gains of commercialisation in the colonial period. The cash crop producers (peasants) since independence have been subordinated to the state marketing boards (another continuation from the colonial period) in effect paying a high rate of tax to these monopsony organisations. While in Marxian economic terms the peasantry obviously is an exploited class, it is a class without common consciousness or organisation. Peasants, however, can mount an effective enough resistance to exploitation at the hands of the state: such resistance tends to be desperate, by withdrawing from commercial agriculture in favour of subsistence crops or by leaving the land and migrating to town in the hope of employment.

It is striking that the apparently benevolent official attempts to 'help' the peasantry in West Africa have often accomplished the opposite of the avowed intent. Thus the colonial marketing boards, established to regularise production and (so it was said) to provide an insurance against bad years, have succeeded year after year in remorselessly over-taxing the West African peasantry.[5] Jerry Rawlings has recognised the dimensions of this problem: 'We are acknowledging the historic debt of the whole nation to the farmer and have thus repudiated the monstrous injustice of a past in which we virtually ran the machinery of the state on the tired backs of rural producers and provided little for their basic needs' (in Richard Jeffries on Ghana, chapter 6 below). The Sankara regime in Burkina Faso was similarly committed at least in rhetoric to redressing this wrong, but the institutions established by government in the rural areas were bitterly resented: it is of interest to note here that Rawlings in Ghana appears to have recognised a similar peasant resentment, by abolishing the People's Defence Committees. Like the Revolutionary Defence Committees in Burkina Faso, the People's Defence Committees in Ghana were made up of militants imposed from the centre, and Richard Jeffries very reasonably asks why the peasants' urban benefactors have never considered the provision of genuinely representative institutions for the rural producers.

7

If the categories of social class (bourgeois, worker, peasant) are difficult to adjust to West African conditions, one might perhaps expect a political analysis in terms of ethnicity to come closer to social reality. Some useful reservations are, however, suggested here, in the case of Cameroon, by Jean-François Bayart, suggesting a 'contextual' approach to the subject of ethnicity. Ethnic identification is thus to be understood as always in movement, and as providing the individual with one among many identities. The relation of ethnicity to political action is by no means always close: one excellent example here is that of the political rivalry between Goukouni and Habré in Chad, a segmentary clash among Toubous and not at all rooted in the fundamental north/south division of the country. Bayart usefully distinguishes between commercial networks, which are pluri-ethnic by the necessities of business, and the networks of clientelist politics which are commonly structured along ethnic lines. The position of the head of state is then to be understood, in Cameroon as elsewhere in West Africa, as that of an arbiter between networks, drawing his own power from the discordant ambitions of the commercial and political worlds.

Religious identifications are to be considered in conjunction with those of ethnicity, notably with reference to the coast/inland or north/south divisions which are to be remarked in so many West African states. Here again one has to beware of misleading simplicities: thus the northern region of Cameroon under Ahidjo, as the northern region of Nigeria under Ahmadu Bello, was a 'false monolith' created by a skilful political actor rather than an immutable social reality. The north/south division of Chad is similarly only one aspect of social or political reality: Chad is thus 'multiple' as well as 'double', with dozens of ethnic groups to consider as well as segmentary or personal rivalries. In Liberia, again, it is not enough to think in terms of political conflict between the America-Liberian settlers and the indigenes: since the Doe coup the important political divisions have been between hinterland people, although America-Liberians have continued to do well enough on the basis of their skills, both in the state administration and in the professions (Christopher Clapham, below: this preservation of social position on the part of the America-Liberians is to be compared with the communal self-defence mounted for over forty years by the Krios in Sierra Leone).[6]

The cross-cutting nature of socio-political divisions, ethnic or regional not to speak of religious, commercial or personal, may help to explain the absence of any successful separatist movement in West Africa. It is in any case remarkable that there has been no separatist movement in Chad despite the civil wars in that country since 1969: the suggestion of Robert Buijtenhuijs below is that part of the explanation here must lie in the policies of neighbouring states. Cameroon and Nigeria, each with its own north/south problem, would thus have acted to stifle any would-be independent state of southern Chad. Among the cases dealt with below, and excluding the case of Biafra, the secessionist impulse is most clearly represented in the case of Casamance. But in this case also one may expect a negative diplomatic consensus to be organised by what Julius Nyerere once described as that 'trade union of heads of states', the Organisation of African Unity.

The political party is also an institution capable of a positive contribution to the survival of the West African state. Thus in Cameroon or in Senegal the governing party can be seen as allowing for a very broad alliance of different communal segments of the country's elite, under the overall authority of the head of party and state. Elections within the governing party are, potentially at least, matters of greater political substance than has been recognised by most outside commentators on West African politics. The governing party in such cases may even provide a more effective channel of communication, between the capital and the outlying regions, than the institutions of state administration. Nor is multi-party politics to be lightly derided, even if an opposition party has yet to win a national election in West Africa (with one marginal exception, in Sierra Leone in 1967). Dr Naomi Chazan has drawn attention to the underlying reality of a two-party situation in Ghana from the nineteen-fifties until recent years:[7] a similar assessment could be made of Senegal (Senghor/Diouf versus Lamine Guèye/Abdoulaye Wade). Periodic episodes of multi-party politics in Nigeria have also of course suggested a real continuity of popular political allegiances, from 1959 to 1979. And in Liberia the downfall of the True Whig Party, with the *coup d'état* of Samuel Doe, showed the ex-members of that party to be capable of political survival in a way which also showed the ex-party to be 'more deeply rooted than might previously have seemed to be the case' (Christopher Clapham below).

Political parties in West Africa may indeed correspond to a significant social reality, but it goes without saying that parties have rarely decided the question of succession to the office of head of state. The withdrawal of several democratically elected heads of state over the past decade (Leopold Senghor, Ahmadu Ahidjo, Siaka Stevens) was in each case in favour of a nominated successor. Popular elections then provided a means of ratifying a succession which had already been decided by the outgoing incumbent – a procedure more monarchical than democratic. More commonly in West Africa the succession is decided by military coup, although in the region this need not involve extensive bloodletting: the succession of senior military officers in Nigeria by a sort of Kaduna quadrille is discussed by Shehu Othman (chapter 8 below). But in general terms it remains the case that one can have little confidence in regular procedures for succession in West African states, yet another indicator of the institutional weakness prevalent in the region.

The issue of foreign involvement in the politics of West African states is raised by several contributions below, notably in respect of the continuing role of France in the internal affairs of her ex-colonies. The balance sheet of such dependency is not necessarily a negative one: thus Richard Jeffries, in commenting on the 'catastrophic' financial independence of Ghana in the Acheampong years, contrasts this with the financial stability of the Ivory

Coast – assured among other things by the latter's reliance on the CFA franc. France has not only given a stable currency to her ex-colonies, but military sinews in the form of bases in key states and defence agreements. Such agreements do of course involve a continuing dependence on France, although a dependence which is accepted by West African rulers as some sort of insurance against the *coup d'état*. The insurance is probably of declining effectiveness, due to changes in military technology and in French diplomatic priorities.[8] The dependence should not be seen as going only in one direction: the political career of Hissein Habré is an eloquent testimony to the possibilities of manipulation on the part of the dependant, as he has played the United States against France in drawing the latter more deeply into the conflict with Libya than the French government would no doubt have wished. The manipulation of a dependent relationship by the rulers of France's African client states, notably by the massaging of French public opinion through French journalists who are themselves clients of the African rulers, has been dealt with elsewhere by Jean-François Bayart.[9]

Analysis of African politics in terms of dependency is out of fashion now, and dependency is not a central consideration in any of the contributions below. There is perhaps some irony here, in that the fiscal collapse of many West African states has made them more than ever dependent on loans from outsiders, very often the International Monetary Fund. IMF loans with their attached 'conditionalities' specify a requisite programme of government retrenchment involving the dismissal of many in government service. But while many West African opposition politicians like to emphasise the indignity of having to submit to the IMF *diktat*, there is some evidence that the heads of state have taken to the task of retrenchment with some relish. Thus Félix Houphouët-Boigny uses a programme of government austerity to crack the whip over his over-mighty barons of the parastatals, and Jerry Rawlings finds ground for convergence between IMF requirements and his own populist image, while General Babangida 'imposes monetarist policies which [are] far more radical than the IMF itself required' (Shehu Othman, below).

One may ask finally whether the study of West African states requires a new vocabulary, a radical reassessment of past approaches to the subject. Consider for example the assessment of the PNDC government in Ghana, which 'now gives the appearance of being suspended in mid-air, lacking any institutional social roots' (Richard Jeffries, below), or the assessment of the incapacities of the Liberian state: 'whether the state can actually do anything, in a developmental sense, remains an open question... it has hardly tried' (Christopher Clapham, below). The state in West Africa is thus often of feeble administrative capacity, raising little in the way of taxes, providing little in the way of law and even less of services. It is remarkable here that the most forceful and cogent criticisms of the African state have recently come from young Francophone African scholars, notably from the excellent work of Comi Tulabor and Achille Mbembe. Dr Tulabor sees the 'state of nothingness' in Togo as succeeding only in maintaining the privileges of a ruling elite, and in maintaining itself in being as a tropicalised caricature of the Western state, but this survival importantly showing that in its way the Western graft has taken and must now be allowed to mature. For Mbembe, on the other hand, the subject matter of African politics has become that of who is going to eat: the institutions of the state are presented as 'alimentary deposits and instruments of extortion'.[10]

The overall assessment of the chapters below nonetheless leans well away from a dismal conclusion. The states of the region have often been under considerable stress, but they have survived as juridically independent entities for nearly three decades. One explanation for this survival may lie in the diplomatic consensus of African states against secession or the breaking of political entities. Another explanation would focus on the state as resource, as unique source of power and wealth, as prize. Politics then is concerned with competition for this prize, for access to the resources of the state, and is an activity of those who are qualified (by knowledge or by guns) to compete. But even the unqualified have an important interest in the outcome, and like the voters of Sierra Leone they may take considerable risks in declaring that interest.

The survival of the state, in however approximate a form, and with all its institutional imperfections, remains of great value to the citizenry of the states of the West African region. That would be clear not only to the West African reader of Thomas Hobbes, but also, for example, to the observer of Chadian politics in the warlord period from 1979 to 1982. A popular appreciation of having some sort of stake in the state may then even be inferred from the weakness or non-existence of attempts to dismantle or replace the state. Individual rulers are very often deplored by their subjects, those close to power are often the objects of resentment or even hatred. But the war of all against all is not an alluring prospect: the arbitrary or corrupt manifestations of government not only remain preferable in principle to anarchy and chaos, they are observedly preferred by the citizens of West African states.

2

Burkina Faso: between feeble state and total state, the swing continues

RENÉ OTAYEK

Since the *coup d'état* of 25 November 1980 that brought an end to the civilian regime of the Third Republic led by General Sangoulé Lamizana, Upper Volta (rebaptised Burkina Faso in August 1984) has gone into an infernal spiral of political instability. In a little more than seven years, no less than four takeovers by force have resulted in the replacement of the ruling team.[1] The latest misadventure to date is the fall and death of Captain Sankara and the replacement of the Conseil National de la Révolution (CNR), over which he had presided since his seizure of power on 4 August 1983, by a Front Populaire headed by Captain Blaise Compaoré, once the intimate friend of Thomas Sankara and his second in command within the CNR.

At the time of writing, if the underlying causes of this change are in essentials known,[2] it is still premature to draw conclusions as to the future political orientation of Burkina. But the relative ease with which the regime of Thomas Sankara was toppled, as well as the timidity of the popular reactions which followed his death, are bound to raise disturbing questions about the extent of institutionalisation of a government drawing its legitimacy from its revolutionary character and its proclaimed will to give voice to the people. How could this apparently solidly entrenched regime be swept away so easily, despite its methodical strategy of investing in the state apparatus and a territorial layout system allegedly without flaw, which had put into place a rigorous mechanism of social and political control? To answer this question requires a thorough reflection on the type of relationship that the CNR state maintained over four years with Burkinabè society, and on the project personified by Captain Sankara.

The state in Africa today is in crisis. Numerous works underscore the major pathological symptoms of this situation: political and institutional instability, ethnic and regional tensions, economic difficulties, financial bankruptcy, catastrophic public management, corruption, and more or less accentuated political authoritarianism. Pluralist democracy is the exception, not the rule. Along with a few other rare countries, the former Upper Volta until 1980 (and save for two interludes to which we will return) was conspicuous by its relatively democratic political system. On the strictly institutional plane, its evolution, punctuated by an incessant coming and going of civilian and military governments and the succession of three republics, can rightly be termed 'chaotic'.[3] But it is remarkable that throughout this twenty-year period (1960–80) a certain freedom of expression persisted. Thanks to this, the country appeared as a haven of tolerance in an Africa devoted to the single-party regime. Political and trade union pluralism along with free and competitive elections made Upper Volta a refutation to rigidly developmentalist approaches mechanically linking political authoritarianism and economic underdevelopment.

This situation (let's repeat it, quite uncommon in Africa) suggests that there existed in ex-Upper Volta a sufficiently consistent civil society (to repeat J. Dunn's expression),[4] sufficiently institutionalised to limit the ascendancy of the state and to preserve for itself some spaces of autonomy. To the logic of the state aiming to penetrate society with its 'civilising' values in order to control it (and absorb it into its own sphere), society was able, with success, to oppose its own logic, structures and values. The presence of the contradictory process of 'totalisation' and 'detotalisation' studied by J. F. Bayart is visible here.[5]

Thomas Sankara's seizure of power inaugurated a new mode of relations between the state and society. It is important to make clear at once that this change was not due simply to the military nature (which is in any case itself debatable) of the new regime. Along with others, we consider that in effect the distinction between civilian regimes and military regimes is not totally pertinent to Africa.[6] The logic on which the functioning of the African state is based must be examined in the light of other theoretical instruments, notably through an analysis of political clientelism and neo-patrimonialism,[7] which transcends the superficial differences between civilian and military regimes. Therefore, it is both to the type of society projected by the CNR, and to its modalities of intervention in this society, that we will turn our attention here.

The CNR's project rested on a radical transformation of Burkinabè society on the base of a 'democratic and popular revolution'. This rupture, the first real one in the political history of independent Burkina, postulated the modification of the social alliances on which the previous regimes had supported themselves. For the pact linking the state to the urban salaried strata (in particular those in the civil service), there had to be substituted another with the peasantry, now called upon to become the social base of the regime. The success of this strategy necessarily involved a profound disturbance of attitudes and the dismantling of traditional structures, in particular those of the rural world, capable of competing against the institutions put into place by the revolution, and thus threatening the realisation of the social and economic changes required for the very survival of the process initiated on 4 August 1983. For the cultural and ideological references that have for centuries structured the political make-believe of the existing social formations, the CNR had to substitute its own. It is thus a

14

genuine historical fracture: a fracture which initiated the establishment of a state quite novel in the history of Burkina, a strong state, a totalising state.[8]

It is this process that we intend to analyse in this chapter. Our questions will centre on the following themes. What differentiated the CNR state from those which preceded it? How did it set about imposing its political and social order? In what measure did its multiple structures of training and supervision (*encadrement*) succeed in competing with the traditional structures in which civil society recognised (and still recognises) itself? Confronted with a strategy which threatened to place it under state-controlled tutelage, was civil society able to invent new forms of resistance or new practices of refusal of the total-state (*tout-Etat*)?

The clientelist and neo-patrimonial state: 1960–1983

As elsewhere in Africa, the state which emerged at independence under the name of the Republic of Upper Volta found itself confronted by societies equipped with their own systems of organisation, often ignorant of that form of politics which the modern state entails. One might in this connection speak of a 'multi-polar' political landscape. 'On the one hand, the state, but on the other, a constellation of societies, yesterday still political, masters of their destiny, today accepting with difficulty being lowered to the rank of civil society.'[9] This constellation is made up of three forms of social organisation: those of the lineage, of the village, and of the state.[10] The first two govern a multitude of ethnic groups situated for the most part in the west of the country; the third is the prerogative of the Moogho (Mossi Empire), a massive bloc and a state within a state, it occupies the centre of the country and is the nucleus around which contemporary political space is incorporated.[11] These systems have a considerable advantage over the modern state: they have historical precedence and, especially, they know how to 'obtain allegiances and loyalties, to create and maintain networks of solidarity which, in the best of cases, coexist outside of the state and, in the worst, rise up against it'.[12] Faced with these redoubtable competitors, the state has responded with two successive attitudes, two different modes of intervention, although aiming for the same objective: to enlist society in its development.

The First Republic of Maurice Yaméogo. State of strain: 1960–1966

Under the First Republic, presided over by M. Yaméogo, state-society relations were placed under the sign of confrontation.[13] Faithful to the general tendency that took shape in independent Africa, and to the Jacobin ideal inherited from the French coloniser, the state sought to remodel the political and social construction that it inherited so as to subject it to its order and substitute a national space of identification for particular ethnic or regional solidarities. It thus openly attacked all the opposition fronts, which

15

it intended to blend into the classic mould of the state-party regime. The presidentialisation of the regime, the preeminence of the party (the RDA), the submission of recruitment in the administration, the parliament and the government to criteria of loyalty to the party, these signalled a hegemonic will implying the elimination of any structure capable of constituting a way out from state domination. This strategy was directed particularly at the powerful Mossi chieftaincy as well as the trade union machinery, both of which articulated, each in its own sphere, the refusal of the total state (*tout-Etat*).

Maurice Yaméogo is himself Mossi, but at this time he represented the 'modern' elite of this ethnic group which fought with the customary chieftaincy for political leadership. In order to impose his authority in the rural areas (the 'periphery') which recognised themselves (and still recognise themselves) in customary institutions, he had to dismantle them and undermine the foundations of this power: the suppression of the re-muneration of chiefs, the banning of their replacement in case of death or revocation, their election by universal suffrage, all went in this direction and testified to the willingness of the state to do without the 'relay' represented by the chieftaincy in order to impose its own instruments of domination.

In the urban milieu, the policy of standardisation was applied by bringing the trade unions to heel and integrating them into the authoritarian single party. But, beneath the appearance of unanimity, the state under Maurice Yaméogo was penetrated by numerous clientelist networks which often had a clan or lineage base and indiscriminately combined officials of the RDA, the presidential party, leaders of dissolved or banned political formations, and trade union leaders. In Burkina it is remarkable that familial (in the broad sense) solidarities, notably in the Mossi milieu, are still so influential; they govern conduct so much that one may consider that they have for a long time, at least until 1983, acted as a limitation upon political violence; at least up until 1983. They have in any case been at the origin of a redistribution of resources that, thanks to the acquisition of positions of power, permitted them to limit the weight of state domination.

Be that as it may, 'worked upon' from within by society and subverted by it, the party–state of M. Yaméogo proved incapable of merging the trade unions into its order. The latter were sufficiently numerous, powerful and active to set themselves successfully against the state, assuming that function of 'detotalisation' which signalled the degeneration of the total state into the feeble state. The failure of M. Yaméogo (a popular insurrection supervised by the trade unions forced him to retire on 6 January 1966) signalled the failure of the attempt at resolving the hegemonic crisis of the post-colonial state to the detriment of social groups aspiring to domination.

The 'debonair' state : 1966–1980

The accession to power of General Lamizana led to a modification in state-society relations. This return to a multi-party system was accompanied by a new attempt at resolving the hegemonic crisis through the restructuring of social alliances at the summit of the state. These henceforth (and for many years) linked civilian elites and modern military men, the customary chieftaincy and representatives of the religious hierarchies, Catholic and Muslim. The broadening of political support was accompanied by a redefinition of the modalities of state intervention in society. The army, with Sangoulé Lamizana at its head, remained the arbiter of the political game, but its weight, save for a new but short-lived attempt to restore political monism in 1975, only really made itself felt in the governmental sphere. This curious paradox permits us to speak of 'debonair authoritarianism' when referring to the General's regime.

A system of indirect and more supple control replaced the previous constraint. The state no longer sought to destroy civil society in order to install itself upon its ruins. Its totalising potential had not however disappeared. But, more intelligently and doubtless more securely, it intended to domesticate the institutions of civil society in order to insert them 'smoothly' into its development strategy. The restoration of the prerogatives of the chieftaincy and its association with the administration of the nation, the taking account of the interests of the big cereal merchants (very influential within the Muslim community), the resolution in 1969 of the school crisis which had set the Catholic hierarchy against Yaméogo's regime, and the cooptation of posts of responsibility for academics from minority ethnic groups, all these testified to the state's concern to create links with society. Thanks to these links, an uneven but uninterrupted 'dialogue' came to be established between the 'centre' and the 'periphery', the 'top' and the 'bottom'. Chiefs, brotherhood and maraboutic leaders, natives of such and such a village exercising functions in the administration, a political party, or a trade union acted as the mediators of this relationship. Thanks to their positions of power, they formed clientele networks which they used as bargaining chips in their relations with the 'centre'; first, of course, to their own advantage, but equally to the benefit of their *protégés*. The whole history of the party dominant from 1960 to 1980, the RDA of M. Yaméogo and of S. Lamizana, is the history of this clientelism.

This phenomenon took on an unprecedented scope at the beginning of the 1970s with the stated economic policy of 'Voltaïsation'. This explicitly aimed at creating a national bourgeoisie through the reinforcement of the interests of national entrepreneurs by granting preferential financial and public market facilities. More fundamentally, one may consider that if the state consented to rethink the nature of its interventions in the economic sector, this was with a view to channelling access to the mechanisms of accumulation, and so creating the conditions for the transformation of the ruling class into the economically dominant class. Further, it was, not surprisingly, the high-level bureaucrats who profited from the measures accompanying this new economic policy.[14] This, furthermore, resulted in the generalisation of clientelist practices. The access to financing indeed supposed the existence of

17

a considerable relational capital. This 'primitive accumulation' of relations could no longer be made, as in the past, on an ethno-religious base. The allocation of the advantages provided for by 'Voltaïsation' supposed a minimum of objectification as well as an 'advanced integration' into the sphere of the state, which became the privileged place for the structuring and restructuring of clientelist networks.[15]

But this race to accumulation equally (and especially) involved a competition between the different networks. That the state organisms (*Office de promotion de l'enterprise voltaique,* OPEV; *Office national des céréales,* OFNACER) bore the brunt of this, and were transformed into the stakes of struggles for influence, reflects the incapacity of the government to insert the expected financial facilities into the project of industrial development aimed at by 'Voltaïsation'. The conflicts which were to follow (between officials of the state and 'private' entrepreneurs who saw access to the mechanisms of accumulation close up before them; between millet merchants poorly integrated into the clientele networks and big cereal merchants with solid political backing)[16] testified to the existence of real frustrations due to the dramatically limited character of the economic and financial resources that could be released by the state, a state classed among the poorest in the world. It is in the light of this competition that, according to P. Labazée, the owners of 'relations capital' (*capital-relations*) split into antagonistic networks. The tormented evolution of General Lamizana's regime may be interpreted in its broad outlines in the light of this splitting (two republics, several successive governments, an attempt to return to a single-party regime, multiple social conflicts which determined the intervention of the army under the aegis of Colonel Zaye Zerbo on 25 November 1980).

All things considered, one can say that clientelism and neo-patrimonialism fashioned a certain type of state-society relations which excluded or limited the recourse to constraint. They led to a subtle mode of domination, real but not heavy-handed, and they maintained a permanent 'dialogue' between state and society, each governing its space with its own paradigms but without being cut off from the other. But if this situation allowed ex-Upper Volta to escape the rigorous law of the single-party regime, it failed to resolve the hegemonic crisis of the state. The institutional instability characteristic of this country testifies to the manifest incapacity of the groups aspiring to domination to group themselves around a common project. To this crisis, the CNR claimed to bring *the* solution.

The CNR or the revenge of the state

Up to this point we have hardly mentioned the regime of the CMRPN and that of the CSP. This is not because they do not merit a thorough analysis, but their short duration suggests that their advent constituted a sort of historical parenthesis, a period of transition, of a crystallisation of conflicts and a maturing of ideologies.[17] What should be retained from these two experiences, it seems to us, is that they mark the growing politicisation of the army and its stratification into ideologically antagonistic groups.[18] It is possible to schematically distinguish two factions: that of the top hierarchy, made up of officers who had served in the French army and participated in its colonial wars, and that of middle-ranking and non-commissioned officers, educated and trained in the most prestigious military schools of Africa and Europe, with a strongly nationalist-populist, indeed Marxist-influenced sensibility. Among the second group, a line of cleavage separated the moderates (personified by Commandant J. B. Ouedraogo, President of the CSP) from the more radical elements grouped around Thomas Sankara.[19] It is thus interesting to point out that the evolution leading from the CMRPN to the CNR expressed itself in the victory of the youngest military personnel and in the installation at the summit of the state, by means of the political formations of the extreme left supporting the CNR, of a new generation of 'cadets' many of whom are the children of notables from the Third Republic.[20] One can moreover wonder if one of the fundamental cleavages in Burkina is not the opposition between the old generation, master of the order which still very largely governs civil society, and the younger generation who seized the reins of the state in the forceful takeover of August 1983, and propelled Burkina into an era of ruptures.

Towards the formation of a new hegemonic bloc

The grand design of Sankara's regime consisted of modifying the social base of the state to the benefit of the peasantry, who make up more than 95 per cent of the population. In order to do this, he had first to subjugate the state itself. This was done through a methodical strategy of restructuring the state apparatus. The CNR's attitude broke with that of the preceding military groups which had contented themselves with making the state (which they had inherited from colonial rule) function for their own profit. A wide range of institutional reforms of the decision-making authorities, the administration and the army, permitted the rapid elimination of centres of opposition capable of thwarting the work in progress.[21]

The CNR equally took on the task of dismantling the clientelist networks. It established Popular Revolutionary Tribunals (*Tribunaux Populaires Révolutionnaires* or TPR) charged with conducting public trials of those responsible for the misappropriation of public funds and fraudulent practices. The campaign to brand the former leaders with a stamp of illegitimacy, which grew out of the meeting of the TPRs, permitted the CNR by way of contrast to provide proof of the moral virginity of the artisans of the August revolution.

Master of the political field, the CNR was in a position to set about the reversal of social alliances, on the basis of which it had seized power. Since independence, the social base of every successive regime had been made up of officials from the civil service. The massive recruitment pursued since 1960 resulted in the formation of an overcrowded administration (close to 30,000

19

bureaucrats for a population estimated today at little more than 8 million individuals). The revolutionary regime immediately applied a policy aiming to reduce the budgetary and social weight of the bureaucracy. This was articulated in a set of salary and fiscal measures (like the suppression or reduction of subsidies and the reduction of wages), deductions (for a National Solidarity Fund – *Caisse nationale de solidarité* – or development projects) and more or less 'voluntary' contributions (subscription to the official Gazette, and to the only daily newspaper, *Sidwaya*). Advantages in kind (government car, housing allowances, etc.) for top-level bureaucrats were also adjusted downward. Finally, the dismissal (often for non-conformity to revolutionary ideals) of several hundred officials crowned a plan of action to make considerable budgetary savings, a firmer management of the large economic balances, and a transfer of resources towards the countryside.

The situation of Burkinabè agriculture inherited by the CNR was, to say the least, difficult. To the structural constraints (poor soils, limited water resources, extraversion of the economy) were grafted the dramatic effects of the drought at the start of the 1980s, the slump in livestock sales due to saturation of the Ivorian and Nigerian markets, and the collapse of food production (millet and sorghum) in the regions of the centre and east.[22]

The agrarian reform of 1985 was presented as the solution to all these problems. Reversing the balance between the towns and the countryside, lightening the burdens weighing upon the peasants, instituting new relations between them and the state, eliminating the power basis of the chieftaincy, these were the heart of the reform. The reform meant in fact the installation of a new mode of development resting upon the dismantling of traditional training and supervision (*encadrement*) systems to the benefit of 'democratic' structures favouring a 'scientific' exploitation of the land through 'collectivisation'. In rethinking these modes of intervention in the rural world, the state also gave itself the means to control it so as to merge it into a global, rationalised project embodied in the symbolic importance accorded to 'grand projects' (like the development of the Sourou Valley or the construction of the Kompienga dam near the border with Togo).

In order to ratify the pact that would guarantee the peasantry's support for its project of social transformation, the CNR adopted a set of measures to stimulate agricultural production: suppression of the poll tax, increase of purchasing prices to the producers, revaluation of the role of OFNACER, creation of regulating stocks and 'cereal banks'.[23]

Generous in its intentions, the agrarian reform did not however give the expected results; far from it. If the accompanying measures outlined above did permit a substantial improvement in production, this however also generated a scarcely saleable surplus, inducing a revival of inflation in the urban centres due to the exacerbation of speculation. The implementation of the reform also stumbled on some insurmountable obstacles. The practical measures required to realise the objectives were never defined, any more than the contours of the training (*encadrement*) structure (state farms, village cooperatives, or small family holdings of reduced size) were conclusively established.

But the major obstacle came from the impossibility of imposing upon the peasants the disruption of their traditional hierarchies by the elimination of customary authority. Stigmatised the day after the forceful takeover of August 1983 as 'the number one danger for the revolution', the chieftaincy notably in Mossi country constitutes a potent counter-power whose attitude totally conditions the control of the periphery by the centre. But the ideology of the CNR could not accommodate itself to such an intermediary. It thus repealed the texts codifying the prerogatives of the chieftaincy, in order to confide the latter's administrative and judiciâry power to the CDRs by means of installing in each village a Popular Tribunal of Conciliation (*Tribunal Populaire de Conciliation*) 'charged with judging minor offences and "all anti-social behaviour" even undefined by the law'.[24] The CDRs were equipped with wide-ranging repressive prerogatives, 'from the seizure of land and livestock, up to the right of collective punishment inflicted upon villages'.[25] If the peasants in general voluntarily mobilised themselves around small infrastructure projects (construction of primary health-care posts, small dams, etc.) planned within the context of the *Programme populaire de développement* realised between October 1984 and December 1985, on the other hand, they rejected this 'revolution of mentalities' on which the agrarian reform rested. Their attitude epitomised the relation that the CNR had established with Burkinabè society as a whole.

The imposition of society

'To organise the peasants, to organise women, to organise youth, to organise the Burkinabè in general is a duty, a fundamental task.'[26] These words of the president of the CNR convey the nature of the revolutionary regime's ultimate project: to remodel society. This ideology was systematised in the *Discours d'orientation politique* (DOP) [Political Orientation Speech], a sort of charter of the revolution, delivered by Captain Sankara on 2 October 1983.[27] Questions have been raised as to the inspiration of this speech: is it Marxist, and to what extent?[28] The question is doubtless pertinent, but it seems to us that the essential lies elsewhere.

It lies in the fact that the CNR was the first regime in the political history of Burkina to produce a mode of speaking about society and to appropriate for itself the medium (*parole*) for this, eliminating from the debate all other currents of thought. The function of this mode of speaking was to produce a 'social memorandum' founded on a normative analysis of society 'taken from the position of each class or social stratum in the relations of production and in mechanically defined economic interest'.[29] The class analysis that the DOP sketches is an illustration of this. Functioning by exclusion and inclusion, this public discourse attributes to each social group a defined place in the revolutionary process, isolating the 'people' on one

21

side and its 'enemies' on the other. The Manichaean social categorisation which follows from this confers upon this discourse a further implicit function: to freeze society in a symbolic system justifying *a priori* the selective allocation of the *parole* as well as the control of its content.

Armed with this instrument of legitimation and delegitimation, the CNR set about imposing its system of domination. To the traditional networks of solidarity, it opposed the Comités de Défense de la Révolution (CDR) [Committees for the Defence of the Revolution]. Declared the 'authentic organisation of the people in the exercise of revolutionary power', the CDRs were accorded preeminence over all other mass organisations and were allocated the task of structuring social space in its totality; in the administrations, at the work places, in the neighbourhoods, in the villages. To them equally reverted the responsibility of mobilising each social group into the structures provided to this effect: Union Nationale des Paysans du Burkina (Burkina National Union of Peasants), Union Nationale des Anciens du Burkina (Burkina National Union of Elders) (a structure charged with re-establishing communication with the older generation and to which the Mogho Naaba, S. Lamizana and M. Yaméogo belong), Direction de la Mobilisation et de l'Organisation des Femmes (Department for the Mobilization and Organisation of Women). The young were subjected to civic instruction based on the teachings of the DOP and endowed with a 'pioneer movement' destined to form a 'new man' and to teach this new man community life in the *Keeogo*, place of initiation to social values like 'patriotism, discipline, love of work well-done, spirit of sacrifice'.[30] This was a tight system of social control, by a standardisation of codes, social rites and behaviour; an orgy of slogans and watchwords 'which seem to be a veritable permanent conditioning'[31] striving to concert the political make-believe of 'a few artisans' of the forceful takeover of 4 August 1983 into a dominant ideology.[32]

In parallel fashion, the CNR devoted itself to homogenising the social field in order better to assure its control. The reform of the judicial machinery is to be seen in this context, notably with the creation of the Tribunaux Populaires de Conciliation, which were, in each urban sector or village, henceforth authorised to settle conflicts which had previously been resolved by customary regulations. A new family code (suppressing or limiting polygamy – the problem had not yet been decided – and modifying rules of succession), on the point of being promulgated just before the coup of 15 October 1987, would confer upon the state a further instrument for the unification of the juridical scene. The reform of the educational system ('splintered' in Burkina between official establishments, missionary schools and Muslim *medersas*) followed the same logic.

Finally, the CNR developed a hyper-sophisticated strategy for the control of space. The national territory was redivided administratively into thirty regions roughly coinciding with ethnic boundaries. Ouagadougou and Bobo-Dioulasso were divided into sectors (thirty and twenty-five respectively).

Thus strengthened, the administrative network better lent itself to the control of power by the interposed CDRs.

In Ouagadougou, this strategy has been prolonged by a gigantic project of urban reconstruction. The 'spontaneous' quarters where close to 60 per cent of the population live, and which account for 65 per cent of the urban surface, have been progressively levelled, to the benefit of housing around 'modern' developments baptised in honour of the revolution (*Cité du 4 août, Cité de L'An II, III, IV*), and organised at the community level with CDRs, management structures and tenant committees.

Besides being at least in aspiration a solution to the problem of housing, the recomposition of the urban landscape was intended to undermine the foundations of the customary authority which controlled the allocation of land. By coincidence, it also resulted in the dismantling of traditional networks of solidarity by dislocating extended families into nuclear families on the basis of the authoritarian allocation of plots or units by person or household. Other works fitting into the same scheme (like the destruction of the old central market and the construction, as yet incomplete, of a new one on the same site) likewise reveal the obsession with 'modernity' that seemed to haunt the CNR and reflect the 'civilising mission' which it assumed.

Finally, the last facet of this strategy of urban control was the supervision of economic activities. The state has sought to circumscribe the informal sector by a national survey (January 1987) involving the allocation of professional identity cards. If this measure testified to the search for economic rationality, it also implied a struggle against a certain form of 'marginality' which is the very nature of the 'informal', a sector that functions 'in its own manner' and regroups 'those who have abandoned school, migrants, the unemployed, workers expelled from the formal sector...'[33] The will to eradicate begging through the creation of re-habilitation centres (*centres de réinsertion*) stems from the same concern. As for the formal or modern sector, it has been called upon to organise itself into Groupements d'Intérêt Economique (GIE) by branch of activity and subjected to a surplus of constraints and taxes. Under the cover of 'rationalisation', the state thus gives itself the means to enlist the private economy in its planning operations.

The revolution at a dead end

In view of this impressive organisational and juridical mechanism, one would have thought the CNR was protected from all serious dispute. Proof was furnished to the contrary on 15 October 1987. In fact, by dint of wanting to reorganise everything, the CNR finished by destabilising the society *against which* it had constructed itself. Its agrarian reform, for example, resulted in the opposite of the expected results; in the urban *milieu*, housing reconstruction policy drove the majority of the *déguerpis* (the urban poor, literally 'those chased off') to the periphery of Ouagadougou where they

23

themselves reconstructed those 'spontaneous' neighbourhoods that the reform proposed to suppress, whereas the 'modern' housing projects, due to the high cost of rents, benefited wealthier social strata. In the countryside, the abolition of customary regulations was translated into a multiplication of conflicts (between livestock breeders and farmers, between migrants and indigenous occupants of the land) that had previously been resolved thanks to these regulations. The CNR obviously did not have the means to realise the changes it desired. Without a real grip on society, it found itself alone and confronted with itself.

'*Making do*' with the revolution

Excluded from the institutional areas where it had expressed itself, society formed other areas, even recreating new spheres of autonomy and resistance. It deployed the discourse of the government to this end, reappropriating the latter for itself by diverting its original function. By means of humour (a caustic humour recognisable by the Burkinabè), it subverted the content of the slogans hammered out by the government, making apparent the gulf between its own cultural codes and those which were imposed on it.[34] The refusal to participate in collective sports activities or to wear cotton fabric (as was highly recommended) likewise assumed the character of an implicit protest.

The revolutionary project failed equally on its most sensitive point: the dismantling of customary institutions. In the urban milieu the chiefs, who controlled the allocation of land plots before the agrarian reform, knew how to use the reform to safeguard their authority, either by having land parcels allocated to several members of their family through the state, or by having a parcel on each new site successively allocated to themselves. In a more general fashion they succeeded in neutralising the CDRs by means of different familial or lineage strategies, for example in getting elected themselves or having their sons elected to the bureaus of the CDRs; this frequently led to the dissolution of a *bureau* and the election of a new one. When this was not sufficient, recourse to sorcery was the ultimate path for the preservation of the traditional social order.[35] Its effectiveness was such that the CNR believed it had to make a war cry of the struggle against fetishism, 'one of the principal social hindrances that plunge our countryside into obscurantism...thus preventing minds from liberating themselves and opening themselves up to the progress brought by the August revolution'.[36]

Religion seems furthermore to be more and more a refuge from the total state (*tout-Etat*) and a response to the 'problems of living' (*mal de vivre*) experienced by the young, disappointed by a revolution of which they had however been the most ardent partisans. In the Christian milieu, prompted by a Catholic clergy worried about the Marxist-influenced discourse of the CNR, the catechism movement has for some years now taken on unparalleled dimensions while the 'grassroots communities' have become the place of expression for spiritual 'expectations' all the more pressing due to the social disorientation generated by the action of the CNR.

An identical phenomenon can be observed in the case of Islam. Burkina is not generally considered a land of Islam, but rather the bastion of animism in a region, the Sahel, profoundly marked by the message of the Koran. Burkina, it is true, is not Senegal or Mali but the opinion evoked above must today be substantially qualified. A very clear Islamic renewal has manifested itself there for some years. If at present this has little influence on political life, it very much permeates the social field. Further, this awakening rests on a hidden Muslim mistrust of the CNR, a mistrust aroused by direct attacks against Islam the day after 4 August 1983 and then sustained by more or less veiled criticisms in the media, the destruction of a number of mosques in the context of urban reconstruction, or certain provisions of the new family code. The development of the associative movement (Association des Étudiants Musulmans du Burkina – Association of Muslim Students of Burkina), mutual aid structures (like those in Bobo-Dioulasso that undertake the ceremonial organisation of funerals for the more destitute), or collective activities of a festive character (excursions, animation) or a cultural one (seminars of reflection) or the attempts at unification of the Communauté Musulmane[37] and the rise of a reformist movement somewhat influenced by Wahhabism, all articulate popular attitudes that reflect the search for a sociability which does not blossom in the organisational forms of a solidarity imposed from 'above'. The *medersas*, whose number is rapidly growing, moreover welcome more and more tightly-packed contingents of students. Their success stems just as much from low schooling costs as from the concern of Muslims to merge 'profane' teaching with that of religion. Given this, the *medersa* is also a place for the formation of a sort of Arabicised counter-elite whose cultural and ideological references differ appreciably from those of the Westernised elite, socialised in official or Catholic teaching establishments controlled by the state since independence.

It is advisable, however, to point out a certain ambiguity in this Islamic resurgence. On the one hand, it indeed expresses the process of defining an autonomous space of identification against the state's wish to bureaucratise Islam, to the profit of a 'legalist' Islamic discourse more in keeping with the political and social options of the democratic and popular revolution. The more or less forced association of Islam with the struggle against begging and *maraboutage*, or with the promotion of teaching by means of lotteries, corresponded to this logic. But on the other hand this awakening reflects the concern of Muslims to insert themselves more as a group into the political arena, an arena from which they have been largely excluded up to the present.[38] The discussions of the *shari'a*, the place of women in society, the education of the young, and various Islamic practices that are expressed during 'seminars of reflection' thus reflect an attempt at an Islamic 'rereading' of the social reforms undertaken by the CNR.

The coincidence of religious renewal with the advent of the CNR reflects

25

the capacity of the latter to impose its referential system, a referential system on the basis of which a new, 'ideal' society would be constructed. By cutting itself off from the ideological machinery (the chieftaincy, Catholic hierarchy, Muslim community, whose loyalty to the old RDA party, one should remember, was largely responsible for the political longevity of General Lamizana) that established communication between state and society, the CNR condemned itself to being based exclusively on the minuscule and fragile political coalition that its accession had propelled to the summit of the state.

Political disintegration

One of the elements that most contributed to sustaining an enormous surge of sympathy outside of Burkina for the CNR (in particular among Africans in the younger age brackets and a good number of Western, *tiers-mondiste* intellectuals) was incontestably the battle against corruption that the CNR undertook upon its accession. The TPRs, which sat virtually without interruption from 1983 to 1987, were the instrument for this. At the beginning of 1987 the CNR established a People's Commission for the Prevention of Corruption (Commission du Peuple pour la Prévention de la Corruption, or CPPC) before which political and administrative officials had to declare their possessions (Thomas Sankara, moreover, was the first to do so). This action shook the bases of the clientelist networks and was a precondition for the redefinition of relations that the state intended to maintain with society; it furthermore illustrated the 'redeeming sensibility'[39] that is personified today in certain (so-called) radical military regimes, like that of J. Rawlings in Ghana; the comparison of Rawlings' regime with that of T. Sankara would certainly be very instructive.

This is not of course to pretend that clientelist and neo-patrimonial practices disappeared as if by magic. But it is undeniable that the ideology of the CNR, turned entirely towards moral integrity and the revaluation of the ideal of public service, acted as a brake in this area, permitting at least a partial realisation of the modernist-authoritarian project of the August revolution.[40] The reserve shown by commercial interests, as well as the transfer to Lomé or Abidjan of the activities of numerous large Muslim merchants, formerly major beneficiaries of the clientelist and neo-patrimonial state, testified to this.

But in doing this, the CNR was undermining its own foundations. By short-circuiting clientelist networks, it put an end to the vertical redistribution of resources that these allowed; a redistribution which would have compensated the heavy sacrifices demanded of salaried workers. The confrontation with the trade unions illustrated the incompatibility between the revolutionary ideal and socio-economic constraints.

When the CNR installed itself in power, the trade union landscape was composed of three large centres: the Organisation Voltaïque des Syndicats Libres (OVSL), the Union Syndicale des Travailleurs Voltaïques (USTV), and the Confédération des Syndicats Voltaïques (CSV), as well as a string of autonomous unions. Of the three cited, only the CSV (later becoming the CSB), which defined itself as a 'class struggle' trade union, supported the new regime unconditionally. The two others maintained an attitude of prudent reserve.

The first skirmishes between the unions and the government came a bare few months after 4 August 1983. The occasion was provided by a strike led by the Syndicat National des Enseignants Africains de Haute-Volta (SNEAHV), a teacher's union, motivated by the government's salary policy. Confronted with this opposition, the first truly organised one, the CNR opted for a showdown. It summarily dismissed close to 2,500 primary school teachers. From this moment on, its relations with the unions steadily deteriorated. The point of no return was reached with the promulgation of the statute instituting the primacy of the CDRs over all other mass organisations. The unions saw this as an attempt to marginalise them, notably within public and para-public enterprises and the administration; just where they did most of their recruiting. Their analysis was not mistaken. In trying to reduce or even eliminate trade union influence, the CNR in fact attacked one of the principal civilian opposition fronts. Its offensive also involved coercion (arrests of union leaders, interventions by the forces of order during union meetings) and a violent press campaign against *petit-bourgeois* unions and 'anarcho-syndicalism'. This confrontation culminated with the arrest of Soumane Touré, leader of the powerful CSB, and several other trade unionists. This step at once provoked a hardening on the part of the unions whose critiques of the CNR's economic policy were henceforth accompanied by a denunciation of the attacks on democratic liberty. Reduced to a clandestine existence, the unions did not as a result disarm. Strengthened by their past experience, they continued to make themselves regularly known through tracts, meetings, or celebrations that paralleled the government-organised ones marking the 1 May workers' holiday. Conscious of its powerlessness to bring down the unions, the CNR from the beginning of 1987 opted for a different attitude: it was no longer a question of dismantling the union organisations but of imposing leadership acceptable to the government at their head. This then led to the holding of several extraordinary congresses that resulted in the election of 'safe' leaders whose legitimacy, however, was relatively insubstantial. The result was a divorce between the state and the unions, and through them, the urban wage-earners.

But most serious for the CNR was the impact of this showdown upon the political coalition which sustained it. The first sign of this came in 1984 with the eviction from the government of the Ligue Patriotique pour le Développement (LIPAD). An outgrowth of the old Parti Africain pour l'Indépendance (PAI), LIPAD was (and remains) the most powerful political formation of the extreme left. Professing a Marxism faithful to the Soviet model, it was alone in practising a very active 'workerism' (*ouvrièrisme*) in the name of which it maintained close relations with the CSB. In fact, if it actively supported Thomas Sankara at the time of his march toward power, LIPAD also had its own objectives: it hoped in doing this to orient the action of the CNR to options of its own making. The strategy of infiltrating the state apparatus that it adopted soon after the CNR was installed corresponded with this design. But the hegemonic ambitions of LIPAD stumbled upon the hostility of other political groups forming the CNR, while the 'peasant' option of the regime accentuated the divergences between it and the nucleus of Thomas Sankara's followers; the anti-union offensive forced LIPAD to choose between the support of the government and its solidarity with the CSB. Showdown was inevitable. But in separating itself from LIPAD, the CNR also lost the only formation of the extreme left that was capable of giving it a minimal social base.

The confrontation with LIPAD as well as the 'domestication' of the unions did not however settle the 'trade union question' within the CNR. In fact, it is clear that this was largely responsible for Sankara's fall. One of the subjects of discord between the head of the CNR and Blaise Compaoré was the attitude towards the trade unions: Sankara was the partisan of a brusque effort to subdue them once and for all, by force if need be, while Compaoré favoured the reestablishment of a dialogue with them. The tragic end of the first president of Burkina Faso may thus be seen as a resounding revenge for the trade unions.

The confrontation with LIPAD, contrary to what was expected from it, did not result in the 'clarification' desired by the government. It on the contrary accelerated a process of decomposition and recomposition of alliances and influence within the CNR. After the dismissal of the 'LIPADist' ministers, the government was formed only of representatives from a few groups of the extreme left (Union des Luttes Communistes or ULC; Union des Luttes Communistes 'Reconstruite' or ULCR, product of a split within the preceding group; Groupe Communiste Burkinabè or GCB, formed by renegades of the Parti Communiste Révolutionnaire Voltaïque or PCRV, the only group hostile to the CNR from the beginning), who were deeply divided between themselves as to what internal or external political options to favour. But in fact the power of decision lay in the hands of Sankara's closest followers, grouped together in a mysterious Regroupement des Officers Communistes (ROC) which was replaced by the Organisation Militaire Révolutionnaire (OMR) a little after August 1983. Within this ideological nebula, Sankara in fact represented a point of equilibrium which permitted the maintenance of a seeming consensus. But this could be so only as long as decisions remained collegial and each group could hope to direct them towards its own preferred options. Yet Captain Sankara cropped up more and more as the unique centre of decision, lone instigator of the revolutionary process. In order to impose his views, he played the different cliques or *groupuscules* in the CNR against each other, drawing successively and alternately for his support on one or the other. But in order to provide himself with a reliable intermediary organisation, he brought about the creation of another *groupuscule*, the Union des Communistes Burkinabè (UCB), which, in a fateful irony, soon escaped his control only to fall into the hands of the CDRs. This failure signalled his growing isolation within the CNR.

In the face of this political fragmentation, Captain Sankara's solution was the creation of a single party. Placed in the minority on this point within the CNR in June 1987, he returned to the attack a few months later. And without any further result, except that of convincing his opponents that it was time to intervene. For them, this decision was premature. More fundamentally they may have feared a complete seizure of power by Sankara through this party.

The first president of Burkina Faso was also in this isolated position in his relation to the army. His authority, resting on his renowned heroic stand during the first war with Mali in 1974, was eroded by his direct calls to the rank and file to denounce counter-revolutionary officers. In spite of its transformation into a 'popular army', the Burkinabè armed forces retained a remarkable *esprit de corps*. The army had other areas of dissatisfaction, in particular Sankara's project to equip the Ministère de l'Administration Territoriale et de la Sécurité with an autonomous intervention force (FIMATS); to be placed furthermore under the command of a non-military figure, loyal to Sankara and responsible for a number of political assassinations. With FIMATS, Sankara would have had *his own* military unit at his disposal, just as Blaise Compaoré had the commando unit at the town of Po, the most powerful in the Burkinabè army, at his disposal.

The fall of Thomas Sankara is linked to a range of factors stemming from economic difficulties, the rise of social opposition, the crystallisation of political divergences within the CNR, and from personality conflicts that the excessive personalisation of power by Sankara had progressively exacerbated. More fundamentally, the failure of the CNR is also the failure of a certain political order which was unable to gain legitimacy to the extent that it insisted on trying to ignore the deep forces of the society it intended to govern. With the demise of the CNR, the latter had its revenge.

Conclusion

The evolution of the state in Burkina under the CNR underscores a problem that goes well beyond the Burkinabè case and to which few African states have found the solution: how to insert (or in the celebrated expression of G. Hyden, to capture) the peasantry in the process of development? The CNR however failed just where it was justified in thinking it had to succeed: in making the peasantry a partner in its project of social transformation. It failed not only because of the resistance to which its authoritarianism gave rise, but also because the social structures that it wanted to substitute for the traditional structures revealed themselves to be empty shells, without a grip on reality. It multiplied structures for training and supervision (*encadrement*) but these failed to train and supervise many people. 'This revolution finished by existing only in speeches', acknowledged the national press the day after 15 October 1987.[41]

Will the Front Populaire that has replaced the CNR be capable of reinstituting less conflictual relations between the state and society? For this, it will have to revise its conception of society and its modes of intervention within it. It will also have to regain the confidence of urban wage-earners without renouncing, at least symbolically, the peasant orientation of the previous regime. Finally, it will have to enlarge its political support beyond the few tiny *groupuscules* that monopolise power. The first proclamation of the Front seems to indicate that the new team is conscious of this situation: it has sent out a call to 'all patriotic and revolutionary organisations' to join forces in the process of 'rectification'. Contacts have moreover been established with the 'centre-left' opposition personified by the historian Joseph Ki-Zerbo, exiled in Abidjan, and it has been said that the business community, although still prudent, was not unfavourable to the change that took place. If the Front Populaire really has the will and the means to bring about the promised relaxation, Burkina might find its way again to a certain political stability. If not, one fears an acceleration of the infernal spiral.

3

Cameroon

JEAN-FRANÇOIS BAYART

On 4 November 1982 President Ahmadou Ahidjo, head of the executive since 1958, suddenly stepped down in favour of his constitutional successor, Prime Minister Paul Biya. Although on several occasions he had hinted at his intentions not to remain in power forever, and it had been obvious that his health had taken a turn for the worse (his speech and gait often becoming difficult), Ahidjo took both the public and foreign observers by surprise. The transition was nonetheless seen as exemplary and the press did not hesitate to praise it, comparing it to the retirement of President Senghor. Since at this time Cameroon had a growing reputation on the international economic scene, the image of its 'stability' and 'moderation' thus reached its apotheosis. This was no doubt an ideological and excessive image of Cameroon, just as the one of sudden deterioration would be in turn when difficulties began to accumulate. For on 18 June 1983 an unexpected cabinet reshuffle confirmed what the rumour mill *Radio-Trottoir* ('pavement radio', the popular grapevine), and its white-collar counterpart, *Radio-Couloir* ('corridor radio', the bureaucrat's version), had been murmuring for several months: President Biya dismissed four 'barons' of the old regime, Messrs Sadou Daoudou, Eboua, Ayissi Mvodo, and Bwele, and from this moment the rupture between the former president of the republic and his successor was complete. The pace of events began to accelerate. On 22 August, Biya solemnly announced the discovery of a plot against the government. Some days later Ahidjo, who had settled in France since July, began a virulent polemic on the airwaves of Radio-France International. Meanwhile, a movement of student and 'elite' elements, if not popular ones, gave its support to the head of state and pressured him to become a candidate for the presidency of the Cameroon National Union or CNU (Union Nationale Camerounaise). Ahidjo had kept this position for himself but had to resign in order to avoid the humiliation of a dismissal.

Then in rapid succession came the CNU extraordinary congress in Yaoundé on 14 September; the early presidential election of January 1984; the trial, death sentence, and pardon of Ahidjo and two of his collaborators implicated in the plot of February–March; and on to the dramatic events of 6 and 7 April when an uprising of the presidential guard had to be put down

31

violently; the model succession had indeed turned into a nightmare. In order to come to grips with these developments, observers were not short on explanations: Biya had lacked the necessary 'reconnaissance' regarding his predecessor; he had been indecisive and poorly advised by his entourage; he had, out of a spirit of revenge, driven the north to revolt. These interpretations are striking in their inability to think about Cameroonian society in a political and historical fashion, and are guilty of reducing it to a dimension that is either strictly personal, 'tribalist', or 'regionalist'.[1]

It is certainly premature to attempt an exhaustive analysis of the 'succession' crisis while so many crucial points remain obscure. It is important nevertheless to begin to place the transition period of 1976 to 1987 under the light of the Cameroonian state's own historicity. The essential question then concerns the evolution of the 'vast alliance regrouping the different regional, political, economic and cultural segments of the social elite' over which Ahidjo had presided, and of which 'the single party is as an emblem'.[2] The day of reckoning over the succession was all the more worrying from this point of view because coercion appeared to constitute the principal instrument, for all the organisational work carried out over more than twenty years; this to the point where one would have to doubt that it was truly a question of a 'hegemonic search' in the Gramscian sense of the term.

From founder-president to successor-president: an institutional, political and economic conflict

It is certainly possible to find phenomena of a psychological, ethnic or regional nature in the web of events from 1982 to 1984.

Once retired from the political life to which he had devoted the last thirty-five years of his existence, Ahidjo, not having the resources of a Senghor, may have felt a bit disoriented, and since his health returned after a few weeks of rest, all the more anxious to reenter the ranks. One can just as easily imagine that Biya, one of Ahidjo's principal collaborators since 1967, had built up a particular idea of his boss's actions and perhaps still more of his methods. Regional stakes also weighed heavily on the perception, or at least possible perception, of the conflict. If the Cameroonian reaction to some French journals which developed this line of analysis was so pointed, was it exactly because they wished to ward off a danger they knew threatened them just below the surface? And, in a certain manner, have these fears been confirmed by the revival of the ethnic problem since 1986?

The problem of succession had been posed in such terms due to a rumour, probably unfounded, which had circulated in 1975. According to the rumour Ahidjo had wanted to step down in favour of Sadou Daoudou, his defence minister and fellow northerner, but ran into opposition from the 'southern' members of the Political Bureau.[3] More seriously, the transition organised in favour of Paul Biya in November 1982 appeared in the month of December to be a decoy intended to placate the Centre–South. The new president's entourage quickly gained the conviction, most likely justified, that everything would be done so that Biya would fail and have to cede his place to his Muslim prime minister, Bello Bouba Maïgari, Ahidjo's true *dauphin*.[4] Furthermore the latter half of the 1970s had witnessed the rise in power of Muslim business interests which were not all that strict as to the means of their enrichment; in the public eye they were stigmatised regionally as much as religiously as *alhadji* and 'Hausa'. Ahidjo's abrupt departure deprived them of their political support and 'straddling' resources, and these interests were thus plunged into disarray.

The regionalist colouration of the succession crisis thus became almost inevitable. The ex-president of the republic was responsible for contributing to these tensions by seeking to obtain, on 18 June 1983, the resignations only of those ministers native to the 'North'. Ahidjo made this move knowing that a similar manoeuvre against the then prime minister, André-Marie Mbidas, had worked so well for him two decades earlier, and knowing that he was not without support in the rest of the country. Since Biya had refrained from restructuring the presidential guard in order to avoid charges of 'tribalism', the list of people wanted by the authorities on the day after the uprising was only too revealing in the proportion of names originating from the northern departments. While underscoring this fact ('All the rebels were from the north'), Andze Tsoungui, minister of the armed forces, and General Semengue, talked of 'rope in the house of a hanged man'; they were later reprimanded in no uncertain terms.[5] It was also said that Muslim merchants in Yaoundé's 'Briqueterie' quarter had informed their clientele of the imminence of the drama on the eve of its eruption and were thus accomplices.

At the same time the ethnic groups of the 'south' ('south' in the broad sense of the term), or at least the 'elites' who speak in their name, did not cease to affirm their identity nor to perceive in this political shift the opportunity to settle some old scores according to this broad 'north–south' distinction. This is true of the English-speaking population whose original autonomy had been confiscated as government centralisation increased; they did not hesitate to make their expectations known from 1982 onwards, and their discontent was effectively expressed in a variety of ways around 1984.[6] This is equally true of the Bamiléké, whose business interests displayed a healthy, expansionist 'dynamism' on a country-wide scale, and of the Bassa, who were quick to point out the victimisation they had suffered for their political stand during the nationalist struggles of the 1950s as justification for their advance in the public sector. This is perhaps still more true of the Beti and the Bulu who, fortified by their prosperity and the large number of children they had in school, aspired to the political direction of Cameroon, and who have always regarded Ahidjo's eviction of André-Marie Mbida as a usurpation of power. It follows that in one of his first acts as president of the republic, Paul Biya had to show the door to a Bulu delegation that had come to congratulate him on his accession to the presidency. Nevertheless, this pedagogical act did not in the least dissuade certain elements from seeing the succession as an opportunity for revenge against the north; one intellectual close to the new regime even pointing to a threat of 'ethnofascism' developing from the aforementioned 'Bamiléké dynamism'.[7]

No sector of society has escaped from this resurgence of the ethnic problem, which had been overshadowed first by Ahidjo's authoritarianism and later by popular mobilisation in favour of 'renewal'. Not even the Catholic Church was spared, as it split in harsh polemic over a plan for the 'Bamilékisation' of the clergy imputed to Mgr Ndongmo![8] In this way the last decade has subjected the 'hegemonic alliance' to severe centrifugal pressures, to the point where, in the case of an economic crisis, one can no longer rule out the possibility of these pressures bringing on a political rupture.

However it would be erroneous to reduce the cleavages of the last few years to a clash of ethno-regional identities. First, it is important to recall that the 'ethnic group' (at least as we imagine it in its current usage, in the form of a given entity, homogeneous and corresponding to a defined territory) does not exist. The demonstration of this for Cameroon has been carried on at the edges of the great debates that have taken place in anthropology.[9] Following the example of all cultural identifications, ethnic consciousness is contextual and not at all exclusive of complementary or competing identifications. It serves as a vehicle for political, religious, and economic interests while at the same time helping to conceal these from the view of the observer. Moreover ethnicity is a complex and relative phenomenon, not a static or timeless structure. Inter-ethnic relations are the products of history and not a combination of stable invariants. Yet commentators on the Cameroonian contemporary scene fell back on a type of explanation that was cruder still, giving great importance to dichotomies between 'north' and 'south', or between the 'south' and the 'west', without seeing that the terms of these binomials were hardly homogeneous entities.

The north in particular is shot through with societal cleavages; Biya has known how to use these with great skill. Colonial rule, in an officially recognised fashion during the time of the Germans and in a more nuanced manner during the French period, relied on the support of an ethnically composite power bloc controlled by the great Fulani families and cemented by the 'Islamic way of life'.[10] Although he had secured his rise to power against the wishes of the principal Lamidos (lamibé) of the region, then imposed the creation of a Western-style political party upon them, and in the early years of his regime limited the *Lamido* prerogative, Ahidjo, year in, year out and right up to the moment of his resignation, pursued this same policy, perhaps giving up ground gained on the chieftaincies as a result. His intentions were transparent, and ultimately quite similar to those of the Sardauna in Nigeria, this despite the difference in their social origins. Reaching power in 1958 because he appeared to be in the best position to ward off the spectre of a secession being entertained by the Fulani aristocracy, Ahidjo set the political division of the 'south' against the arbitrary construction of a vast and unitary 'north' under the control of an irremovable governor, Ousmane Mey. This hinterland base always continued to represent a major political resource for him and was a permanent guarantee of his position in power.

From 1983 on it was this false monolith that Biya, by making use of the frustrations it engendered, set out to dismantle. There were frustrations in Maroua and Ngaoundéré where, between 1958 and 1963, the Lamidos had been hit very hard for having opposed Ahidjo's rise: they subsequently found the city of Garoua being systematically favoured over them. There was anger from the masses of pagan and Christianised peasants, exploited by a canton chieftaincy that was Islamicised and integrated into the socially dominant bloc of the region. There was the irritation of the Christian churches (principally the Catholic Church) which were engaged in the task of developing the countryside but were persecuted in an underhand manner by a chieftaincy which little cared to see its peasantry rise above its condition. Finally there were the frustrations of a substantial part of the elite who were integrated into the regional social hierarchy, but who knew its corruption and economic Malthusianism too well not to feel it to be doomed. A whole series of measures was taken to respond to these expectations: a reminder of the secular quality of the state during Biya's visit to Garoua in May 1983; the breaking up of the former northern province into three administrative units and the creation of new departments which resulted in the establishment of Maroua and Ngaoundéré as provincial seats; the nomination of top-level bureaucrats from the south to posts in the region; social and economic investment, particularly in Maroua. But Yaoundé, probably haunted by the Chadian precedent, was careful not to attack the Fulani power bloc and its cornerstone, the canton chieftaincies, directly, contenting itself with checking abuses. The Lamidos continue to be pampered, and in all probability financed, by the central authorities; the role these latter play is both subtle and constrained and thus reflects the complex social realities they face.

The southern half of the country does not present a simpler configuration: the English-speaking Cameroonians are split between the south-west and the north-west; the Bassa between the Nyong and Kelle and the Maritime Sanaga (which itself includes a Bakokoko minority); the Bamiléké between rival historical chieftaincies; the Beti between different families according to the ethos of lineage emulation. But there is no point in multiplying the examples. When all is said and done it is the notion of *terroir*, or 'native soil', which must predominate, in Cameroon as in the rest of Africa, if we want to understand the historicity of the state and politics. There is nothing exotic in this observation. After all, the emphasis that Fernand Braudel places on the description of the constituent 'countries' of the French nation (paradoxically celebrated for its 'unity') illustrates the universality of this analytic imperative in political sociology.[11]

While overshadowing the plethora of historical circumstances that furnish the framework for contemporary politics, interpretations of the 1983–4 crisis in terms of 'regionalism' or 'tribalism' also push aside some other crucial dimensions. The conflict between Biya and Ahidjo was above all political, and has been experienced as such by Cameroonians. It bore in the first instance on the institutional order and the allocation of spheres of influence provided by the party on the one hand and the state on the other. Announcing his resignation on 4 November 1982, Ahidjo was pressured by a delegation from the Central Committee (which included Paul Biya) to hold on to the national presidency of the CNU.[12] Beyond the emotional pathos behind which they camouflaged themselves, the 'barons' who initiated this move were pursuing a specific objective: to limit the power of the new president, to deprive him of control of the party and thus leave 'open' the nomination of the candidate for the 1985 presidential election.

Be that as it may, the former president of the republic, having exited by the front door, quickly gave the impression of wanting to return through the window of the party. Under the pretext of wanting to reinforce the authority of his successor and to counter the factional manoeuvres of his former companion, Moussa Yaya (excluded from the CNU on 10 January 1983), Ahidjo started upon a tour of the provinces during which he was received (against his will, he claimed) as a veritable head of state, this even though Biya had yet to make an official tour in the country. In the first interview he gave following his resignation, questioned on the existence of a 'bicephalism' Ahidjo insisted strenuously on the 'confidence' he placed in Biya; he apparently viewed this confidence as the only source of legitimacy for Biya's power. This came through when he blandly retorted:

> I naturally remain National President of the CNU...However, there is no dualism nor bicephalism in the exercise of power. The party and the government each have a well-defined and distinct domain of responsibility. The party...defines the orientations of national policy. The government applies these in taking account of our potential, with the adjustments necessitated by particular realities and circumstances. If everyone loyally plays their role within the framework of collaboration that our governing democratic regime implies, there could never be any ambiguity.

So that things were perfectly clear, he added in conclusion:

> Any misunderstanding would be due to the fact that some people may no longer wish to see me in Yaoundé. However, they'll have to get used to my presence and resign themselves to seeing me. Indeed, as former president of the republic, I have a right to lodgings and offices in Yaoundé where furthermore I will continue to preside over meetings of the higher party authorities at the headquarters of the CNU any time this is necessary. For my part, I have been vaccinated and immunised against slander for a long time. Equally, I believe President Biya sufficiently intelligent to be able to avoid such crude traps.[13]

'Who governs Cameroon?' public opinion wondered, thus assuring the great sales of a book which didn't answer this topical question at all.[14] Anxiety was now at its peak. The preeminence of the party, which Ahidjo now intended to affirm, would have completely changed the configuration of the political construction that he himself had built up, and which had since the Ebolowa Congress of 1962 guaranteed the primacy of the state, from the point of view of the Constitution and of governmental practice.[15]

From quarrels over precedence in cabinet reshuffles to talk of plot rumours, the conflict grew more acrimonious. A point of no return was reached when Ahidjo managed to secure control of the nominations of candidates for the May legislative elections; then, at the price of a veritable takeover by force, he did his utmost to pass a law institutionalising the single party. Biya suddenly thwarted this manoeuvre through the unexpected Cabinet reshuffle of 18 June. The former head of state having lost the struggle (militarily as well, during the dramatic night and early morning of 18 and 19 June, the eve of President Mitterrand's official visit), the way was now open for his successor to take over as head of the CNU in September and to receive the unction of universal suffrage in January of the following year. Although his own personal practice was often different, Ahidjo had pleaded for twenty-three years without respite in favour of a strong and institutionalised state. The crisis of 1983 showed that 'the Word was finally made flesh'. When Ahidjo wanted to retake control of his creature, it escaped by explicit reference to constitutional legitimacy and 'republican legality'. These events, discussed in a manner suggesting catastrophe, have in fact contributed to the stiffening of the Cameroonian political fabric, and henceforth they define the scope of the possible. In the current working plan, the place of the party is destined to remain second. Furthermore this line of ideological structuring has prevented ethnic and regionalist identification (at the strength of which we have hinted) from prevailing over strictly political identifications; it has equally weighed in favour of the army's reserve, notwithstanding the decisive part it took in the tense moments of June 1983 and April 1984.

Nevertheless the bitterness of the conflict between Biya and Ahidjo was not limited to the constitutional sphere; it was also related to two opposed political projects. Throughout his successive mandates Ahidjo had been more feared than loved, whatever might have been the sense of pride in his regime's achievements. To tell the truth he was never more popular than on the day of his resignation, and this thanks to the lesson in civics he seemed to be giving to the rest of Africa. Still it must be pointed out that a number of Cameroonians lived that Friday in the obsessive fear that the head of state was going to go back on his decision before the transfer of power ceremony.[16] The regime had relied too much on intimidation and self-censorship to gain the allegiance of a country in full cultural and economic vigour; and since the middle of the seventies it had been a country intoxicated by expansion in the petroleum sector. 'Africans, whether they be Guineans, Cameroonians or others, simply ask their historic leaders, on the one hand, to reflect a bit on "life itself", they are not eternal; and on the other, to realize that a people is like a child who has grown up; at 25 years old, excluding disability, he can no longer wear the same trousers that he wore at 12 months...'; so the editorialist of the *Messager* later wrote.[17] Biya's great political wisdom was to understand these expectations of an *ouverture* and to go out and meet them during his 1983 provincial tours. Through allusions well-suited to his listeners, Biya rendered more and more explicit the drift of the change in his relations with his predecessor.[18] The Cameroonian people understood without the situation having to be spelled out for them, and they didn't withhold him their support when the rupture exploded in July/August 1983. Probably for the first time since independence, a mobilization was spontaneously triggered off in favour of the established power.

What did this project of Biya's consist of? In the beginning at least, and perhaps essentially in style, it was that of a simple and reputedly honest man.[19] Beyond that was the outline of a more precise programme, and one cannot dismiss the notion that this led to a misunderstanding between the president of the republic and his 'rank and file'. The declared objective was the construction of a

> new social order founded on a realistic democratisation of the state and party. In a word, it's in the last analysis to a profound change in national life that history has summoned us since 6 November 1982; a change to undertake resolutely and in close collaboration with the people, that's certain, but also to undertake in a spirit of responsibility, of realism, and of method with a view towards progressively giving birth to a more authentic democracy and a more open society.[20]

Already by the end of that 1983 rainy season, increased freedom of expression, and more particularly the proliferation of private press material, rendered this shift in political life tangible. But in an inevitable fashion the head of state found himself torn between the expectations of those who wanted to increase the pace of 'renewal' and the apprehensions of members of the old order. Some people for example wanted to see Biya create a new party in place of the CNU or as a counter to it. No doubt wishing to avoid a political void, or realising the real strength of his adversaries, the president of the republic preferred to be the head of the existing formation, although it did mean announcing an internal democratisation. In doing this, he disappointed a portion of his base. Even so, he liberalised, in a Platonic manner for the time being but holding promise for the future, the conditions for candidacy in the presidential elections while judging the reestablishment of a multi-party system somewhat premature. This implicitly contradicted remarks that *Le Monde* had attributed to one of his ministers.[21] It was not long before Biya's middle course engendered a similar uneasiness in the economic sphere, and in that of the recruitment of political personnel. Ever eager for upheaval, the public found it easy to raise objections against increased corruption and the maintenance of ministers suspected of misappropriating funds in the name of 'rigour'; a rigour, it was said in jest, that was very expensive. Finally, declarations Biya made with regard to political exiles during his official visit to France in February 1983, although certainly scaring Ahidjo's partisans and even Ahidjo himself, were a long time in materialising and were obviously not destined to lead to the legalisation of the UPC, as the latter pretended to believe.[22] But it was the occasion of Ahidjo's trial and that of his collaborators which exacerbated the divorce between the head of state and his rank and file. In making public the affront in the form of a discovery of a plot, one might say that Biya condemned himself to follow ordinary judicial procedure. The authorities in Yaoundé conducted a fairly poor investigation of a case that was not however unfavourable to them.[23] The head of state, whose image had just been altered by election results that were just too good to be true (concocted for him by the political bosses of the party) and by a Cabinet reshuffle which was poorly viewed by public opinion, collided with the latter head on by pardoning his predecessor and codefendants. He had already done too much to avoid pushing his adversaries into playing their trump card. The uprising of the presidential guard erupted in a rather general indifference, at least until the rebels' radio declaration revealed its real tone: that of a '*putsch* of Papa's boys', quite irresponsible and incompetent, wishing to regain their privileges. The fallout from this episode damaged the presidential project's credibility for many months.

In reality, the breach between Biya and Cameroonian public opinion proceeded from a naive conception of politics and from a refusal to consider yet another dimension of the succession conflict. What was at stake was not only a 'good' democratisation versus a 'bad' perpetuation of the past, but also the distribution of the fruits of economic accumulation; one knows that in Africa this is indissociable from the control of power.[24] Neither in Cameroon nor abroad has it been sufficiently understood that the president of the republic was dependent on a connection with forces that were not always to his advantage and whose resources were heavily financial. 'Rigour', the watchword so dear to Biya, here takes on its full meaning. Certainly it was a question of moralising an economy which had been perverted during the last years of the Ahidjo regime, and which had taken a suicidal bent. Equally, by shutting down the fictitious warehouses at the port in Douala, by increasing customs control operations, or by enjoining Muslim merchants to repay the indulgent loans so liberally granted them, it was a matter of finding a new equilibrium for the excessive influence of certain national business interests, to the advantage of other networks.

Addressed to Biya, this motion from the 'community of Cameroonian businessmen', meeting at the Chamber of Commerce, Industry, and Mines in Douala shortly after 22 August 1983 (and within which Bamiléké interests are influential), is explicit in this regard:

> Considering the disorder which reigned in the Cameroonian economy at the time of your accession to the supreme magistrature, disorder characterized by: (1) a scandalous favouritism in the regulation of goods and service imports consumed in Cameroon; (2) a wilful disregard of true businessmen to the benefit of adventurers without licenses or other proper titles, these adventurers having profoundly upset commercial circuits and this giving to our country the

appearance of a sound economy [*sic*]; (3) a lenient granting of bank credits without guarantees or possibilities of reimbursement; (4) a tolerance, indeed an encouragement of organized customs fraud; (5) a generalisation of contraband trade by land, sea and air; (6) a free circulation in our national territory of a currency that was not legal tender in our banks [clearly the Nigerian *naira*]... we thus approve your policy of moralization in Cameroonian society, a policy which generates the social peace indispensable to the life of business.[25]

Nevertheless this policy of 'rigour', insofar as it began to reach them, was not long in disappointing those who saw it simply as a weapon against their Northern competition, a competition simultaneously weakened by the demonetisation of the *naira* and by the closing of the Nigerian border. Disappointment to such an extent that there was a good deal of concern about a collusion of Bamiléké and Muslim business interests being behind the attempted *coup d'état* of 1984; an hypothesis which diverse indices, notably a shortage of basic goods or some of the arrests, seemed to suggest. These socio-economic ramifications of the conspiracy seem in any case to have been more important than the regionalist ramifications insisted on by the foreign press. It was really the problem of accumulation, of the state's relation to this and its capacity to transcend the patrimonial dynamics of the 1970s, that had dramatically come to the fore. Conscious of the suspicions which hung over them, the Western entrepreneurs led by Kadji asked to be received by the president of the republic, during his official visit to Douala in December 1984, in order to express their loyalty. The sumptuous banquet they insisted on offering the Bamenda Congress had a similar meaning. But these testaments of good will clashed with the suspicion that the political class from the Centre and South intended to take huge advantage of its positions in power. This hidden competition between the head of state and Bamiléké entrepreneurs was at one point impeded by the intrigues of certain political personalities. Thus, just below the surface mistrust seems to persist between the government and businessmen from the West, the latter being accused of preferring the informal financial networks of the *tontines* to banking institutions and of indulging in frantic contraband trade as well as capital flight. The objective of the Minister of Commerce and Industry, Nomo Ongolo (from the Centre-South and married to one of Foncha's daughters), appears to have been double: on the one hand, he intended to set the growing power of economic operators native to the South against interests from the West; on the other, he hoped to cut back on the influence of French interests by favouring the diversification of the country's foreign relations and by developing trade with Canadian, American, German, and Asian partners. Destined to clash sharply with established practices, this strategy is all the less convincing as it has been applied without much subtlety; further, it has tended to sacrifice the industrial sector to commercial activity with the support of some outsiders who are more inclined to ostentatious consumption than to productive investment. Be that as it may, competition with a view towards the accumulation of wealth and power is getting more intense, particularly in the banking sector, public enterprises, and even at the university.[26] A sign of this competition is the development of corruption among bureaucrats who demand more and more often to be 'motivated'. 'Yesterday the goats were tied up and they nibbled. Today the goats are tied up and they nibble. Tomorrow the goats will be tied up and they will nibble!', so exclaimed a participant at a 1986 information meeting of the new party, the Cameroon People's Democratic Movement (CPDM).

However, it would be another error if one were to exaggerate the strictly regional connotation of these tensions. These are almost necessarily multi-ethnic networks of political and economic interests that confront each other without threatening the cause of national unity or even giving place to significant popular mobilisation. (Although it is true that the clientelist distribution of the fruits of accumulation does operate according to largely ethnic criteria.) Within each region the competition is not any less than that at the national level. For example, the 'Bamiléké business interests' that are so readily described as a homogeneous and threatening entity are in reality associated with non-Bamiléké operators (and not only through the Cameroon Mutual Credit firm founded by Tchanque) and are themselves divided by sharp cleavages. The easiest to detect are those which split along generational lines: on the one hand, there is for example Kadji's generation, originally favoured by Ahidjo to counter the UPC rebellion and composed of nearly illiterate 'self-made men' with a multiplicity of activities;[27] and, on the other hand, there is Tchanque's generation, better educated and more modernist. In this case the contradiction had repercussions on political developments: from January to March 1986, during the revival of the CPDM's grassroots activities, Messrs Kadji and Koloko no doubt supported the candidacy of Kuoh Tobie, and Tchanque that of Ekindi.[28]

One sees the advantage the head of state can draw from these network rivalries as soon as they pledge an allegiance to him. He thus places himself in the position of referee, on the watch that no group distances itself too much from the others, and contributes to the growing power of a generation of entrepreneurs on which he can count. (This was done notably by coopting them into the inner circles of the party at the Bamenda Congress.) All this assures Biya's own autonomy from a political as well as economic class structured by twenty-seven years of independence. Hence the 'renewal' project appears under a different light. Biya certainly has given sufficient proof of his sincerity and tolerance, from the relative liberalisation of elections and the press to containing the repressive fury following 6 April 1984, so that one doesn't doubt them. Yet through these means (and one can never draw enough attention to the fact that he preferred them to others, in contrast, for example, to Daniel arap Moi in Kenya), he has also sought to establish his authority to the detriment of the influence of the regime's 'barons', who sometimes scarcely concealed their own desires. This aspect of things is all the more important since the presidential succession was despite appearances open, and since the Bamenda Congress was to lead to a

Jean-François Bayart

redistribution of party membership cards. In this respect and *mutatis mutandis*, the Cameroonian political system is very comparable to that of the Ivory Coast, Senegalese, and Sierra Leonian regimes; it amounts to a strategy of maximisation of power for the head of state, an objective which had been previously pursued through authoritarian control, and which is today suffering from the corrosive virtues of universal suffrage.

The reciprocal assimilation of segments of the elite

The dynamic of the growing autonomy of presidential power and the conflicts which have accompanied it have not until now really impeded the process of reciprocal assimilation of segments of the elite; for several decades this process has merged with the construction of the Cameroonian state. It is of course advisable that we be on our guard against a teleological interpretation of history, to a greater or lesser degree implying the idea of a dominant class in formation.[29] However, one has little choice but to recognise that the highly conflictual episodes of the transition were in the end resolved through compromise, and a fusion that no doubt enhanced segments of the social elite. Seen from this angle, economic and political antagonisms in Cameroon are often only the expressions of this process, especially when the holder of supreme power uses ambiguity as an art of government.

The crystallisation of a civil society which is now more autonomous *vis-à-vis* the state than in the past (as a result of liberalisation) is liable to further the reciprocal assimilation of segments of the elite. The formation of powerful financial networks outside the banking system and the increased role of an associative fabric of interests (of which the double Fronde of architects and lawyers furnished an interesting example in 1986) are important stages in this evolution. Important arrangements, those requiring traumatic measures, are still concluded within the state apparatus; the mutation of the party and the cooptation of the new Central Committee in 1985; the holding of competitive elections (renewal of rank and file party organs in 1986, municipal ones in 1987, legislative ones in 1988); and the redistribution of top-level administration and public sector posts within the government; all these are characterised by a double tendency that is falsely paradoxical and thus poorly understood by the public.

On the one hand, the 'men of the renewal' have indeed shown themselves to be, harking back to terminology in vogue in Cameroon during 1984–85, 'new men'. At the close of the Bamenda Congress the composition of the Central Committee was profoundly modified: forty members out of sixty-five and fifteen deputy members out of twenty had not belonged to the corresponding organ of the CNU. The renewal rates of the CPDM's party cadre and women's organisation were furthermore respectively, 54.30 per cent and 53.06 per cent in 1986. One year later, in October 1987, the municipal elections confirmed this breakthrough of new political personnel

42

by recording the victories of its fastest rising spokesmen, Ekindi in Douala and Melone at Edea. Although in a certain manner these two embody the heritage of the Union des Populations du Cameroun (UPC), it would certainly be too much to conclude that the great schism that tore the country apart between 1950 and 1964 (which Ahidjo's suspicious authoritarianism had not helped to cauterise) has healed. Nevertheless, the regime slowly reconciled itself with the nationalist past through small symbolic gestures (for example, dedicating new classes of officers with the name of Rudolph Douala Manga Bell and Martin Paul Samba; the nomination of Victor Kanga, an ex-minister imprisoned by Ahidjo, to the head of a public organisation; the return to Cameroon of Mgr Ndongmo, accused of plotting against the government in 1970). Simultaneously, the resurgence of a nationalist consciousness (whose principal target, as is proper, is France) has combined with a fever for money and consumption that renders the nightmares of clandestine militancy, to which certain exiled members of the UPC continue to adhere, rather empty. In just a few years the political spectre of the country has in this way been constrained but falls short of being truly appeased.

On the other hand the opening up and enlargement of the political elite has not resulted in the elimination of personnel who managed the state during the time of Ahidjo. Such is the case naturally of Biya himself, General Secretary to the presidency of the republic from 1967 to 1975 and then prime minister from 1975 to 1982. But he confided some of the key posts of his regime to other highly-skilled 'barons', even though it meant leaving his liberalisation project with a credibility gap in the eyes of those who believed that 'one couldn't put new wine in old goatskins without running the risk of losing it'.[30] In spite of some tangible signs of an opening up that were concealed in Biya's general policy speech, the first impression that emanated from the Bamenda Congress was that of victory for the 'old guard', or at least a defeat for the 'innovators'. The CPDM Political Secretariat, and its Secretariat for Organisation in particular, remained under the control of the old hands Sengat-Kuoh, Doumba and Mengueme; whereas personalities stamped with the seal of change like Messrs Ngango, Labarang and Njoh Mouelle only reached the Central Committee as deputies. The 'barons' considered hostile to 'renewal' (for that matter, often excessively so) didn't always succeed in securing ministerial terms. All the same, this did not stop them from holding some crucial portfolios, like that of Territorial Administration. And in a manner still more shocking to the public (insofar as some among them are renowned for their misappropriation of funds and their close collaboration with Ahidjo), men such as Ayissi Mvodo, Youssofa Daouda, Eboua, Sadou Daoudou, Yadji Abdoulaye, and Sadi found themselves entrusted with more or less important or honorary functions.

It is a false dilemma that systematically opposes change and continuity. The strategy of taking small steps, pursued by Biya to the great displeasure of his initial partisans, corresponds to that fundamental logic of the 'hegemonic search' which wants no significant fraction of the ruling class to be cast aside from the system. In a revealing fashion, *Le Messager*, usually quick to push the wheel of change, emphasised soon after the revival of the rank and file organs that, henceforth, it was 'urgent to wait' if the regime wanted to avoid 'finding itself faced with an uncontrollable army of panic-stricken opponents'.[31] As in the preceding decades the dynamic characteristic of political life, including conflict, has been a privileged vector of this process of reciprocal assimilation.

It remains necessary to outline the contours of this much-discussed 'dominant class in formation'. During the Ahidjo epoch, it was linkage to the state which gave the actors their capacity to enrich themselves and to dominate the social field; the profile of the 'hegemonic search' was definitely bureaucratic, organised around positions of power.[32] Certain people have deduced from this the patrimonial character of the Cameroonian state.[33] This label, however, does not seem to take account of a whole type of reasoning from the Weberian model of 'sultanism'. The positions of power in Cameroon furthermore do not absorb the totality of the channels of accumulation, along the lines of the Soviet Union or the People's Republic of China. From this point of view, state appropriation of numerous means of production and exchange is not unduly striking. It is not of the same nature as in a socialist or mixed economy; this although the mediation of the state in Cameroon is stronger and more specific than in Kenya, Nigeria or even more so, Uganda; and although the activity of private enterprise still closely depends on state power insofar as it rests on administrative authorisation (import licences, industrial assent, price sanctions) and on special dispensation from the law (customs and fiscal fraud). It manifests rather the will of the Prince; if not in monopolising commercial exchange as in the old Asante kingdom,[34] then at least in keeping track of those who could gain advantage from it and thus decrease the Prince's power. Now, when all is said and done, only the gangster politics of a Touré family in Guinea or a Nguema family in Equatorial Guinea have been able to come near to a *de facto* confiscation of the means of enrichment, without however actually achieving this. Everywhere else a more or less consistent layer of entrepreneurs has managed to differentiate itself; even in the highly patrimonialist regimes of Mobutu and Houphouët-Boigny.[35] In Cameroon this development is all the more pronounced because of the solid merchant tradition that existed in the west and north before the arrival of the state.[36] Thus it is quite tempting to discern in Biya's project a wish to represent this 'business bourgeoisie' and to water down the bureaucratic tenor of the regime. At the Bamenda Congress, eminent patrons such as Messrs Kondo, Tchanque, Sack, and Onobiono were in fact made members of the CPDM's Central Committee; the concern exhibited in Cameroonian diplomacy for a diversification of its foreign economic partners also appears to display this readjustment.

Examining it more closely the reality becomes nuanced, and all things considered, one scarcely perceives the radical otherness that neatly differentiates the 'business bourgeoisie' from the 'politico-administrative bourgeoisie', and which would make these 'two distinct groups', whose 'conflict' would be 'potential but...still concealed'.[37] Certainly the background of a Monkam, or a Kadji, or a Kondo is different from that of a minister or top-level bureaucrat, even though this is already less true of a Tchanque, who was general secretary of the Central African Customs and Economic Union before founding Nobra Breweries. Further, the big merchants and especially the industrial merchants have their own preoccupations that lead them to criticise the administration's grip on the way firms conduct their business, the orientation of the government's economic policy, or the increase of imports which compete against national produce. Last but not least, before he was beaten by Ahidjo in the 1960 presidential elections and withdrew from the power struggle, Paul Soppo Priso, the nationalist (but not 'red') multi-millionaire from Douala, had embodied an authentically liberal political philosophy; the extreme opposite of Ahidjo's state authoritarianism. But at the end of the day 'bourgeois' and 'bureaucrats' drive in the same Mercedes, drink the same champagne, smoke the same cigars, and meet up with each other in airport VIP lounges. The cleavages between the two activities, economic and politico-administrative, do exist and are in part projected under the form of personal rivalries. Nevertheless they convey antagonisms of role rather than those of status or class. They are not inevitably more acute than the factional confrontations which divide the political class, the conflicts of authority which paralyse administrations, or the contradictions which set major businessmen against each other.

In other terms, both the private and state networks of accumulation broadly share the same ethos of personal enrichment and munificence. And, conversely, nothing indicates that their interrelation is by a principle of exteriority. It is not in the end important that the fortunes of Ahidjo and Moussa Yaya were amassed under the cover of their political responsibilities; that those of Soppo Priso, Kuoh Tobie, and the late André Fouda go back in the main to the decades of the colonial period; nor is it important that Kondo's fortune rests on a genuine industrial occupation. Neither is it crucial that Kadji had long benefited from the deliberate myopia of a regime that wanted to set Bamiléké businessmen against the rebellions of the UPC and that the big merchants of the north had also profited from a similar calculation; nor is it crucial that M. Monkam works in the wake of a foreign brewery and that M. Fotso entrusts the administration of his companies to repatriated managers, where in the same place others dream of doing battle with French investments. Nor, finally, is it crucial that some opt for capitalist management while others believe that 'looking after one's self is not stealing'. For the moment, the maelstrom which sweeps along all the discords and ever-changing alliances returns to a field of interests which have been intermingled through the years by contracts, by loans, by acquisitions and by marriages. In this whirlwind, private operators and state operators act in complementary fashion (when they aren't simply merged together), being content to change hats according to the circumstances.

As in Kenya,[38] the central place of 'straddling' mechanisms between salaried employment (notably in the public service) and private investment gets to the heart of the progressive unification of the sphere of domination. J. Iliffe suspects that these 'straddling' lines are less salient and systematic in West Africa than in East Africa.[39] This is not evident as concerns Cameroon. Despite the existence of pre-colonial commercial networks in the west, the biographies of contemporary Bamiléké merchants show that, for them also, the salaried class has been 'the obligatory departure point' in the formation of their capital.[40] To this it is necessary to add other modalities of interrelation between private and public channels of accumulation. We already know that the majority of those entrepreneurs coming from the Grassfields region, following the example of their Muslim colleagues, have at one time or another been the object of the solicitude and indulgences of power (especially as regards banking). Beyond this, some among them have been, and in all likelihood remain, the direct associates of eminent members of the political class with whom they compete to recycle stored-up prebends. As on the rest of the continent, merchant circuits and political circuits mutually reinforce themselves and make a system.[41] Instead of a relationship of exclusion or competition, there is a complementary and hybrid relation between private capital and public capital, between the 'business bourgeoisie' and the 'bureaucratic bourgeoisie'.[42]

In order to conceptualise this dominant class both in its potential unity and in its plasticity, most authors accept the notion of a 'national bourgeoisie'.[43] In the case of Cameroon the epithet 'national' is singularly out of place, whatever may be in other respects the 'nationalist' acrimony of businessmen as regards foreigners and, in particular, French firms. Not that this 'bourgeoisie' is divided along ethnic lines, as is often harped upon: on the contrary, we have seen that the networks of accumulation almost necessarily transcend regional particularisms. But the label suggests an irreducible contradiction between autochthonous business interests and foreign capital, where in reality ties of association and overlapping assert themselves. These links of interdependence naturally do not exclude the conflicts of interest or strategy which are inherent in the business world. Nothing however authorises one to read these in teleological terms. Confrontations can in fact lead to a greater integration of indigenous and foreign capital, this being the fruit not of a defeat of the 'national bourgeoisie' but of a deliberate choice on their part. And from this point of view, neither is there anything that permits us to distinguish in Cameroon a 'national' bourgeoisie from its 'comprador' ugly sister. G. Kitching notes this in a similar way: all businessmen, all bureaucrats find themselves sometimes under one of these categories, sometimes the other; this depends upon the activities one takes into consideration and their motivations, as well as the particular alliance, which corresponds to precise stakes, into which he has momentarily inserted himself.[44] The majority of Cameroonian entrepreneurs deal daily with Western operators, Nigerian operators, and more and more, 'Asiatic' or Israeli operators. The substantial amount of 'extraterritorial bank deposits from the non-banking sector' coming from the country suggests that they consider the Western world economy as their natural field of expansion and accumulation, well beyond narrow national boundaries.

Further, and the objection is all the more fundamental because it bears on the very concept of 'bourgeoisie', this dominant group searching for an identity and gathering together under the cover of the state does not preside over the destinies of a productive economy which is based on veritable class exploitation in Marxian terms. Whatever the strength and stability of the dynamics of social reproduction from the 1930s up till today, the stratification scaffolding remains unstable and no doubt quite close to the scene that S. Berry paints of the Yoruba.[45] The Cameroonian agricultural and industrial fabric was fragile and uncompetitive even before the serious crisis which was unleashed in 1985, a bit later than on the rest of the continent.[46] In the process of domestic accumulation, diverse loans and predation practices have won the day; they do not have much to do either with the spirit of capitalism or with its necessary institutional vector, the bureaucratic state.[47]

Conclusion

It would be as well to recognise that this process of forming a dominant class still remains very uncertain, as shown in the historical trajectory of the state in Cameroon. This is not at all exceptional on the West African scene. It corresponds more or less to the 'fusion of elites' that R. L. Sklar marked out in Nigeria, or to the 'reciprocity model of African politics' that M. Kilson sets forth from the case of Sierra Leone. It has its equivalents in Ivory Coast, in Senegal, in Niger and even in Liberia, since President Tubman's policy of 'unification', soon after the Second World War.[48] This middle course, halfway between conservative modernisation and social revolution, seems to constitute the rule as a limited number of exceptions confirms, on the modes of social continuity (Mauritania) or of rupture (Guinea, Zanzibar, Rwanda). The altered scale of colonial rule rendered the multiple compromises of which it is woven more or less inevitable, this by bringing about the differentiation of the social foundations of the state from one region to the other.[49] At the very most one can say that for thirty years Cameroon at best has exemplified this fundamental scenario of reciprocal assimilation of elites owing to institutional stability and to its relative economic prosperity.

But the epoch if not past seems then at least subject to divergent dynamics. Plunged into a structural crisis that the diminishing income from petroleum, the lasting devaluation of Robusta coffee and the formidable competition of Malaysian cocoa will ultimately worsen, sucked up more each day into the

47

field of attraction of the Nigerian giant, prey to deleterious factional struggles that exacerbate the hazards of a sometimes contradictory liberalisation, paralysed by the hypertrophy of the presidential function and of the administration, the country is entering a storm zone. This will not necessarily be fatal to the hegemonic search. It will nevertheless render its outcome more hazardous. In order to conceptualise the historical compromise between the diverse sediments of the social hierarchy in the shadow of the post-colonial state, and its procedures of coopting counter-elites which might be capable of leading a sizeable popular mobilisation, the Gramscian notion of 'passive revolution' imposes itself upon the mind.[50] Now, without absolutely excluding it, in the eyes of the Italian theorist this scenario did not constitute the royal road to the institution of a genuine hegemony. From the episode of the Risorgimento in the nineteenth century to the 'bastard' and fascist state in the twentieth century, the development of the peninsula suggests on the contrary that two major traits of the 'passive revolution' – the preservation of the influence of the old dominant strata and the spatial asymmetry of inequality – instead were the basis for authoritarian tension. Only the future will tell us if the dominant class project in Cameroon is in this way doomed to incompleteness and compensatory coercion.

4

Chad: the narrow escape of an African state, 1965–1987

ROBERT BUIJTENHUIJS

John Dunn offers some particularly relevant remarks about Sahelian political entities:

> The states of the interior, the southern fringe of the Sahara...are highly distinctive political formations. Some of the least viable states in the world, weakly integrated into the world market because endowed with so few resources worth exploiting, they have also endured in the last decade an ecological trauma in the shape of drought and famine of a highly distinctive character. The most placid and optimistic observer of post-colonial political capabilities will hardly escape a measure of dismay in the face of this experience...it takes today a real ideologue, whether of the right or of the left, to see with any confidence a happy political future for the Sahel.[1]

Being neither a placid and optimistic observer nor really an ideologue, of whatever tendency, and having studied Chadian politics for some years, I emphatically agreed with this diagnosis when I read it for the first time. Today, about ten years later, the Chadian experience attracts even less in the way of boundless enthusiasm or blind commitment. Since the publication of *West African States*, Chad has almost disappeared from the political map, and even in 1988 doubts about its survival as a political entity are not without foundation, in spite of the patient's slow recovery over the last few years.

In this chapter I will first briefly describe the slow but steady disintegration of the Chadian state from 1965 till 1982, as well as the slow, but again steady, recovery that has taken place since Hissein Habré came to power in June 1982; then I will try to analyse why this process of withering away occurred and why, finally, it was called to a halt just before total collapse. A few words about the future will be said at the end of the chapter, but I would ask future readers not to use them against me should my predictions fail.

The withering of the Chadian State: 1965–1982

The withdrawal of the state, founded in August 1960 by President François (later Ngarta) Tombalbaye, began in 1965–6 with a series of unorganised and rather loosely connected peasant revolts in the central and eastern parts of

49

Chad, to be followed in June 1966 by the creation of Frolinat (National Liberation Front of Chad), aiming to organise the peasant movements in the field and represent them to the outside world. State disintegration gathered momentum in 1968, when the northern BET *préfecture* (Borkou-Ennedi-Tibesti) joined the rebellion.[2] The people of the BET were principally Toubous, whose unruly reputation dates back to the French conquest, and they had their local reasons for joining the Frolinat rebellion.

The rebellion spread like wild-fire through the whole north of the country from 1967 to 1969, chasing the national army out of considerable parts of the countryside. With the army, the state disappeared with equal speed: in spring 1969 the government controlled no more than fifteen *postes administratifs* out of a total of about a hundred in the central and eastern regions of Chad, and such was the insecurity even on the main roads that the *préfets* of the besieged areas had to travel by air in order to report to the central government on the state of anarchy in the circumscriptions they were supposed to rule. Contemporary confidential documents provide some idea of the extent of the disaster:

> Goz-Beida [a small provincial town in the East] is an island comprising the military post and nothing more. During daytime state authority does not extend for more than 3 or 4 kilometres beyond the camp gates...There are no merchants left at Goz-Beida as the road is unfit for any traffic.[3]

The situation improved slightly in 1969 due to French military intervention, but when the French soldiers left at the end of 1971 the central and eastern regions slid back to a state of total anarchy. The same situation prevailed in the BET: in the beginning of the 1970s the armed forces of Chad only controlled a few fortified camps in the northern desert, which had to be supplied by air and out of which they did not dare to venture, even for occasional patrols. State authority was thus about nil for the whole area in revolt.

Things took an even worse turn at the end of the 1970s, when Frolinat, or rather some of its military commanders such as Goukouni Weddeye and Hissein Habré, thanks to a complex process of military victories and peaceful negotiations, came to dominate the central government in N'jaména.[4] The southern-dominated army, beaten by the insurgents in the very streets of the capital in March 1979, then retired to its home areas beyond the Chari river, to be followed by most of the civilian administration. Momentarily Chad was thus cut into two parts, but after negotiations at Lagos in August 1979 sponsored by the Organisation of African Unity, all parties to the conflict were persuaded to sign an agreement. This led to the formation of a Provisional National Union Government (GUNT) in which all the political and military factions, from both north and south, agreed to participate.

This compromise unfortunately did not last for long. As early as March 1980 a new civil war flared up when Hissein Habré, Minister of Defence and leader of the FAN (Forces Armées du Nord), challenged the leadership of his

50

President (and fellow Toubou) Goukouni Weddeye. During this war, which was largely a confrontation between the most powerful Frolinat commanders, Habré after several months of bitter combat seemed to be near victory, only to be beaten at the end of 1980 when Goukouni asked Colonel Qaddafy for Libyan military intervention. Qaddafy did not need to be asked twice: within a few weeks Libyan soldiers poured into Chad and chased Habré's forces from all their strongholds, including N'jaména.

As was to be expected, the foreign 'liberators' did not retreat immediately; for about a year they maintained garrisons in the most important centres in northern Chad, taking over some of the duties normally incumbent on the national administration. Colonel Qaddafy finally withdrew his army in November 1981, following a request by President Goukouni and due to pressure from France, the US and OAU, but Goukouni unexpectedly proved unable to hold the ground on his own. Habré's FAN, which had sought and obtained refuge in the Sudan, took advantage of the new situation to turn the tables. After a few months of fighting they took control of the northern provinces, and in June 1982 they marched into N'jaména. Goukouni and most of his fellow GUNT leaders had to flee into exile in their turn, ending up in Tripoli, where they maintained a rival puppet government heavily dominated by their Libyan 'friends'.

During this whole period state authority had been almost non-existent. In the realm of politics and administration the central government lost control of almost the whole country, with the exception of parts of the capital. In the north Frolinat disintegrated into several *tendances*, each with its own 'fief' where leaders ruled in true warlord style, admitting no government intervention whatsoever. In the south Colonel Kamougué, who had emerged as the strongman of Chad's armed forces during the events of 1979, founded a Comité Permanent in May 1979, with the consent of the majority of the southern politicians and senior civil servants. This Comité Permanent 'acted as a fully-fledged government in the southern areas',[5] although it refrained from using a governmental label. Goukouni Weddeye, the official president, recognised his own lack of authority. In March 1981 for example he 'deplored the fact that Chad is ruled by the military factions participating in the GUNT',[6] and a few months later he used even harsher words: 'GUNT does not dispose of any power, or finances, or regional administrative authority over factions that constitute real states within the state. GUNT is a government only in name.'[7]

His declarations were confirmed by leading Frolinat warlords. When some of them agreed to disband their armies in May 1981, in order to reunite under the Frolinat banner (a promise they never kept), they committed themselves to 'transfer to the GUNT all the administrative powers in their respective spheres of influence'.[8] The central state had thus lost its executive privileges: in the southern *préfectures*, relatively well administered at least until the end of 1980, executive officers continued to officiate but they were nominated and controlled by the Comité Permanent; the northern provinces were not

51

administered at all, and certainly not by staff obeying the orders of President Weddeye.

The same situation prevailed in the economic field. Between March 1979 and June 1982 the south functioned under a regime of near total autarchy. Cotton, Chad's main export commodity and cultivated only in the south, was transported directly to the Central African Republic, while the town of Garoua (Cameroon) served as the main banking centre. The Comité Permanent moreover levied all taxes and import-export duties and soon decided not to transfer them to the central government in N'jaména, which in turn suspended all payments for civil servants posted in the south. In April 1980 Colonel Kamougué even had a fully-fledged regional budget worked out, which was carried over in 1981.

Disposing of the majority of Chad's civil servants, the south thus managed to maintain economic activities to a reasonable standard, while the warlord-dominated north relapsed into anarchy and a subsistence economy such as had prevailed in ancient times. Economically the ruling military commanders were kept afloat by foreign subsidies (mainly from Libya, although some minor warlords allegedly were in the pay of Nigeria and the Sudan) and by levies enforced at local markets and road-blocks all along the main traffic routes. Political and economic anarchy also took hold in the south in 1981, notably with the appearance of numerous road-blocks manned by unruly and irregularly paid (if at all) soldiers. It can finally be said that the central state had lost all its economic prerogatives to the leading politico-military factions.

As for the currency, the Libyan dinar had been used, at least since 1978, as the only means of payment in the BET. It is quite irrelevant whether this should be interpreted as a sign of Frolinat allegiance to its Libyan protectors or whether this was merely a practical device due to the difficulties of replacing the wasting stock of CFA francs, as has been suggested by M. Brandily.[9] The important point here is that the central state had lost control over part of the cash circulation. During the Libyan occupation of the north in 1981 the dinar also briefly took over in the central provinces, as well as in eastern Waday (where the local population strongly protested against its use).

From February 1979 on, Chad did not dispose of a genuinely national army, although Colonel Kamougué's southern forces continued to claim military 'legitimacy'. In reality the political *tendances* each maintained their own armed forces, and nobody in N'jaména, not even President Weddeye, could claim to command these irregular bands. The monopoly of legal violence also was thus lost for the central state authorities.

Other facts, perhaps less important but highly significant in this context, can be quoted to illustrate the almost total breakdown of the state. Colonel Kamougué and his Comité Permanent did not hesitate to send envoys to international conferences such as OAU summits, in order to express their points of view. Twice, moreover, in 1979 and 1980, the southern authorities managed to organise final secondary-school examinations in the area under their control, while the central authorities were reduced to total inactivity in the educational field. Other state activities disappeared (the central bank) or were taken over by private organisations, such as road maintenance (by the Coton-Tchad Company) and the postal services by missionary societies.

For several years, in short, the central state of Chad was no more than window-dressing and, as has been argued by M. P. Kelley,[10] only the ongoing recognition of the N'jaména authorities by the international community prevented those authorities from losing face all along the line.

The slow recovery of the patient: 1982–1987

As intimated in the introduction to this chapter, since June 1982 the predicament of the central state has improved under the presidency of Hissein Habré. (History goes fast in Chad. During 1987 the Libyan armed forces, in spite of their sophisticated weaponry, suffered a humiliating defeat by Habré's more rustic guerrilla fighters, which caused them to retreat hurriedly to their home bases. In March 1988 only the contested Aouzou strip remained under their control.) Even in the beginning of 1987, to be sure, the central government did not control the entire national territory. Libya was still entrenched in some parts of the northern BET, while in remote areas of central and eastern Chad Frolinat insurgents remained in hiding, making communications by road sometimes hazardous. President Habré however has controlled large parts of the country, in contrast with the reign of Goukouni Weddeye. The south has been conquered by FAN troops, rather ruthlessly at first, with the help of some southern forces hostile to Colonel Kamougué; since September 1985 an uneasy truce has been maintained south of the Chari river. Economic autarchy has been ended and taxes and levies flow again directly into the central state's coffers. Habré moreover has appointed new *préfets* for all the fourteen provinces, which clearly indicates his will to re-establish undisputed central authority. During the *conférence des préfets* in April 1984, the first to be held since 1976, they were recognised by the President himself as, *l'autorité suprême hiérarchique*, in their circumscriptions,[11] which was interpreted as a guarantee against the undesirable military interference that had been the rule since 1979.

Compared to the GUNT era, Habré has thus obtained significant results, and it can be said that the situation prevailing in 1984 looked rather like the one described for the period 1965–8 (i.e., the first years of the Frolinat revolt). The central state, although weak and still convalescent, existed once again in most fields of national life. Since 1984 Habré has earnestly pursued his policy, putting the central state back upon the political stage. The foundation of a new party, UNIR (Union nationale pour l'indépendance et la révolution) in June 1984, and the simultaneous dissolution of the FAN, not only represented gestures of goodwill to southern Chad, which could not give enthusiastic allegiance to a movement which was 'northern' by its very name. It also meant an attempt to curb the ardour of the FAN guerrilla veterans, whose conspicuous presence at state functions and in civil life hampered the smooth flow of administrative business; only a minority of members of FAN's Command Council were co-opted into the UNIR Central Committee, and such a change of personnel seems to have occurred at all party levels. This too is a significant improvement on the 1979–82 situation when Chad lived under what I have called *le règne des combattants*.[12] Habré's Toubou fighters still take too many liberties with civil rights, especially in remote areas of the countryside, but they are slowly being pushed into the background, fading away as old soldiers should, to be replaced by competent and well-trained civil servants, many of them from the old southern *nomenklatura* that lorded over Chad before 1979. Habré really means business, and he has had some success in rebuilding central state power.

The background to the breakdown

Why is it that Chad, unlike its neighbours with the notable exception of Sudan, has had to face persistent civil war almost from the very beginning of its career as an independent state? A first important point has to be noted. Chad has been France's Cinderella colony, utterly neglected economically and (especially) educationally. Thus Chad suffered from a dramatic lack of well-trained civil servants in the beginning of the 1960s, people to man the state apparatus, especially at the regional and local level. In 1959, with independence nearing, crash programmes were indeed organised to train Chadian nationals to take over the civil service. Many of the lucky candidates, who were hurriedly sent to France and elsewhere for upgrading courses, were primary school teachers with no previous experience in administration; they soon proved to be below standard when left to rule the country.

This certainly was not a unique situation at the time, and one wonders whether neighbouring Niger, for example, was much better off here. In Chad however the effects of under-administration and mismanagement were worsened by the fact that the great majority of the newly promoted civil servants were from the southern, cotton-growing areas. This was where France, for obvious reasons of immediate profit, had concentrated most of its admittedly insufficient development projects, and where the local population had enthusiastically responded to new opportunities in the field of schooling and education. In the absence of northern counterparts, quite a few southern *évolués* had to be posted outside their home areas, which soon led to trouble.

As Le Rouvreur[13] remarks, *Le Tchad est double*, meaning that a cultural rift separates the Muslim northern parts of the country (some three-quarters of the national territory with about half of the population) and the southern areas. Islam did not take hold in the south, where agriculture is the only economic activity, unlike the north where most people are full-time or part-time herdsmen. This cultural and economic cleavage has always been present in the background of Chadian history, from the nineteenth century when there was no political entity known as Chad, but when the northern Muslim Sultanates regularly went slave-raiding beyond the Chari river, and then latently during the whole colonial period.

Even if J.-P. Magnant[14] were right in affirming that the north–south ethnic conflict was not really an issue in 1960, latent animosities were soon resuscitated by the arrival in the north of the first batches of southern civil servants. These administrators had not been prepared, either by their cultural background or by their superficial training, to behave according to the standards current in the north for 'good' rulership. Some of them moreover behaved as though in 'conquered land', and fell to the temptations of corruption and contempt of the local population, which soon made them despised as representatives of an 'alien' government. It is this tense atmosphere of cultural and ethnic conflict that produced the first peasant revolts in 1965–8.

Chad moreover is not only 'double', but 'multiple'. The north, although indeed united by Islam, comprises dozens of ethnic groups, some of which like the Toubous and the Arabs have been hostile to each other from time immemorial, while the segmentary organisation of many northern societies easily gives rise to internal strife,[15] as when Habré and Goukouni, both belonging to the Toubou cluster, started to quarrel, first in 1976 and again in 1980. This is one of the reasons why Frolinat splintered into a dozen *tendances*, a situation of which certain foreign powers greedily took advantage, thus worsening and prolonging the civil war.[16]

This very rough sketch of the background factors to the withering of the state in Chad leads to an interesting question, namely: how far is Chad representative of other African countries, a kind of forerunner? Some scholars have suggested, seemingly without hesitation, that Chad basically had to be seen as a trend-setter. Michalon in 1979 thus prophesied that:

> The entity shattered in N'jaména is the same one which in other African countries has been unable to improve the lot of the masses: the nation–state, on the standardising Jacobin model. Colonial ideology, substantially adopted by African elites at the time of independence, relied on centralised institutions of European origin to break up traditional societies…and thus allow the emergence of national feeling and the 'modern' African.[17]

Michalon argues that this ideology failed mainly because the Jacobin nation–state has no sociological substratum, rests on no national consensus: 'The professedly unifying function of these authoritarian or even dictatorial states seems to have resulted in an acute exacerbation of ethnic rivalries and internal tensions.'[18]

Michalon's thesis however is over-simplifying matters when trying to reduce Chad's problems to the simple failure of the nation–state, a failure moreover that supposedly will occur elsewhere in Africa. Chad may not differ intrinsically from other African states, but the country suffers a severe quantitative handicap in that certain cleavages and conflicts that do occur elsewhere none the less all present themselves together in Chad, in a particularly dramatic fashion. This is also the opinion of S. Decalo who says that 'though not unique to Chad, the dimensions of these problems certainly appear monumental in this former French colony'.[19] The withering of the Chadian state thus does not necessarily portend the breakdown of political entities all over the continent. How acute problems are, and how they combine and interact in each particular situation, will be important in deciding whether African states go 'over the brink' or not. More research is needed in this field. Why did some African states fail, politically and/or economically, like Chad, Uganda, Sudan and the Central African Republic, while others managed to survive and even settle into cruising speed? A study of Chad in isolation cannot answer this question, although one point seems to stand out: Chad (like Sudan) had to cope with a basic north–south division between two demographically equal cultural-religious blocks. This is not Chad's only problem, but many others would probably have remained latent and 'manageable' in the absence of this burning issue.

Why has there been no fatal outcome?

Another question needs to be answered before concluding this chapter. How has Chad managed to survive, if not as a nation, at least as a state, in spite of the gloomy prospects prevailing from 1979 till 1984? A first and superficial answer would refer to the political zeal and administrative capacity of Hissein Habré and the crew which now mans the ship of state. This is undoubtedly an important factor, but it could not have been decisive had it operated in a political vacuum.

Another basic factor has to be stressed: all through Chad's civil wars, nobody ever openly professed any inclination to break away from the national community and to favour separatism. Even Frolinat, although a northern movement by its recruitment and by the world-view of the great majority of its 'privates' (and even military commanders), never claimed a separate independent state, and the same holds for Colonel Kamougué's southern followers, although in the latter case thoughts of an independent République du Logone may have stirred some hearts and minds. Even in the south however such unspoken desires never came to the surface, and all parties and factions loudly proclaimed allegiance to the national state, even if some southern leaders did (and still do) argue for a federal solution, or at least a decentralised administration that would give the separate regions a much larger command of cultural, linguistic and educational matters. This sets Chad apart from Nigeria (during the Biafra war) and from Sudan (where the southern rebels did claim independence during the first phase of hostilities, until 1972).

Another reason for Chad's survival is to be sought in the international environment. We have seen that foreign intervention, by Libya and France but also by the United States, Sudan and Nigeria, has had decidedly negative effects on the situation in Chad, and has hindered national reconciliation. Libya's role has been particularly damaging in this field, and it remains so. This however is only one side of the coin, as has been argued by M. P. Kelley:

> Post-independence governments were not required to exert authority through-out the territory under their jurisdiction because their legitimacy was guaranteed by international recognition following upon the wave of self-determination. They were not required to develop empirical statehood.
>
> Consequently, states such as Chad have persisted not because they have been able to stand on their own, but because they have been provided with political, financial, and military support from the outset by former colonial powers and with the moral-legal forms of international society guaranteeing their survival.[20]

This is quite true, and apart from the rather abstract level of the international community as a whole, it can moreover be said that a unilateral declaration of independence by southern Chad would have provoked the ire of some of its neighbours, such as Cameroon and Nigeria which both have latent north–south tensions to cope with and which would certainly not have been enthusiastic about Chad creating a dangerous precedent. Their anger would immediately have materialised in an economic boycott which could have strangled a land-locked country like Chad within a few months. This threat also has helped to guarantee Chad's survival.

Conclusion

Finally, one more question is to be asked in the context of the Chadian experience of the seizure of power by armed and allegedly revolutionary guerrilla movements. As this is the first case of its kind in *independent* Africa (Uganda having more recently joined the category of guerrilla-led govern-ments), one would like to know whether the rather unrepresentative background of the present incumbents has any consequences in the realm of politics and methods of ruling a country. In the case of the Habré regime the answer is that there are no major differences setting it apart from African governments that came to power by more traditional, although rarely democratic, means. Contrary to what one might have expected on the basis of the revolutionary language he used during the nineteen-seventies, Habré has been an essentially pragmatic politician who has made no attempt whatsoever, since June 1982, to revolutionise the political life or the economic situation of his country. Ideologically he seems to be nearer to Senegal's Abdou Diouf (or to his own predecessor, Tombalbaye) than to radical Marxist-Leninists such as the leaders of Lusophone Africa. On a more practical level he has established close relations with Mobutu, for whom he has expressed his admiration on several occasions and whom he seems to take as his model, in so far as his pride permits him to refer to any

57

models at all. All that can be said here is that his coming to power did not in any way represent a break with the past, and that he did disappoint some of his earlier supporters.

Nor does there seem to be much difference as far as Chad's political personnel is concerned. During the first two years of his reign, many of Habré's past military commanders held office. Some of them are still present – conspicuously or in more or less concealed advisers' roles – at the highest levels of the state. The days of most of them are however numbered since the creation of the UNIR, and they are slowly giving way to a new category of competent but pragmatic managers, some of them from the previous southern incumbents. The regime and the army nevertheless have a markedly northern outlook, and those observers who characterise Habré's coming to power as *la revanche du Nord*, are not entirely wrong. Regionally and ethnically speaking a redistribution of political power has occurred, from which the Toubous (a minority group representing 5 to 6 per cent of the population) have benefited most. It should however be emphasised that the new regime does not stand for *une revanche de l'Islam*. Although Arabic is now Chad's second official language, theoretically at least, Habré steers a neutral course in religious matters and tries to refrain from too close relations with Muslim 'patrons', be they Libyan or Saudi Arabian. Here too, differences do exist compared to the situation during Tombalbaye's reign, but it is all a question of fine tuning rather than dramatic upheavals. About twenty years of sometimes fierce and bloody civil war have thus boiled down to remarkably little.

One ray of hope may be discerned. Habré has been able to exorcise the spectre of total collapse of the central state, and his presidency is to be judged in this positive respect also. Will he be able to ride the storm and steer the ship of state to calmer waters over the coming years? Many problems still remain. National reconciliation advanced in 1985–6, but not all Habré's Chadian opponents have been won over. Those that continue the struggle might in future still receive the lavish support of Colonel Qaddafy, who sees Habré as a dangerous threat to his regime, a straw man of US interests. Economic life has slowly been reactivated since 1982, but drought and locusts still endanger local food production, while the price of cotton, Chad's main export crop, recently plummeted on the world market to below production costs. Habré, finally, has no political heir, and Chad's present precarious equilibrium depends to a great extent on his continuing presence on the political scene. John Dunn's general remark on Sahelian states still holds for Chad in 1988: a really happy political future will not be reached for quite some time, and total failure is still a possibility, even if the patient's recovery has set in.

5

Côte d'Ivoire:* analysing the crisis

YVES A. FAURÉ

In contrast with the situation in the majority of African countries, the Ivory Coast until the end of the 1970s achieved an economic growth of the order of 7 per cent per year (and this without any mineral resources). This was obtained by an expansion of the economic orientations inherited from colonial rule. The years 1977/8 marked the high point of an economic boom that had been maintained until then by the price explosion of coffee and cocoa on the world market. Ivorian ruling circles appear from the mid-1970s to have been seized by a financial euphoria which led to a substantial inflation in public investments. Large agricultural development operations were launched and managed by a rapidly expanding public enterprise sector. This expansion was accompanied by an apparent concern to redistribute the fruits of this growth according to region, with some particularly extravagant consumption propensities and an expensive policy of infrastructure creation and capital goods purchases. This unbridled expansion was bound to increase the country's foreign debt, as a large chunk of the investment financing came from Western banks. The deterioration of some balance of payments items (services, transfers) ensued as the heavy equipment installed during this fever meant increased imports.

With the least drop in the markets the country would thus be in a very difficult financial situation. This is what happened from the second half of 1978: the collapse of coffee and cocoa prices (as sharp and profound as the preceding rise had been steep and exciting) exposed all the components of an internal and external crisis. Over the next eight months and in a very intense manner, a certain number of factors were to combine with tremendous effect upon the Ivorian economy: to the drop in the market there was added the rise in imported goods (notably due to the second petroleum shock), the rise in interest rates, the rise of the dollar, and, because of export quota practice established by the International Accord, the impossibility of selling all the coffee produced. Up until 1980 (and in certain spheres even later), the Ivorian authorities reacted sluggishly to the quickly deteriorating situation: a recovery programme was indeed established in 1978/9 with the aid of a

---

* The government of the Ivory Coast has recently instructed international organisations to use this French language designation, rather than any translated form, in all official documents. We respect this preference for the title of this chapter (eds.).

fiduciary fund but it proved to be quite insufficient and, in any case, expansionist policy by and large continued while the ambitious public investment operations went on. One did not have to wait long for the results: the deterioration in terms of exchange produced a growing balance of payments deficit, and the drying up of resources at the Caisse de stabilisation (the organisation which controls coffee and cocoa marketing and has traditionally acted as an important source of taxation) placed the financing of state budgets (operating and investment) in peril; finally debt servicing became much more onerous.

The Ivorian government then had to call upon International Monetary Fund and World Bank assistance, beginning in 1980. In return for new credits, these lenders made the government adopt a severe programme for financial recovery. But the tendency to deny the evidence of the crisis, illustrated amongst other things by greatly exaggerated official hopes for oil production, prolonged and deepened the imbalances. The drought of 1983, with its effects on the level of agricultural production (the coffee harvest which followed was scarcely one-third that of the preceding year) and on the decline in industrial activity (due to numerous electrical power cuts), also gave new impetus to the crisis.

The difficulties of day-to-day existence, until then unknown in the capital, in the end convinced the Ivorian leaders that the crisis was real. After the good export receipts of 1985 (drawn from a brief recovery of the markets and record harvests), the suspension of debt payments (recently declared by the government) testified to some very serious difficulties in the country, although perhaps there is a tactical aspect to this affair, aiming to obtain better financial conditions from the Paris and London Clubs for the recycling of the debt. This announcement of insolvency at the end of 1987, although not surprising to specialists of the Ivorian economy, does however appear highly symbolic and significant: in the country where economic growth has continued at the pace of a forced march; in the country of conspicuously displayed wealth, of huge development projects and luxury goods; in the country where, according to the official formula promoted by the dominant class, there was no room for 'cut rate Africanisation'; in this country the impossibility of paying the foreign debt put an end to any remaining illusions.[1]

The economic crisis and the numerous and painful adjustment measures that have been decreed in order to restore the large macro-economic balances, and to rehabilitate particular sectors of economic activity, have constituted not only the framework of economic evolution in the Ivory Coast, but also that of its social and political evolution. The object of the present analysis is to go back over the modalities and components of the crisis, and to examine the various explanations that have been advanced for it. Due to a previous general and unfortunate underestimation of socio-political variables, we also propose to clarify the crisis through a look at the evolution of the Ivorian patrimonial system.

Some interpretations of the Ivorian crisis

It is possible to pinpoint two broad types of interpretation in the economic analyses of the Ivorian crisis. This binary distinction should be considered here as simply indicative: it is based upon the emphasis given to either situational content or structural content in the explanation. This examination will allow us to be more specific about the economic vicissitudes of the country over the last ten years.

Official versions

These do not provide the best possible understanding of the crisis. Governmental speeches are either blind, or partial, or contradictory because they respond to immediate political interests. What is essentially at stake here is the question of political control, survival in power and the legitimacy of those in office. Thus one should not be astonished, for example, by ambiguous declarations from the Ivorian president at the same time complaining about the rise and fall of the dollar.[2] Equally, one must note with prudence the bluster of the authorities in Abidjan regarding speculators hidden behind the markets, who prevent the establishment of the 'just price' so ardently called for by the Ivorian government for coffee and cocoa. Specialists in the marketing of these commodities have clearly shown that prices correspond to the balance between production and consumption.[3] Finally, one remembers the hasty announcements of the 'end of the crisis' which were made by the Ivorian leaders towards the end of 1985, although the improvement in the situation was only temporary.[4] The analysis of the official positions over the crisis, interesting more from a political point of view than an economic one, merit meticulous examination. Between 1978 and 1980 the crisis was denied by government circles, and the type of economic policy which was then applied perfectly expresses this refusal and/or blindness. In a second period (1980–2), the crisis was recognised but only in a euphemistic fashion as regards its scope, the government being inclined to see the imbalances as a result of economic jolts of external origin (unfavourable international environment). However, the first batch of austerity measures was put into place at this time with the assistance of the IMF and the World Bank. The crisis only seems to have been recognised as such on the occasion of the severe and quite exceptional drought of 1983; the government resolved after a lot of hesitation to solicit the first recycling of its foreign debt. The first improvements in export receipts (1985) soon encouraged people to think that the crisis was a thing of the past. But the return of very weak world markets (scarcely higher than the prices paid to the producers) obliged the authorities to face the facts by declaring the country's insolvency in the month of May 1987.

This oscillation from fundamental blindness to partial lucidity, interspersed with uneasy denials and circumstantial underestimations, is revealing. The hesitancy of the diagnosis betrays, at the highest level of power, the

61

anxieties attached to some of the ideological and even economic foundations of a regime which has long prided itself on being able to bring about expansion and assure social integration. The sudden impossibility of fulfilling the 'contract' (whose terms were of course fixed by the authorities) and of respecting the challenge (one recalls Houphouët-Boigny's public challenge to Nkrumah at the time of Ivorian independence) helped to produce a phenomenon of cognitive dissonance in the perception of the crisis among the Ivorian ruling class. These fluctuating stands also show a set of dispositions which had been taken in circumstances of strong growth and which therefore prevented clear thinking in the new situation.

Situational interpretations

In an abundant literature, one may give particular attention to the analysis of Neil B. Ridler.[5] According to this author, the Ivorian crisis paradoxically originates with the boom market for coffee and cocoa between 1975 and 1978; the effect of this was greatly to improve the country's balance of payments and, as a result, the surplus accumulated by the Caisse de stabilisation. This gold mine helped to finance the investment and capital goods budget. But the rise in the markets of course did not last, quite considerable downturns ensuing until 1981. However, public investment operations were undertaken on the basis of these formidable export receipts. All analysts agree upon the perils of financial investments made on the basis of exceptionally advantageous coffee and cocoa prices, and they underline no less unanimously that many development and capital goods deals were made hastily, regardless of official plans, and often from motives of political opportunism or considerations of prestige, with poor prospects of profitability.

The consequence of these decisions, as Ridler notes, was a very significant increase in public spending (from 187 billion CFA francs in 1975 to 530 billion CFA francs in 1978), according to World Bank sources. In order to complete the financing of these ambitious programmes, Ivorian officials resorted to foreign loans, principally from private financial institutions. Thus is explained the tenfold increase of the external public debt (of which close to 50 per cent was drawn in dollars) during the same years.

While the downturn in the coffee and cocoa markets persisted, the dollar soared upwards (with a corresponding depreciation of the French franc and consequently the CFA franc) as did interest rates; as a result debt servicing became more and more of a burden. The ratio of debt servicing to annual export receipts went from 9 per cent in 1975 to 11.2 per cent in 1977 to 25.9 per cent in 1981 and reached 37.3 per cent in 1983. If the debt had not been recycled in 1984, the repayments for that year would have approached 500 billion CFA francs or more than 60 per cent of export revenue. The recycling negotiated with the Paris and London Clubs, in reducing the service on the debt by around one half, brought the authorities in Abidjan some initial financial relief.

Ridler recognises that this outcome gives some apparent justification to those analysts who doubt the possibility of development based on an economic policy of a maximisation of comparative advantage. But he principally blames the behaviour of Abidjan authorities fascinated by the price explosion in the commodities markets. He furthermore sees a certain importance in the delay of the Ivorian rulers in reducing the level of public spending at the time of the market fall; he estimates this delay at two years. Other authors developing a 'situational' explanation strongly insist on the nature of economic and financial decisions taken during the years of the market downturn, which appear to them to have been largely out of step with the rapid deterioration of the country's principal indicators of resources, debt, and economic activity.[6] Many experts agree on this point, whatever their interpretations of the crisis might otherwise be. Investment continued to develop as spending in the public sector rose until 1982; the surpluses stored up during the peak of the boom were thus entirely squandered, the authorities behaving as if the high markets were going to last forever (or reappear). They did not modify their economic policy even after the gold mine had disappeared. The pursuit of these programmes accentuated the call for foreign loans precisely because of the drying up of state revenues and the paucity of local savings. These vicissitudes are obviously not all the direct consequence of the comparative advantage model.

This type of analysis then insists on the circumstantial status of those factors selected as having provoked the crisis, which does not appear as inescapable or insurmountable. More judicious internal financial and economic choices, and quicker responses to the ups and downs of the international situation, would thus have limited the size of the imbalances and permitted the model of growth to perpetuate itself.[7] The over-investment and over-indebtedness of the years 1975–8 are thus among the situational factors most often called into question in this type of explanation.

Structural interpretations

In his mission report of 1978 the expert assigned by the World Bank, B. den Tuinder, had already drawn attention to some profound imbalances created or accentuated by the mode of growth in the Ivory Coast.[8] Put together before the advent of the crisis, the analysis had the merit of pinpointing the limits being reached by the country. Its author most notably indicated:

that the necessary diversification in agricultural production had henceforth to extend to areas where comparative advantage was less;
that the cost of industrial development, though necessary, was rising more and more, and was correlated to a process of import substitution that was stifling;
that the exhaustion of forest resources would lead to a substantial loss of export earnings;
that foreign investments would become rarer and more costly, the best opportunities for profit having already been taken.

However, while developing a serious critique of the Ivorian economy, den Tuinder expressed confidence in the possibility of adapting economic policy to the new challenges and old constraints, as well as making business management more rigorous. This would allow the country to 'get over the hump ... The essential flexibility of the Ivorian economy and the record of its management suggest that it will find an adequate solution.'[9]

One of the best examples of a fully structural type of interpretation is the analysis of G. Duruflé.[10] This expert is fully aware of the immediate factors which damaged the international environment of the Ivorian economy after 1978. This deterioration, perceptible from the end of 1978, is however only seen as the trigger mechanism or amplifier of existing imbalances in the Ivorian economy that had been concealed by the extremely favourable economic situation between 1976 and 1978.

The genesis and components of the blockage according to this analysis can be summarised as follows: foreign trade created a regular rise of imports (of goods and services but also of factors of production) provoking a progressive deficit in the balance of payments which was accentuated by the increased burden of debt servicing. This irresistible rise of imports (of goods and services but also of factors of production) is explained through the basic orientations of the Ivorian economy: extroversion (for labour and capital); stifling of the industrialisation process by import-substitution; very high (and thus very costly) standards for infrastructure and capital goods; European-style consumption; large disparities in revenue, etc. As a result there ensued massive profit repatriation, revenue transfers, and the increased burden of debt servicing. Yet it is also noted that the structure of national production has been little modified since independence. Efforts (however real) at diversification in agricultural production, and the processing of commodities (with the setting up of large farm produce complexes) did not prevent the country from remaining dependent on the traditional export crops for the bulk of its receipts: in 1981, for example, coffee and cocoa represented close on 80 per cent of the value of Ivorian agricultural export products.

Potential impediments were however hidden by the very favourable evolution of the commodity markets at certain periods and by public spending during the time of dynamic growth. Thus for a long time the realities of a country remaining for the most part an exporter of a few agricultural foodstuffs did not appear, the limits reached by the industrialisation process were masked, and the non-competitiveness of Ivorian products was hidden.[11] The decrease in economic efficiency moreover is explained by the growing role assumed by the Ivorian state in the 1970s: support for agricultural growth; industrial policy; intervention to reduce some of the serious disparities created by economic expansion; development of social, health and educational services; capital goods financing (notably in urban housing) for the benefit of civil servants.[12] Consequently, the costs attached to the development of public power had a tendency to increase the search for external financing. This financing, only slightly productive, generated basic imbalances attested to by the increase in public spending as compared to GNP (this ratio reaching 42.7 per cent in 1978)[13] and the expansion of foreign borrowing.

Duruflé sees blockage factors as deep-seated and long standing, corresponding to the model of accumulation and growth. The existence and weight of situational factors are not ignored, but they are denied an explanatory power for the crisis; from this perspective, the way out of the crisis presupposes profound structural modifications.[14]

The affinity of this analysis with Samir Amin's famous study in the early years of Ivorian independence is obvious.[15] In the eyes of Samir Amin the conception of the Ivorian crisis (of which there was then only a premonition) rested essentially on external financial imbalances irresistibly provoked by exporting a large part of national savings in necessary payment for foreign capital invested in the country, and for repayment of loans contracted outside the country. But, more qualified than other analysts, and aware of a capacity for reorientation amongst the Abidjan authorities, Samir Amin saw the Ivorian *impasse* as probable and not inescapable. In this presentation, however, the crisis most certainly takes on some structural dressing in the sense that difficulties with outside finances were perceived as the compulsory counterpart of the modalities of Ivorian growth.

Other recent analyses of the blockages in the Ivory Coast economy have insisted on different factors and mechanisms. Some authors emphasise the overcapitalisation of industry and the subsequent urban underemployment, against which the Ivorian government struggles with measures that are inevitably very expensive and superficial.[16] Others see in the financial crisis simply the present manifestation of fundamental contradictions in the prevalent mode of accumulation, with enormous transfers from the agricultural sector to the foreign dominated industrial sector; the stagnation of the revenue of rural producers thus prevents the broadening of the internal market, and drains the traditional financial resources of the state.[17] Thus the original conditions for reproduction in this model of growth may no longer be assured. From this perspective, the crisis that has occurred since 1978, clearly visible in the financial indicators (balance of payment, debt, state budgets, etc.), is a more or less necessary historical fulfilment.

Levels of analysis: sub-Saharan and Ivorian

The number and diversity of the explanatory outlines of the Ivorian crisis no doubt testify to its real complexity, and to the difficulties of grasping its nature and meaning, beyond a general agreement (outside of official spheres) on the gravity and seriousness of the country's problems. Analyses of a situational type tend to neglect the tendency to imbalances in the model of Ivorian growth (stressing dependence, risk of reversal in the financial flow, growth of external indebtedness, exacerbation of social and spatial disparities, etc.), which render it vulnerable to sudden changes in the international environment. We acknowledge that the obscurities and confusions in the various attempts at comprehending the Ivorian crisis will not disappear of themselves and that a supplementary effort of clarification appears necessary. Several sets of problems are, in effect, left hanging by the various interpretations.

One wonders for example whether the vicissitudes of the Ivorian economy since 1978 really comply with those foreseen by the dependency theory of Samir Amin. For Samir Amin the scissor effect that was to stifle the Ivorian economy would come from the reversal of financial flows inevitably created in peripheral countries moving from the stage of development (when economic growth 'miracles' are possible) to the stage of exploitation: the inevitable value transfers to the exterior would thus necessitate not only the maintenance but even the increase of private foreign capital investment and external public aid. For Samir Amin, the improbability of an unending rise in external capital thus necessarily led to the impossibility of self-sustained growth and to a blockage of growth.[18] This scenario is seductive and internally coherent, but one must not ignore the fact that all this referred to the international financial framework of the 1970s, a decade characterised by a high rate of inflation and by the problem of recycling the dollars that the oil economies could not absorb. This resulted in a relatively low cost of indebtedness and easy access to credit. Many Third World countries thus responded to (and the Ivory Coast was more attracted than other African countries by) the propositions of American and European private banking institutions. The quick and persistent downturn in the commodities market and a global movement towards deflation, components of a veritable reversal of the economic situation after 1978, aggravated the consequences of debt contracted in the preceding period. These external fluctuations have thus weighed rather more on the Ivorian economy than have those 'objective laws' of accumulation at the centre which lead the dependent country to a net capital export.[19] These external vicissitudes do not appear to be inscribed in the 'genetic programme' of the Ivorian model of growth, even if the latter is naturally more sensitive to the erratic movements of the world economy, due to its extreme extroversion.

The second consideration which should be taken into account is the continental dimension of the crisis. Most African countries have been deeply affected by structural adjustment (irrespective of whether the programmes of stabilisation have been conducted with the IMF and World Bank) whatever their productive structures, economic orientations, or political tendencies. All African states know the painful problems of foreign indebtedness; all or almost all are grappling with deficits in their balance of payments and their public finances as well as blockages in their production. The stifling of the industrial process, sometimes perceived as inherent in the Ivorian crisis,[20] is generally acknowledged by other specialists to be a continent-wide phenomenon.[21]

The problem then is to know how far one can attribute these phenomena to the Ivorian model of economic growth alone. A lot of confusion and misunderstanding arises from an insufficient precision concerning the level of analysis and explanation. Some observers have a tendency to reproach the 'Ivorian system' for a certain number of developments which are also the lot of other countries with a quite different mode of growth and system of accumulation. On the other hand, one might submerge the products of properly Ivorian economic orientations in a globalising approach. This is why the identification of two types and two levels of model, the sub-Saharan model on the one hand and the Ivorian model on the other, appears likely to improve our knowledge of the Ivory Coast crisis.[22] The sub-Saharan model is characterised by extensive production, an important agricultural export sector, some highly protected industries, an eminent role played in the economy by state power, etc.; the Ivorian model is distinguished by an extreme openness to the exterior, rapid growth, a liberal policy for capital movements, etc. From here on in we must follow the biblical adage 'render unto Caesar that which is Caesar's' as we try to detect which elements of the crisis in the Ivory Coast are products of blockages observed on the continent as a whole (decreasing output, non-innovative overprotectionism, narrowness of the internal market, excessive taxation of the primary sector, and most especially, the difficulty of reaching the intensive stage of production, etc.)[23] and which are the results of imbalances, contradictions and blockages unique to the mode of accumulation in the Ivory Coast (external over-indebtedness, excessive imports in domestic production, a greater vulnerability to external hazards). With this double definition of the operating conditions of the African economy in general and of the Ivorian economy in particular, we believe it is possible to make some advances in understanding the crisis which has rocked the country.

The crisis of the patrimonial system

For a recognition of socio-political variables

Refined and nuanced though they often are, economic analyses of the Ivorian crisis clearly cannot satisfy those who want to understand the shift from a situation of growth to one of recession in all its rich complexity. Constructed at the level of economics and finance, these analyses take account of the behaviour and decisions which have provoked and/or accompanied the ups and downs of the economic situation. But elucidation and treatment of the socio-political variables, seen as external to the economic field, are then expelled from the well-defined universe of economic and financial expertise, and assigned to the specific investigations of the sociologist or political scientist, conforming to the principle of the division of intellectual labour into juxtaposed and tightly compartmentalised disciplines. Yet thus to push aside social and political considerations, which are linked to the mounting crisis of the country, but seen as outside the field of comprehension of 'pure' economics, may deprive us of an opportunity to understand this crisis.

Let us argue from two practical examples. In the first place, all observers[24] have noted that during the 1970s the Ivorian authorities, abandoning the principal industrial projects of the Third Plan (covering the 1976–80 period), embarked upon some operations which were not in the programme and which revolved around prestige amenities or operations that resulted in the development of the service sector, of a very uncertain profitability (building an inland capital city, at fabulous cost, in the President's home town of Yamoussoukro, is only one of many very costly projects), or equally, as in the service sector, operations whose direct financial effects were to deepen the balance of payments deficit due to the large import content in the growth of this sector.[25] This departure from the plan of public investment, this all-out spending explosion, obviously incited by growing liquidity drawn from the coffee and cocoa markets and from easy recourse to foreign credit, cannot however be understood without reference to the specific internal political conditions in this period. When one remarks that the Ivorian leader, over the years between 1971 and 1980 and within the scope of Loi-Programme investment alone (leaving aside other financial sources and procedures that were used), succeeded in mobilising for the sumptuous edification of the new capital 8.5 per cent of total budgetary grants while the demographic weight of the new city, according to the most favourable estimations, was in the neighbourhood of 1.5 per cent of the country's total population,[26] one must conclude that the economic and financial situation in the Ivory Coast cannot fully be grasped independently of the models of conduct which prevail at the summit of state power, and pervade the entire politico-administrative structure.

Let us now examine the vast financial waste of the sugar industry programme (whose accumulated losses amount to hundreds of billions of CFA francs). Although it is several years since this scandal was disclosed, the affair continues to weigh upon Ivorian public finances (debt transfers, subsidies, etc.). No one would contest that it is one of the elements of the crisis. One might think, following a structural approach, that this type of programme (hastily conceived, ambitious, poorly prepared technically, economically and financially) was in some way the inevitable mechanical counterpart of the Ivory Coast's extreme openness to the exterior (which is to say, extreme vulnerability). It clearly represents the kind of risk engendered by the basic orientations of the 'Ivorian system'. But one must also admit that the waste created by the sugar industry programme is especially remarkable in its scope. Yet this does not necessarily appear to be linked to the model of growth; amongst other things, it is to be seen in the context of the political climate reigning during the years of expansion, notably, favourable to misplaced enthusiasms (the desire for economic growth in the northern savannah zones), haste (poor preparation of the dossier), and blindness (errors of foresight regarding world sugar consumption).

This 'affair' indeed comprises a political dimension which comes to overdetermine or to markedly shift the orientations of the Ivorian model, until now understood strictly on the economic plane. In other terms, in elaborating models of exclusively economic and financial components, the available analyses on the Ivorian crisis reveal the limits of their deductive capacity. The social and political parameters are not reducible to simple external variables, all too conveniently brushed aside; neither do they constitute a simple 'backdrop' with the economic and financial crisis unfolding on the countryside in the foreground, it alone important and worthy of interest. The accountable large-scale developments stressed by interpreters are the economically constructed result of multi-dimensional social practices (systems of action and belief) and indissociable from these systems. This is why the evocation of things which occurred in the 1970s on the plane of politico-administrative behaviour and power relations will allow us to complete the set of internal determinations of the crisis that the identification of an Ivorian model enabled us to put together.

The explosion of patrimonialism

The deficits of the external accounts of the country and of state finances, the breathtaking rise in foreign debt, both essential indicators of the Ivorian crisis and obvious targets for the diverse programmes of structural adjustment,[27] seem more understandable if one recognises the social and political conditions in which these imbalances appeared, and especially the practices which generated them.

Beyond the formal and official institutions, organisational charts, and machinery which serve as supports to the regime, beyond the appearance of behaviour oriented by principles of bureaucratic rationality (in the Weberian sense of the term) or activities deployed according to universalist norms (in the Parsonian sense of the term), we know very well that social and political relations in general, as well as the models of behaviour within or around the state, come under the heading, 'patrimonial'. This latter term covers the clientelism characteristic of relations between persons and groups (relations of dependence generating an exchange between persons or groups controlling disparate but complementary resources) as well as a specific logic of the management of collective or public resources. This logic tends to efface the boundaries ordinarily established by bureaucratic rationality between the domain of the duties of office and the domain of personal affairs, and between the private and public spheres of activities, interests, and patrimony.[28] These classic concepts shed light upon the Ivorian situation. After the pioneering works of A. Zolberg, the analyses of M. Cohen, and the observations of J.-F. Médard,[29] the most interesting later studies of Ivorian political society entirely confirm the good health of the patrimonial system.[30] On the one hand, the whole of society is well and truly framed in a vertical manner by the structure (profusion of networks) of clientelism, and on the other, particularly as concerns the politico-administrative sphere, one observes behaviour whereby public resources give way to quasi-private appropriation.

69

The majority of the administrative and parapublic positions that carry any weight are allocated according to only vaguely meritocratic criteria, and the operation of the machinery is clearly that of a predatory economy. Yet a very important portion of the Ivory Coast's financial imbalances (and, thus, an essential contribution to the crisis) comes from the public enterprise sector (state firms, public establishments and mixed economy firms), precisely where patrimonialism is found in an almost ideal state. One may, for example, point out that at the beginning of the 1980s more than half of the public external debt was attributable to ten or so parapublic concerns.

Some very appreciable transformations, which have affected this system over the last fifteen years, can be summarised with the following schema. Until the end of the first decade of independence the clientelist structure was of a neatly pyramidal type, tightly run and controlled at the top; thus, for example, the financial monopoly then constituted by the Caisse de stabilisation guaranteed that the central regulation of the patrimonial game was in the hands of the national leader. The rapid accumulation of available funds, brought about by the enhanced value of export receipts and the abundance of foreign credit (to which, notably, the managers of parapublic firms succeeded in gaining direct access) sharply modified this initial configuration. The pyramidal structure was transformed little by little into a segmentary structure, each agent who controlled a network and each holder of a resource in the universe of patronage claiming a growing autonomy.

This process of segmentation reflects the exponential liberation (truly remarkable after 1975) of the strong patrimonial tendencies at work in the Ivorian public sphere. This was precisely when the Ivorian economy became overheated, and was taken over by inflation in all areas: public spending and investment, external debt and internal consumption, imports and deficits, etc. Yet a structural interpretation of a strictly economico-financial nature, even if it does allow for the explanation of the compelling and linear rise in imbalances, only imperfectly accounts for their very strong accentuation in the 1970s. The feverish evolution of the indicators can, by contrast, be easily understood from modifications in the patrimonial formula. The crisis in the Ivory Coast as described in the first part of this study is also, in a certain sense, a crisis of the patrimonial system in its two dimensions: crisis of patronal authority but also crisis of the patrimonial economy.

The principal decisions and public policies that have attracted attention these last ten years, and which can be analysed as so many attempts to revive presidential control, correspond to a recentralisation of the patrimonial regime on the part of its leader. These comprised ministerial changes on 20 July 1977;[31] electoral reform from 1980 with the abandonment of the single national list practised for twenty years and the transition to a semi-competitive regime; numerous modifications in the ruling authorities of the single party at the 1980 and 1985 congresses; the disgrace of the party's secretary-general, its veritable boss, in 1980; successive alterations of the constitutional text in its dispositions governing presidential interim and succession.[32] Houphouët-Boigny's reorientations aimed to arrest the patrimonial explosion, both cause and consequence of the remarkable increase in public spending. There was also a reduction in positions of power supported by networks of accumulation (of people and wealth) which had profited from the general stability of posts and functions. This evolution finally called into question the highly centralised regulation and unique leadership of the system.

The factional struggles of this period (commonly described as 'the battle of the barons') bear witness to the clientelist and patrimonial acceleration among the political leadership. They also bear witness to the competitive logic which brought about this agitation and which threatened to sweep away *le grand patron* by eroding the core of his institutions. Other 'bosses' had emerged who controlled powerful networks and reigned over fortunes that allowed them also to accumulate resources and followers.

This interpretation implies that many analyses of the Ivorian regime of this period, by emphasising its strong personalisation and its authoritarianism (no doubt still very real), have tended to overestimate the presidential control exercised over the political system.

The various scandals (embezzlement, misappropriation of funds, etc.) since the 'spirit of July 1977' officially opened the fight against corruption (Logemad trial, the dismissal of mayors in large towns such as Man and Korhogo as well as secretaries of party sections, 'scandals' like that of E. Dioulo, etc.)[33] have probably made high officials surrender to the reaffirmed leadership of the Ivorian president, reminding them, if need be, that the means existed to deprive them of benefits that would only be renewed on grounds of proven loyalty.

The very important reforms implemented in the parapublic sector from the summer of 1980 can also be understood as a response to the crisis of authority. The segmentation of patrimonialism had engendered financial excesses under the form of tremendous liberties and liberalities progressively captured by the people in charge of numerous parapublic bodies.[34] The evolution of this sector shows the metamorphosis of the Ivorian patrimonial system and its financial consequences, with practices placing the economy of the country in real peril and justifying the adoption of a particularly drastic structural readjustment programme.

In his battle to reimpose his leadership, Houphouët-Boigny has known how to meet the circumstances remarkably well. In an economic situation of austerity and rigour, he has had the tactical sense to let the electors do some of the 'dirty work', by entrusting them with the task of ousting the extravagant prebendalists of the political class whose stability was threatening the presidential monopoly.[35] He knew how to make 'good use' of the crisis, at a moment when the serious economic disturbances which had been denounced or revealed by financial sponsors provided an opportune pretext for taking the political and financial situation in hand. The coincidence of the political struggle, which aimed towards the domestication

71

of the ruling personnel, and the new requirements of the economic restructuring policy, were not as superficial as might appear. Financial stabilisation and recovery came through the recomposition of the patrimonial system, the redefinition of roles, and through the recentralisation of its regulation. The cause was largely identical (and it is probably this which explains Houphouët-Boigny's responsiveness) to the reforms advocated by the IMF and the World Bank; these also fitted the requirements of his political survival.

The bringing to heel of the country's political class and the drying up of the sources of clientelist enrichment which had put such a heavy strain on national finances constituted two axes of preoccupation. These can explain virtually all of the reforms and reorganisation (and not only at the political level) which have taken place these last few years in the Ivory Coast: the liquidations and reorganisation of public enterprises; the establishment of a strengthened system for their economic and financial supervision; the systematic trimming of management organisational charts in parapublic and administrative structures; the suppression of a variety of important material advantages within numerous parastatal organisms; the suppression of high cost property leases to the administrators (one of the essential sources of enrichment for the Ivorian bourgeoisie); the increased power of the Direction du controle des grands travaux directly attached to the Ivorian presidency and extending its powers over all ministries to the extent that it is generally thought of as a government in miniature; the concentration, also around the presidency, of old and new means of control of government services (financial control, general inspection of public services); the recent decision that the duties of a manager of a company with public financial participation are incompatible with the status of a deputy; the enlargement of the grounds for intervention of the Accounting Office of the Supreme Court; the redefinition of the conditions for granting government backing for loans, etc.

The Ivorian president's plan to regain firm control over the whole of the patrimonial system appears to have succeeded, even if the new austerity and the rationalisation of economic and financial management have necessarily reduced the usual means of presidential patronage. Thus the inclusion in the budget of a growing part of the resources of the Caisse de stabilisation, made inevitable by the financial needs of structural adjustment, has created serious tensions between Houphouët-Boigny and the IMF.[36]

Recourse to the schema presenting the transformations of the Ivorian patrimonial system has permitted us (we hope) to shed more light upon the conditions of the crisis in the country, and better to understand the nature of certain responses to it. But a final qualification is necessary if we are to avoid erecting the patrimonial outline as the exclusive explanation of what has occurred in the Ivory Coast for the last ten or fifteen years. The reality of the crisis quite obviously goes beyond the strictly patrimonial stakes presented above. One of the truths of this crisis is the social violence that it comprises: employment has dropped sharply and state revenue has clearly diminished.[37] Meticulous inquiries have furthermore shown very clearly the sharp deterioration of the resources of the dominated layers of Abidjan society between 1979 and 1985.[38] There is no need to multiply examples. The crisis defines new (and difficult) modes of sociability, new conditions of social differentiation and distinction, new forms of struggle, new relations to the state, which has until now been the effective instrument of transferring benefits to certain categories of Ivorians.[39] Investigation and interpretation in terms of classes promise a rich inspiration, in an Ivorian society which now faces a crisis of real gravity.[40]

6

Ghana: the political economy of personal rule

RICHARD JEFFRIES

The facts of Ghana's agricultural and more general economic decline, from shortly after independence until 1982–3, provide an especially clear illustration of the superior explanatory power of liberal political economy, with its emphasis on mistaken government policies and interventions in the market, over neo-Marxist theory with its emphasis on imperialist exploitation. Yet it is far from clear that such liberal political economy, as presented most notably by Robert Bates, can adequately account for the really very sudden onset in 1975 of so calamitous a decline in fortunes as most Ghanaians were to experience over the next few years.[1]

Even allowing for the distinction between short-term and long-term effects, it is a little difficult to see how the continuing adherence to economic policies which hurt nearly all urban socio-economic groups so severely in 1975–8 can be explained by the government's especial political concern and rationally conceived measures to cultivate or maintain their support. There is in fact a possible line of defence here and I will present it a little later. But, if one is to understand what happened in Ghana during this period, Bates' perspective certainly needs to be supplemented by a view of government as a highly personalist (or neo-patrimonial) machine, seeking to benefit individual favourites or networks of clients with varying degrees of concern for larger social aggregates.[2]

Moving to the more recent past, the very force of the argument developed by Bates for African states in general, and by Rathbone and myself for Ghana, made the prospect of any radical departure from statist, heavily 'urban-biased' policies, as of say 1982, seem exceedingly slim.[3] Flt. Lt. Jerry Rawlings' return to power at this time hardly appeared to lower the odds, since the most prominent, organised group of his supporters consisted of a neo-Marxist intelligentsia, strongly opposed to dealings with such 'imperialist' agencies as the International Monetary Fund and the World Bank, and to the sort of liberalisation programme we had (independently) advocated. Yet, within twelve months, agreement had been reached with the IMF on an economic stabilisation and recovery programme (ERP) as radical as one might ideally have envisaged, and this has since been implemented with quite remarkable consistency and determination.[4] It has also been

75

implemented without resort to any very great degree of political authoritarianism. The revolution has eaten some, though really very few, of its children.
There have been several coup attempts. But the regime has survived, and not
only survived but emerged with what most recent visitors estimate to be
considerable good will even in the urban areas.[5] How has this been managed?
On a practical level, the answer is likely to be of wider continental interest
because the (to many) surprising, if only partial, degree of success of the
Ghanaian experiment has, amongst other factors, influenced the negotiation
of similar IMF agreements by the governments of several other African
states.

On a theoretical level, the whole experience obliges one to reconsider the
view of African government as being quite tightly constrained by the local
configuration of social forces, a view shared with obvious differences of
specific formulation by neo-Marxists and liberal political economists.[6] It is
arguably at the historical level, however, or at least with a historian's
sensitivity to the limits of social determination, that the beginnings of an
answer need to be sought.[7]

The beginning of the deterioration of Ghana's economy can be traced
back to the early 1960s and the 'socialist' phase of Nkrumah's regime. I have
argued elsewhere that this derived from a huge increase in government
expenditure on vastly expanded and largely non-productive government and
para-statal employment: expenditure which was financed by excessive
indirect taxation of Ghana's main foreign-exchange earner and source of
government revenue, cocoa.[8] In addition, policies of, for example, responding
to balance of payments deficits by import-licensing rather than currency
devaluation, encouraged a large increase in administrative corruption and
monopolistic profiteering, at the same time rendering agricultural production, whether for the local market or for export, hopelessly un-
remunerative. Whilst such policies were initially adopted partly on
'nationalist' grounds and partly out of a concern, for political reasons, to
protect the living standards of urban consumers of imported goods, in the
longer term this was bound to be a self-defeating exercise.

So far, so Batesian. The argument is premised, of course, on the
assumption that agricultural smallholders are free and inclined to respond to
price incentives or disincentives. Marxists sometimes respond that the model
fails to consider the elements of class inequality, coercion and exploitation
involved in almost any mode of production, as well as the importance of state
intervention and transfers of surplus from agriculture to industry in most
historical instances of rapid economic development. This is partly correct,
but mostly misconceived. It is true that Bates' argument is phrased in
perhaps excessively universal terms and that, in many historical instances,
one must take account of the facilitating or obstructive role of quasi-feudal
or proto-capitalist rural landlord classes in surplus appropriation and capital
accumulation. The distinctive character of smallholder petty-commodity
production in most African societies, however, lies precisely in the absence of

any such landlord class, or at least in its very incomplete development. Most important, the continuing right of access of virtually all family heads, under customary land tenure arrangements, to sufficient land (in normal years, at least) for subsistence means that there is no sizeable landless class forced to sell its labour power on a regular basis merely in order to subsist. Consequently, price incentives are the *only effective means* currently available to induce increased agricultural production for the market. It is for this reason, and under such conditions, but not necessarily under other conditions, that Bates' argument is broadly valid for black Africa.

This entails of course a rather special limitation, quite apart from considerations of bureaucratic competence, to the ability of African governments, fiscally dependent on agricultural export production, effectively to pursue a policy of rapid, state-sponsored structural transformation.[9] Moreover, attempts to expand the size and extend the role of government too rapidly on this basis are likely to rebound, inducing a decline in its tax base, reducing its effective control over much of the economy, and threatening its financial ability to perform even such basic functions as maintaining the transportation system.

This is clearly, in very broad terms, what happened in Ghana after independence, as indeed it has happened to somewhat lesser degrees in many other African countries. Yet this was, up until 1974–5, a fairly gradual if also steady process; and if one might in retrospect say that the collapse which then engulfed the economy was the logical outcome of policies pursued for some while, there were few who anticipated so dramatic a collapse at the time. The Acheampong regime's so-called 'honeymoon period' of 1972–4 admittedly depended economically on a combination of a fortuitous rise in the world market price for cocoa with an increase in the production of local foodstuffs; and the latter arguably owed more to the previous Busia government's initiatives than to Acheampong's 'Operation Feed Yourself'. The regime's political popularity at this time accrued, in addition, partly from its bold nationalist stance towards the repayment of foreign debts, and partly from its spooning out short-term economic benefits to virtually every socio-economic group it could identify.[10] One can no doubt perceive in the latter strategy the recklessly irresponsible attitude which later informed the resort to printing extra money to throw at any immediate economic or political problems. There are nevertheless good grounds for thinking that the regime not only appeared to be but actually was reasonably honest and patriotically purposeful: 'a boy-scoutish CPP in army uniforms', as Rathbone aptly described it.[11]

From approximately 1975, however, Ghanaians experienced a self-reinforcing downward spiral of political decay and economic deterioration. Somewhat irritatingly oft-repeated as the 'spiral' metaphor has become, the experience itself has thankfully not been repeated on anything like the same scale in more than a handful of African countries. We have to explain, then, a really rather extraordinary economic and political débâcle. By 1978, the

Ghanaian economy was characterised by negative growth, huge balance of payments and budgetary deficits, an acute shortage of foreign exchange and hence a shortage not only of imported consumer goods, but also of essential agricultural and industrial inputs for local commodity production. The transport system, once the pride of Ghana, was literally in ruins, restricting food production for local markets. Inflation had acquired a momentum, pushing 100 per cent, which reduced the mass of the population, especially in the urban areas, to an appalling level of destitution and demoralisation. At a conservative estimate, the purchasing power of a worker's wage had fallen to one-quarter of what it had been in 1972.

This was closely associated, both in the public mind and in reality, with the increasing dominance of the 'black-market', and with an escalation in governmental corruption and commercial profiteering – especially clearly related in the allocation of import licences – which, significantly, gave rise to the coining of a new word to describe it: *Kalabule*.[12] It is important for an understanding of subsequent developments that one appreciates just how seedy and sordid Ghana's 'commanding heights of the economy' became during this period, as 'top officials issued chits to young women who paraded the corridors of power offering themselves for libidinal pleasures in return for favours'.[13] After the experience of previous regimes, Ghanaians were under no Weberian illusions as to the steady historical development of rational-legal bureaucracy and authority. There were many of them nevertheless quite genuinely shocked by the blatant disregard of official rules and popular sensitivities displayed by the Acheampong regime in its later years. The literary skills of the novelist are far better suited than an academic's prose to convey the stench of moral and political rot.[14]

The venality of government leadership exerted its most direct damage on national economic fortunes through the diversion of foreign exchange earnings from cocoa into private bank accounts overseas. In one instance, a whole shipload of cocoa was supposed to have vanished at sea. For the spread of *Kalabule* lower down the scale, Flt.-Lt. Rawlings was later to offer the explanation, 'Fish starts rotting from the head.' Political economists and sociologists are professionally bound to seek an explanation rather in the way in which policies and processes created structural incentives for suitably placed people to pursue their rational self-interest in highly anti-social ways. This approach is certainly better suited than generalised observations of 'moral degeneration' to explain, amongst other things, the timing involved; and it undoubtedly does illuminate why certain types of *Kalabule* practice became very common. It is necessary to disaggregate *Kalabule*, however, if one is to understand the causation of the various phenomena popularly subsumed under this term. It is even more necessary to do so if one is to distinguish mere symptoms from important contributory causes of Ghana's economic disaster during these years.

One policy decision in particular was crucially important here and well illustrates both the mixture of causes and the several ramifications. In 1974

Ghana incurred a large balance-of-payments deficit, primarily as a result of the previous year's OPEC price increase. Acheampong decided, however, not to devalue the cedi but rather to re-introduce comprehensive import licensing. He did so because the public rationale of his *coup d'état* had been the unacceptability of devaluation, which he had presented not only as a confession of economic failure but as an insult to Ghana's masculine independence. It is perfectly possible, even probable, that he had little or no idea of the destructive force he was thus unleashing. But, in any case, the nationalist mystique which subsequently developed around this increasingly symbolic issue was, together with the myth that to devalue was to commit political suicide (a myth whose sole factual basis was provided by Acheampong's own coup against Busia!) far more important than rational calculations of group interest in continuing to deter a sensible approach to Ghana's economic problems, until Rawlings' PNDC government eventually smashed it in 1983.

The OPEC price hikes of 1973 and 1980 have, both directly and indirectly, inflicted appalling damage on the economies of most non-oil-producing African countries. This fact often seems to be allowed to fall between the two stools of liberal political economists' focus on government-induced decline and neo-Marxists' ideological association of 'international factors' with 'Western' (or 'Northern') imperialism. In one sense, Ghana's deteriorating foreign exchange position in 1975–78 cannot be attributed to her inflated oil bill. The international market price for cocoa rose by 150 per cent during this period, reaching historically unprecedented levels. Together with buoyant prices for her other main exports (gold and timber), this more than offset the effects of oil prices and of international inflation on her terms of trade. The fact that one fortuitous benefit cancelled out, as it were, another unfortunate loss does not mean, however, that the latter was causally unimportant, and should not be allowed to obscure the massively destructive blow to any purposeful development planning exerted by such uncontrollable swings and turns of the world economic roundabout. The morale-sapping psychological impact of the OPEC increases on the conduct of government leaders has arguably been more important than the direct economic impact. Moving forward to the 1980s, the experiences of African governments, including Rawlings' PNDC regime, which have remedied many of the policy failings identified by the IMF and World Bank, have painfully demonstrated the continuing obstacles to economic recovery erected by the governments of OPEC members in combination with commercial banks recycling these governments' surpluses in the form of high-interest loans.

Paradoxically, however, it was Ghana's relative independence rather than 'dependence' which made possible the catastrophe of 1975–8. Acheampong was able consistently to refuse to devalue during this period, and at the same time to remedy revenue shortages simply by instructing the Central Bank to print more money, precisely because Ghana did possess an independent Central Bank and her own currency, unlike the members of the CFA franc zone.[15] Liberation from the requirement that convertibility of the domestic currency be maintained also freed government to inflict more damage on the local economy. Acheampong's decision induced a rapidly widening differential between the official and 'black-market' value of the cedi, which partly reflected the loss of confidence in Ghana's currency and partly the economically unjustified increases in the money supply. The differential widened from approximately 1:2 in 1972 to 1:10 by 1978, whilst the annual increase in the money supply rose from 7.5 per cent to 135 per cent over the same period. It has been estimated that, by 1978, 80 per cent of economic transactions in Ghana took place at the 'black-market' rate. The proportion of Ghanaians (even urban Ghanaians) who benefited from so artificially low an official exchange rate was therefore very small, though those who did gain possession of imported goods at this rate were able automatically to make profits of 1,000 per cent. Quite a few of them formed a new class of 'cedi millionaires'. The Ghanaian government found itself in a position where it was levying taxes at the official rate of exchange and at official prices, whereas it was having to purchase many of its requirements at black-market rates. As, at the same time, an increasing proportion of GDP shifted from productive (and relatively easily taxable) to distributive (and relatively non-taxable) activities, the state machinery itself was characterised by dramatic impoverishment and a consequent inability to perform basic functions of, for example, infrastructural maintenance. Mansfield estimates that government's revenue-to-GDP ratio fell from 20.5 per cent in 1970/71 to 15.5 per cent in 1974/75 and then, precipitously, to 6.5 per cent in 1977/8.[16]

This economic structure provided strong incentives to the various transactions popularly known as *Kalabule*. Some of these can scarcely be considered 'extortionate' or 'anti-social' at all. For example, one can hardly blame cocoa farmers for smuggling some of their crop into neighbouring Ivory Coast or Togo when 'real' prices (and in CFA francs!) were respectively six and four times higher than in Ghana.[17] Again, the rising price of imported goods sold by market-women arguably did no more than reflect the increased cost of importing them from neighbouring countries at black-market rates of exchange. In a situation where hyper-inflation rapidly outran increases in salaries, demanding a bribe (or a higher one than previously) was an understandable reaction of junior or middle-ranking government officials to the problem of feeding their families.

Such practices should surely be distinguished from the racketeering operations centring on import-licensing, lorry-loads of rice being driven across the borders on the instructions of military officers, or the straightforward pocketing of 'cocoa money'. Why did the 'boy-scouts' turn into 'mafiosi'? There were strong incentives, to be sure, just as there are to heroin trafficking. Political accountability has been at least very weakly institutionalised in Ghana as in most post-colonial African states.[18] But some heads of government have seen that this not only makes greater demands on, but also increases the importance of, their personal integrity. Somewhere along the line of social determination, the buck has to stop; and taking on the government of a country is surely equivalent, whatever the constitutional variations, to saying that it stops here. Rawlings' 'rotting fish' analogy is surely not entirely beside the point.

Whilst some strategically placed senior bureaucrats undoubtedly made small (or not so small) personal fortunes from *Kalabule*, and others were able to defend their standard of living through involvement on a lesser scale, most members of Ghana's professional middle classes experienced a catastrophic decline in real incomes.[19] If one thinks in terms of relative deprivation, the near non-availability of many imported consumer goods hit them the most severely of all urban-dwellers. Increasingly, they voted with their suitcases. By way of an indication of the scale of the exodus, from 1975 to 1981 some 14,000 trained teachers left the Ghana Education Service, of whom approximately 3,000 were university graduates.[20]

It is accordingly empirically insupportable to suggest that 'the state' under Acheampong was the instrument of the 'bureaucratic bourgeoisie' and its interests. There are of course a number of alternative neo-Marxist formulations of the nature and role of the state in African LDCs, but they all suffer from obvious empirical exceptions and/or serious logical objections. Too many ruling regimes have transparently not furthered the supposedly 'ultimately determinant' interests of metropolitan or 'core' capital, and such capital has all too often failed to establish reliable or subservient successor regimes. The notion of internally divided and ideologically ambivalent 'petit bourgeois' regimes, quite apart from making a broad residual category out of Marx's more specific and very different class designation, turns out to be quite empty because capable of accommodating almost any conceivable ideological or policy orientation. Similarly, the 'relative autonomy' of the ruling bureaucratic class turns out to approach so closely to the 'absolute' that one is left wondering just what constraints other classes are supposed to exert. Even the somewhat abstractly Poulantzian concept of the state as 'the instant ensuring the reproduction of the social relations of production' can be accepted only if interpreted so loosely as to mean that no African regime, however bloodily tyrannical, has yet succeeded, to the best of my knowledge, in significantly lowering the rate of population increase. Assessed by any more specific criteria, it is obviously wrong in that a regression from commodity towards subsistence production is extensively apparent.

Professionals and students led the opposition to Acheampong, demanding a return to civilian rule. A students' demonstration in May 1976 initiated a series of confrontations, including a notably effective professionals' strike in July 1977, courageously maintained and repeated in the face of fairly brutal government repression. In September 1976, Acheampong first mooted the idea of a 'union government' (UNIGOV) which, he claimed, had suddenly come to him in a dream. He then had to be pressured, however, into taking each next step: to appoint the Koranteng-Addow Committee to formulate a more specific proposal in the light of civilian views; then to agree to a referendum on this proposal; then to name a date (1 July 1979) for military withdrawal.

Through all this, and with the economy collapsing around him, Acheampong steadfastly maintained his belief that no-one could govern better and that, even more certainly, no-one else was going to get the chance. Deliberately vague as government presentations of 'Unigov' invariably were, the notion was commonly perceived as a thinly disguised attempt to limit (non-party) civilian representation to one element, along with the military and the police, in a tri-partite structure and to ensure Acheampong's own 'election' as president. One might perhaps be forgiven for suggesting that his opponents were spurred on not only by their anger at his destruction of their country's economy, but also by the absolutely infuriating way in which he consistently insulted their intelligence. The whole show became increasingly farcical. Public meetings of the People's Movement for Freedom and Justice (PMFJ), formed by leading civilian political leaders to canvass for a 'No' vote in the referendum, were broken up by variously titled groups of pro-government activists, the financing of which must have accounted for a substantial part of the year's 135 per cent increase in the money supply. At one stage, an American evangelist, Clare Prophet, was wheeled out to declare that 'Unigov' was obviously divinely inspired because its tri-partite structure corresponded to the Trinity. The Electoral Commissioner was obliged to flee for his life on the night of the referendum when he tried to insist on the legal arrangements for the counting of votes. It seemed more than purely coincidental, therefore, that most of the results – supposedly producing a majority in favour by 54 to 46 per cent – were announced on 1 April: 'April Fool'.

This was thankfully to prove Acheampong's last real stand. Not only had injustice been done, it had been seen to be done. Following a wave of protests and detentions, he was displaced on 5 July 1978 by a 'palace coup' led by Lt. General Fred Akuffo, who promised, more credibly than his predecessor, an early but orderly return to civilian rule. The student-professional alliance thus achieved a notable degree of success and certainly demonstrated that civilian attitudes remained a force of some consequence in Ghanaian politics. At the same time, one should note that this alliance was distinctly fragile and increasingly conditional as many student activists, under the influence (direct or indirect) of Western academic 'dependency' theory, turned to a radical neo-Marxist perspective on Ghana's economic decline and political decay.[21]

It is important also to consider why most groups of unionised workers did not actively support the professionals and students or move against Acheampong in any other way. The TUC secretary-general actually came out, on the eve of the referendum, in favour of Unigov. At one level, the simple answer is that the leaders of the TUC, including the general secretaries of most of the component unions, were bought off and that democratic processes within the unions were largely suspended. Acheampong was also adept at timing wage increases. His announcement of a 100 per cent increase in the minimum wage in July 1977, for example, though by no means sufficient to compensate for the erosion of real wage levels in previous years, and soon to be swallowed up by further inflation, did at the time appear sufficiently generous to head off the possibility of a general strike in support of the professionals. This was accompanied by propaganda, to which many unionised workers were by no means unreceptive, stressing the elitist and self-interested nature of the professionals' action and recalling their leading role in the Progress Party regime (1969–72) which had attempted to abolish the legal status of the TUC. At a deeper level, however, the effectiveness of such techniques was facilitated by the general demoralisation of the working class in a situation where the lack of essential inputs meant that both public corporations and many private firms were operating more as social welfare institutions than as genuinely productive or profitable enterprises. The railway workers of Sekondi-Takoradi – historically an especially militant and powerful group – were especially enfeebled by the knowledge that their wages were being paid only through monthly subventions from the government to the railway corporation.

The brief Akuffo regime (Supreme Military Council II, 5 July 1978 to 4 June 1979) had two public faces. On the one hand, it implemented a number of well-intentioned if unpopular economic measures (including a 60 per cent devaluation of the cedi), released the political detainees, dismissed the most notoriously racketeering members of the previous regime (including Maj.-Gen. E. Utuka, commander of the border guard, later to be executed by the Armed Forces Revolutionary Council), appointed a Constituent Assembly to formulate a new constitution and, from 1 January 1979, legalised the formation of political parties to contest general elections scheduled for June. On the other hand, it did nothing to bring to account these same racketeers. Although Akuffo had sought to justify his coup on the grounds that Acheampong had been running the government as a 'one-man show', the latter was merely stripped of his military rank and confined to his home village. None of his assets were to be confiscated by the state and no legal moves instituted against him. Increasingly, Akuffo's rationale was seen as a ruse by the members of the Supreme Military Council II to exonerate themselves from a blame which they shared. As the date of the elections approached, rumour spread to the effect that deals had been struck with the main political parties guaranteeing immunity from any legal proceedings after the handover of power.

The very imminence of the return to civilian rule brought to a head feelings of injustice and frustration which had been mounting within the military. The distribution of privilege had become as grossly unequal within the armed forces as in society at large. The ranks had suffered the hardships caused by the regime of pillage and, in addition, found themselves the butt of insults directed by civilians against the military as a whole. It was in this situation that Flt.-Lt. Jerry Rawlings was arrested for leading a mutiny on the night of 15 May. Amazingly, the state-owned press was allowed to report his court martial at which the prosecuting attorney recounted Rawlings' motives with evident sympathy. On the morning of 4 June he was sprung from gaol in the course of what was less an organised coup than a general uprising of the ranks. Later in the day he was nominated by the ranks as chairman of the Armed Forces Revolutionary Council (AFRC).[22]

Insofar as there was a shared conception of the aims of the coup, therefore, this was provided by Rawlings' supposed views as recounted at his court-martial:

> People were dying of starvation in the teeth of a few well-fed who even had a chance of growing fatter, and when the economy of this country was being dominated by foreigners, especially Arabs and Lebanese whom successive governments had failed to question about their nefarious activities. The first accused then started talking about widespread corruption in high places...[which] could be remedied only by going the Ethiopian way.[23]

The irony of the situation was that Rawlings had been seeking in such statements to convey the attitude of the ranks, not his own preference, which was rather for a non-violent 'house-cleaning' within the military. His point was that, if this were not effected, there might well be a bloodbath. On 4 June the latter alternative seemed all too likely. He set out to try to avert this and to channel rank-and-file anger and energies in more fruitful directions. In this sort of context, it is sometimes difficult to separate a primitive desire for vengeance from an historically progressive assertion of the principle of government's popular accountability. Indeed, it is not at all clear, in some instances, that the same basic drive is not simply being presented in pejoratively different vocabularies. It is nevertheless distressing to find some accounts of this episode equating a desire to kill with a 'revolutionary' position by comparison with which Rawlings was a mere reformist.[24]

It was initially very uncertain, not only to worried observers but to Rawlings himself, just how much direction over the purging process he would be able to exert. Prior to his court-martial, he had been a virtually unknown air force pilot. As of 4 June, the whole of the command structure within the army had broken down and, around noon that day, Rawlings is reported to have sought refuge on the Legon university campus, believing that all officers were going to be shot. His achievement in bringing this potentially anarchic situation under control was undeniably a remarkable one. It required, in the early days, his jetting about from one military base to another around the country, remonstrating with the ranks and defusing potential explosions of violence. It depended critically on the magic of his quite extraordinary physical presence and oratorical powers. And it drew strength increasingly from the extent and intensity of civilian identification with his leadership over and against distaste for acts of violence and arbitrary victimisation by the common soldiery. As the latter implies, his growing idolisation by many civilians fed, paradoxically, on his continuing lack of total control and consequent civilian feelings of insecurity. Such feelings were far from being confined to the 'middle classes'.

Rawlings' control of the 'house-cleaning' process was, then, at least until the end of June, very uncertain. He did, nevertheless, manage to establish certain basic principles and general guide-lines for the punishment of 'exploiters' which roughly reflected his own sense of what was just. In somewhat ideal-typical fashion, this might be summarised as follows. He thought it important to distinguish between the prime responsibility of a few government leaders, the opportunistic self-enrichment of a larger group of senior military and bureaucratic officials together with local and foreign businessmen, and the more or less unwilling participation of very many ordinary people in the system of *Kalabule*. A crucial turning-point here was his negotiation of an agreement with rank-and-file leaders that he would go along with the execution of eight senior military officers, including three former heads of state – Afrifa, Acheampong and Akuffo – only on the understanding that there were to be no further capital punishments. Prior to this, these rank-and-file leaders had drawn up a list of almost one hundred officers whom they wanted to be executed. Subsequently, approximately fifty military officers, senior government officials and businessmen were tried by the People's Court and sentenced to long prison terms. Many more individuals and organisations were ordered to refund to the state larger sums which they were alleged to have embezzled or fraudulently obtained. The 'justice' of the People's Court was undeniably somewhat summary and there was no doubt a degree of unfairness in who was and was not brought to account. Yet it is notable how few accusations of unfair treatment were made at the time or have been since. Equally notable was Rawlings' considerable if imperfect success in curbing soldiers' maltreatment of the alleged 'smaller fry'. If, he argued, all those who had engaged in *Kalabule* in one way or another were to be considered legitimate targets of a witch-hunt, where on earth would the process stop? One unjustly treated group, if my earlier analysis of *Kalabule* was correct, was that of the market-women, many of whom had their goods confiscated and some of whom were flogged in public for refusing to sell at 'official' prices.

There was widespread (urban) civilian support for a period of 'house-cleaning' along such lines so long as it was orderly and so long as it was brief. Some especially vocal and visible civilian groups called for more extreme measures, including more extensive killings – primarily the unemployed and university students whose bloodlust sometimes seemed to be even more hysterical than that of the soldiery. But, more generally, Rawlings' line was approved and respected. It is necessarily a subjective valuation that the judgement he displayed, once he began to exercise a more confident control, was both morally sensitive and socially constructive. But it is not just a subjective valuation that he was increasingly able to exercise such control in large part because his own judgement as to what was morally appropriate corresponded closely to what many ordinary Ghanaians felt to be just.

Equally crucial in consolidating civilian support was his early promise that the period of 'house-cleaning' would be quite brief, and that the elections for the return to civilian rule would proceed as scheduled (on 18 June). To be more accurate, this was crucial because there was a growing public recognition of his transparent sincerity and integrity. The social scientist should perhaps restrict himself to the question of a leader's 'credibility', eschewing that of 'sincerity'. It is arguable, however, that in the context of such sceptical and keenly watchful attitudes as Ghanaian civilians entertained towards the military at this time, only so transparently sincere a young man could have established the credibility that he came in fact to possess. Although, moreover, it was pragmatically sensible to proceed with the return to civilian rule, his commitment to doing so did not appear to be the product of mere pragmatism.

Rawlings sought to channel the 'revolution' along socially constructive lines by speaking frequently on the theme of the need for moral reform, for greater honesty and integrity in government leaders, and for the masses to hold government to account by taking their civil rights and duties more seriously than in the past. Ghanaians, he said, had been 'hitting their heads on the ground like lizards' because they were cowards, closing their eyes to the evils perpetrated against them. Although, as we have seen, this was really rather unfair to the leaders of the People's Movement for Freedom and Justice and other movements of opposition to Acheampong, it undoubtedly struck a deep chord. It also logically entailed that Ghanaians should be exhorted to elect their own government and to hold it to account once elected. As Rawlings put it:

> We are trying to get the public to take up its responsibility about its own government. The armed forces is not a time-bomb behind a civilian government... We want to leave it to the civilians... We want to show you that you have been in bondage. We broke your chains for you, now we leave you to go where you want to.[25]

Rawlings is commonly criticised for the naivety of his 'moralising' during the AFRC period, and for his failure to recognise or address the structural causes of *Kalabule* and economic decline.[26] There is an element of truth here: the AFRC's equation of high commodity prices with 'exploitation' was very naive, and its attempts to produce immediate economic benefits for the man-on-the-street simply backfired. The forced sale of stocks of imported goods at controlled prices proved a once-for-all benefit as these stocks were not replenished. Similarly, the supply of foodstuffs from the rural areas virtually dried up at the height of the soldiers' attempt to enforce low controlled prices in the markets. This experience should be kept in mind when considering civilian attitudes towards the prospect of a return to civilian rule and, later, towards Rawlings' reassumption of power. Beyond this, however, the common criticism of the AFRC's achievements tends to miss the relevant points. First, the causes of *Kalabule* lay structurally, as I have earlier attempted to show, in illiberal economic policies together with an especially degenerate form of personal rule. In attacking Rawlings' economic policies, however, most of his critics have in mind not the need for economic liberalisation, but rather some supposed 'socialist' solution. As regards the role of degenerate personal rule, Rawlings was perfectly correct in identifying the problems of integrity and accountability, and in perceiving no easy answer:

> People talk about capitalism as one mode of development and communism or socialism as another mode, but at least they're both on the move, using different paths. They have something in common, namely a certain level of social integrity, a certain national character, a demand for accountability. All of which is missing in most of the third world. But without it, your capitalism or your socialism, or whatever it is, isn't going to work.[27]

Second, the criticism that Rawlings failed to institutionalise a new social and political order, embodying mechanisms of political accountability, would be a criticism by very demanding criteria even if given a fairly lengthy period in which to attempt it. (I shall return to this point apropos the PNDC regime.) As applied to the AFRC regime with its limited control of the army rank-and-file, the conditionality of civilian support, and the brief time-span and limited aims it accordingly set itself, such criticism is patently unrealistic.

Free and fair parliamentary elections do not often take place in the middle of revolutions. It is, as I have attempted to show, an important commentary on the nature of the revolutionary project favoured by Flt.-Lt. Rawlings, as well as on civilian unpreparedness for any further interruption of the promised return to civilian rule, that the elections arranged by the displaced SMC regime for 18 June should have been allowed to go ahead as planned.[28] Rawlings made no attempt, moreover, to interfere with the established arrangements for electoral competition, which were free and fair by almost any standards, and he carefully avoided any expression of preference for one party over another.

The Constituent Assembly established by the outgoing SMC government in January–March 1979 formulated a constitution which was closer to the American than the British model. As far as the method of election was concerned, members of the single-chamber legislature were to be elected from 140 single-member constituencies on a first-past-the-post basis, while a separate ballot was to be held for the executive presidency. The first presidential ballot was to be held on the same day as the parliamentary elections; but, in the event that none of the candidates obtained an absolute majority of all votes cast, a run-off was to be held between the two leading candidates on the first poll.

The elections were contested by only four political parties of any significance. The People's National Party (PNP) was based on the old CPP networks but put forward a large number of young 'new faces' as parliamentary candidates, more highly educated and perhaps more intellectual in their socialism than most of the 'old guard'. The two groups were united by a shared adherence to the memory of Nkrumah, though it would seem likely they remembered Nkrumah rather differently, the young 'progressives' being more familiar with his somewhat romanticised image than with the realities of the later CPP regime. Imoru Egala, a minister under Nkrumah, was the moving force behind the PNP and was expected to be its presidential candidate. After he was disqualified from standing for office, he secured the election of his nephew, the virtually unknown Dr Hilla Limann, as PNP presidential candidate, employing the arguments: (i) that he was an experienced and highly capable diplomat; (ii) that, in view of the crucial role of the northern vote in the elections, it was best to have a northerner as presidential candidate; and (iii) that the fact that he was virtually unknown at least meant that his rivals would have difficulty in finding charges to bring against him.

The Popular Front Party (PFP) was a direct continuation of the former Progress Party which had ruled Ghana from 1969 to early 1972. It is equally important to note, however, that it was not, as some would have liked it to be, an extension or consolidation of the People's Movement for Freedom and Justice (PMFJ) which had led civilian opposition to the Acheampong (SMC) regime and its proposal for a system of 'Union Government'. The PMFJ had succeeded in bringing together many ex-Progress Party leaders with others determined to restore a fully civilian, multi-party political system – most notably, many ex-leaders of the Ewe-based National Alliance of Liberals (NAL) which had provided the main competition to the Progress Party in the 1969 elections. Significantly, however, Victor Owusu and several other ex-Progress Party leaders had played little or no role in the PMFJ's campaign. At a meeting held in Kumasi in December 1978, William Ofori-Atta (an ex-Progress Party Minister) and Lt.-Colonel Afrifa (ex-chairman of the NLC) argued for the formation of a party based on the PMFJ rather than the old Progress Party with its continuing popular image of Ashanti/Brong-Ahafo dominance and favouritism. The reluctance of many ex-Progress Party leaders, however, to accept the possible demotion of status entailed by their incorporation in a new political entity led to the formation of the Popular Front Party on the one hand, and the United National Convention on the other.

The United National Convention (UNC) was, then, largely a Ga and Ewe-based coalition of ex-PP and ex-NAL elements who had joined together in the PMFJ and were dissatisfied with the oligarchic exclusiveness of the PFP leaders. They hoped, moreover, if not to win the election outright, at least to gain a position of considerable political influence through a combination of the unblemished political record of 'Paa Willie' Ofori-Atta as presidential candidate with the very sizeable financial resources of Afrifa.

The Action Congress Party (ACP) was born of the retired Colonel Frank Bernasko's reputation as a dynamic and dedicated Commissioner for Agriculture (and later for the Central Region) during the early and economically relatively successful years of Acheampong's regime. (He had resigned in time to avoid association with the later, economically disastrous years.) ACP mythology – perhaps not lacking a small element of truth – held that he had been approached by farmers' leaders from all over the country to form a party and stand for the presidency. The presence in the ACP's leadership of the internationally renowned Ewe poet Professor Kofi Awoonor could, nevertheless, hardly disguise the fact that it was otherwise composed almost entirely of Fantes, and of distinctly urbanised Fantes at that.

The elections were conducted in as free and fair a manner as might be considered humanly possible under local conditions, with the Electoral Commission drawing on past experience to simplify the polling procedure and to devise a polling technique which was virtually fool-proof against double-voting or other fraudulent practices. Neither the SMC nor the AFRC government openly proclaimed its support for any of the contesting parties; nor did either attempt to pressurise the Electoral Commission to rig the election results in any way. None of the parties subsequently claimed that the elections had been in any way unfair; on the contrary, even the unsuccessful parties praised the work of the Electoral Commission and accepted defeat, superficially at least, in good grace.

The result of the parliamentary elections was a victory for the PNP quite unexpected in the size of its margin over the PFP, winning an absolute majority of seats at 71 out of a total of 140. In the first-round presidential elections, Limann gained 35.51 per cent of the vote compared to 29.66 per cent for Owusu. In the second round, the vast majority of UNC and ACP supporters now turned to vote for Limann, who won by 61.98 per cent to Owusu's 38.01 per cent.

Differences of substantive policy between the parties cannot have played much role in determining the result since there scarcely were any. The parties did, however, project different images, which carried appeal to lesser or greater degrees in different communal contexts. The regional distribution of the parties' successes immediately indicate a pattern. The PNP was able to win seats in all the nine regions of the country, whereas its closest rival, the PFP, though gaining its forty-two seats in seven regions, won twenty-nine of these in Brong-Ahafo or Ashanti. The UNC won one seat (Afrifa's home constituency) in Ashanti, but its twelve others were in either Greater Accra or the Eastern and Volta Regions, i.e., in Ga or Ewe-dominated constituencies. The ACP won seven seats in the Central and three in the Western Region, all Fante-dominated constituencies. It would nevertheless be superficial to conclude that electoral support, except for the PNP, was ethnically determined in any simple manner.

Neither the ACP nor the UNC possessed the finance or organisational network to be able to make much impact beyond the home areas of their leaderships. They were not self-consciously ethnic parties. For the younger Fante, in particular, the ACP of Colonel Bernasko represented a crusading movement based on normative rather than narrowly instrumental identification, which hoped to demonstrate what could be achieved by collective effort under a dynamic and dedicated leadership. It proved difficult, however, to establish much credence in this self-image – which was, after all, partly dependent on the degree to which it was in fact a mass movement – beyond the confines of Bernasko's home area. Similarly, the attempt of William Ofori-Atta's United National Convention to project itself as the party of proven, if somewhat excessively self-righteous, integrity could be readily countered outside Paa Willie's home area by charges that he was too old to provide the energetic self-assertion required of a president under the new constitution, the more especially in Ghana's dire economic circumstances. On the crudest level, this was done by changing the words of the UNC's campaign song – by far the most 'catchy' – so that Paa Willie was alleged to be bound not for Osu (the Ghanaian 'White House') but for Kibi cemetery. The UNC's failure to sweep the Eastern Region came as a surprise only to those who perceived the Region as a solid communal bloc. The PNP, inheriting the CPP's sensitivity to local communal differences, succeeded in playing on the aversion of the Bosume and others to the dominant Akim Abuakwa, Paa Willie's own ethnic group – as well as reactivating their traditionally powerful networks in the area – to win a majority of seats in the Region.

The greatest threat to a PNP victory was, of course, expected to come from the PFP, the successor to the Progress Party of Dr Busia, and the only competitor possessed of a sufficiently extensive organisation to stand a chance of emerging as the largest single parliamentary party. The most self-confident of the PNP's organisers were more than a little surprised when their party obtained an absolute majority of seats, a feat which was generally considered to be beyond the ability of any party in so competitive a multi-party election. Its success in doing so was undoubtedly the result less of its own positive national appeal than of the abysmal failure of the PFP to win more than thirteen seats outside Ashanti and Brong-Ahafo.

Superficially, there were many factors which favoured the PFP victory forecast by the majority of local and outside observers. It could claim to have been ousted prematurely, in its PP manifestation, by the now reviled Acheampong. A certain kind of logic suggested that it should now be given its proper chance. While several ex-CPP leaders had accepted office under Acheampong, Progress Party people had been at the forefront of opposition to his regime and might now expect to reap the reward for their courage and foresight. Above all, perhaps, the PFP leadership claimed to possess those Western friends through whose sympathetic assistance alone the Ghanaian economy might be revived.

The last mentioned argument backfired, however, in part because of the ideological influence of Rawlings and the AFRC which dented the image of the PFP far more than it enhanced that of the PNP. Rawlings' emphasis on the need for collective effort by Ghanaians themselves, his criticism of the predatory role of foreign companies and foreign 'nationals', and, above all, the widespread anger aroused by Britain's condemnation of the execution of eight senior military officers regarded as especially corrupt by the AFRC, all created a mood antipathetic to the idea of reliance on Western assistance. Moreover, Rawlings' personal demonstration of leadership with the popular touch could only serve to throw into harsher relief the distanced and pompous political style of the PFP leaders. Still, the influence of Rawlings was not in itself decisive. The PFP made no serious attempt to improve its public relations, to project itself as a more responsive, less high-handed party which had learned from its predecessor's mistakes. This lack of self-criticism and the presumptuous lethargy of its electoral campaign was in part a reflection of its overweening self-confidence, a result of the superficial advantages which, as explained above, it initially seemed to enjoy. It was in part, also, a reflection of the style dictated by its notoriously arrogant presidential candidate, Victor Owusu, and of his failure to inspire any great enthusiasm for the PFP cause even amongst the most ardent of former Progress Party activists.

Owusu must also be considered largely responsible for public perceptions of the PFP as an Ashanti and Brong-Ahafo based party. His rejection of a possible alliance with the UNC was seen as reflecting his antipathy to the Ewe – his reference to them as an 'inward-looking people' in a speech made in 1971 was still vividly remembered – and to other ethnic groups more generally. In the light of more recent political and economic experience, such an association could hardly have been more damning. After Afrifa, Busia and, far the worst of all, Acheampong, most Ghanaians – with the exception, of course, of the Brongs and Ashantis – had simply had enough of Brong and Ashanti political dominance. If this was, in a sense, a vote against a particular community and its associated political characteristics, it was also, in an equally important sense, a nationalist vote.

The electoral appeal of the victorious PNP was almost as locally differentiated as that of any of the other major parties. But it did, in addition, contrive to weld together its various local manifestations into a more general image of being the nearest thing to a truly national party that Ghana possessed. This was not least because it clearly did possess, by courtesy of the old CPP networks, a nation-wide organisation of impressive durability and vitality. The PNP activists also inherited from the CPP a sense and an image of being in touch with ordinary people and their everyday problems. The interrelationship between national image and local efficacy was perhaps most clearly, and certainly most critically, exemplified in the North where, as Egala had anticipated, the election was effectively won. The edge which the PNP gained over the PFP in most constituencies was not attributable simply to its presentation of a northerner (any northerner) as presidential candidate. (The PFP had the widely respected Tolon Na as its vice-presidential candidate.) Although little was known of Limann, it *was* generally known that he was a self-made man who had struggled to rise from humble beginnings and a particularly disadvantaged area. This held considerable appeal for the many young northerners whose horizons had been widened by some Western education and the recent expansion of rice farming and

91

associated economic opportunities in the north. It was such people whose enthusiasm as PNP activists arguably swung the balance in favour of their party in most northern constituencies. In this sense, the CPP of the south in 1951–54 – the party of mobility opportunities for the young commoners – eventually arrived in the north in 1979.

There can have been few regimes, in Africa or elsewhere, about which it is so difficult to find anything interesting to say as the PNP regime of Dr Hilla Limann.[29] Conversely, though, it is mercifully easy to say very little, and I will therefore just list a few points of relevance to subsequent developments. First, the new government became so absorbed in internal factional squabbles that it found scarcely any time to address itself to the concerns of most Ghanaians, more especially the state of the economy. Second, insofar as it did find any time, it refused to address or even recognise the scale and structural causes of the problem, preferring rather to solicit additional foreign aid and to contract more debts in order just to muddle through. Meanwhile, mass living standards continued to plummet. This was all the more intolerable when scandals broke showing that some government and party leaders were engaged in self-enrichment through corruption and embezzlement. Third, it seems likely that popular disillusion with the antics of both the ruling PNP and the opposition PFP during this period finally broke the mould, the informal two-party system of CPP vs. NLM/PP, which had shaped Ghanaian civilian politics since decolonisation. Fourth, the Limann government's inept attempts first to buy off and then to disparage Jerry Rawlings, to use intelligence operatives to harass him and his close associates, even to denigrate the whole AFRC episode, simply backfired, lending a touch of martyrdom to his already heroic popular status. Notwithstanding the apparent sincerity of his statement in 1979 that he did not wish to be 'a time-bomb behind a civilian government', few were surprised, therefore, when he reassumed power on 31 December 1981, or questioned the justifiability of his doing so.

At the same time, the popular response to this development was relatively sober, if generally favourable, for reasons that are fairly easy to understand. The AFRC intervention had not produced any widespread economic benefits, rather the contrary; and Rawlings had been the first to admit to his limited education, more especially his limited understanding of economics. It was one thing, people realised, to lead a campaign of moral reform, quite another to run a modern government so as to engineer economic salvation in a decidedly uncharitable international environment. The supposed 'experts' of the Limann regime had proved to be grossly economically inept as well as dishonest. One might as well, therefore, have someone who was at least honest even if he should turn out to be administratively inept. But the nagging question persisted, even amidst the popular celebration of his return to power, whether he could provide anything more than honest government in continuing impoverishment.

During the Limann period, Rawlings had become increasingly close to a group of young people who did at least have a fairly clear and self-confident set of ideas as to what was wrong with the Ghanaian economy. This consisted of neo-Marxist intellectuals, mostly university students and lecturers, but also including some junior officers in the army and a number of activists in the labour movement. For them, the problem of the Ghanaian economy and its management was one of 'neo-colonialism', and the main source of the impoverishment of the Ghanaian masses lay, beyond the depredations of corrupt government leaders and officials, in the alleged repatriation of extortionate profits by multi-national corporations as well as in the neo-colonial structure of the economy more generally. More positively, they aimed to achieve a form of socialism in Ghana, a form not very clearly defined beyond a distrust of the profit motive, a desire to foster a cooperative ethic, a determination to destroy the position of the 'propertied classes' and vague allusions to Libyan and Cuban models of socio-political organisation and foreign relations. This group was not new in Ghanaian politics, though it had previously exerted little influence owing not least to the lack of any widespread popular belief in the practicability or efficacy of its ideas. Deriving its intellectual origins and credentials from Nkrumah's theoretical writings (rather than practice) and from education in the 'dependency' school of political economy so popular in both Ghanaian and North Atlantic university circles in the 1970s, it had dominated the leadership of the National Union of Ghana Students (NUGS) since at least 1977. Though sceptical as to the likely achievements of Rawlings' purely populist measures in June–September 1979, it had provided him with his most actively committed support and had, under the Limann regime, developed its organisational coherence, most notably in the form of the June Fourth Movement and the New Democratic Movement.

Several leaders of these organisations deserve mention as being especially close to Rawlings: the two Tsikata brothers, law lecturers at the University of Legon; their cousin, Captain Kojo Tsikata (retired), at one time Nkrumah's representative with the MPLA in Angola; Chris Atim, ex-NUGS vice-president and chairman of the June Fourth Movement; and Sgt. Alolga Akata-Pore, generally attributed with organising and leading the actual *coup d'état*. Members of this group played a leading role in organising the people's defence committees (PDCs) and workers' defence committees (WDCs) which rapidly sprang up in the wake of the coup, especially in the urban areas. They also dominated the Interim National Co-ordinating Committee (INCC), later retitled the National Defence Committee (NDC), charged with coordinating the activities of the local PDCs and with directing the course of the 'revolution' more generally.[30] Their influence was reflected not only in the mushrooming of the PDCs, but also in their definition at this time so as to exclude 'middle class' members. It was further evident in the investigations of the Citizens' Vetting Committee and in the encouragement given to WDCs to take over the management of their firms.

It was in this context that I wrote:

It is at the time of writing impossible to predict, with any degree of confidence or precision, just what economic policies the PNDC will adopt. The composition of the recently announced Cabinet suggests that it is concerned at least not to alienate foreign capital or international financial institutions completely. The eventual acceptance of an IMF package therefore remains a possible, if somewhat unlikely, scenario. As has been argued, the adoption of such a radical liberalization strategy would be to the long-term benefit of the majority of Ghanaians. The problem, of course, is that such measures would be likely to encounter intense resistance not only from vested urban economic interests but from the neo-Marxist preconceptions of many of the students, intelligentsia and radicalized soldiers to whom Rawlings looks for political and moral support. In the absence of a major change of attitude, the implementation of these measures would therefore require a fairly high degree of political authoritarianism.[31]

Yet, in August of the same year, according to an NDC member, 'There was surprise among some of those left-wing elements who had clustered around the PNDC when news leaked out about a possible deal with the IMF.'[32] In the ensuing row, Rawlings sided with the pro-IMF faction. In November the government claimed to have unmasked preparations for a coup attempt in which both Sgt. Akata-Pore and Chris Atim were implicated. Akata-Pore was imprisoned (though only for fifteen months) while Atim fled the country. A number of their associates were also to defect in the course of 1983–84, but the majority stayed on to work with Rawlings.

The defeat of the November 1982 coup attempt helped clear the way for agreement with the IMF on a short-term 'stabilisation' programme, and subsequently an Economic Recovery Programme (ERP). In accordance with this, a series of fundamental economic reforms was announced in the April 1983 budget. These included a 65 per cent increase in cocoa producer prices, a doubling of gasoline retail prices and a hefty cut in the government's budget deficit. Politically sensitive as it was to the widespread urban antipathy to the notion of 'devaluation', the regime chose to introduce its currency measures, which amounted to a devaluation of 990 per cent, as a system of 'export bonuses' and 'import surcharges'. The devaluation was made official, however, in October 1983 and was followed up with a further devaluation and other measures to keep the agreed programme on course in the 1984 budget. If some PNDC leaders initially attempted to square their acceptance of the ERP through an analogy with Lenin's New Economic Policy, any doubts as to the good faith and commitment of the regime's most influential members have since been dispelled by the scale of successive devaluations, the continuing process of economic liberalisation, the steady pruning of the public sector and a determined reduction of budgetary deficits, balance of payment deficits and inflation.

Notable features of the ERP's implementation have been the consistency with which it has been pursued, the realism with which annual targets have been set and the impressive degree to which annual targets have been met or exceeded. Unfamiliar observers might not be terribly impressed by, for example, a GDP growth rate of between 4 per cent and 5 per cent over the past three years, a recent inflation rate of 40 per cent – and falling – or an increase in vital cocoa production from 155,000 tons in 1981 to 220,000 tons in 1986. The significance of such figures can only be properly understood, firstly, in relation to the vicious downward spiral into which the economy seemed to be locked in 1975–81, with negative growth rates and inflation raging by as much as 116 per cent per annum; and, secondly, in relation to the more modest achievements which the World Bank projected as being likely at this stage, given even the most favourable of administrative and international scenarios. On the basis of the same projections, there is at least the possibility, even likelihood, of major and continuing improvements in GDP per capita from now on.

A number of questions obviously arise. First, why did Rawlings, who in the first few months of the PNDC government was still talking in terms of the baneful effects of 'imperialism' and of his admiration for Castro and Ghaddafi, decide to adopt an IMF-World Bank supported economic recovery programme? Second, what has become (and why) of the regime's initial commitment to the enhancement of popular political participation, representation and mobilisation? Third, how has the regime managed to survive while implementing a programme of economic reform which some of us earlier considered to be politically impracticable? More especially here, how has the regime managed its relations with unionised labour and other urban groups which have undoubtedly been required, in the short term at least, to pay a large part of the cost of economic restructuring?

We do not at present possess adequate answers to these questions. The following are therefore intended as merely tentative and very broad suggestions.

The PNDC government inherited a situation of acute economic insolvency combined with a need for a very considerable injection of capital if the rehabilitation of the transport infrastructure and other prerequisites of *any* form of economic recovery were to be effected. Despite their making friendly noises and gestures, neither Libya nor the Soviet Union, nor any other 'socialist' country proved willing to provide much assistance here. Meanwhile, the neo-Marxists in the government failed, perhaps inevitably, to offer any clear, constructive and realistic economic programme. Their newspaper, *Nsamankow*, even declared in August 1982 that, 'the people have shown that, for now at least, they are not very interested in economic demands'. Rawlings became understandably impatient. Only the IMF would provide or, more accurately, would help procure the necessary funding; and the IMF had recently adopted a policy of insisting on very specific 'conditionalities' for the disbursement of loans – conditions which reflected the analysis of Robert Bates and of Elliot Berg's World Bank Report on 'Accelerated Development in Sub-Saharan Africa' (1982).

It would therefore be feasible to explain Rawlings' decision *per se* in terms of his finding himself caught in the pincers of the international political economy on the one side and of Ghana's externally oriented economic dynamics on the other. It is not possible, however, to explain in such terms alone the consistency and even fervour with which his government has taken the ERP on board as an ethical issue, not merely a pragmatic economic exercise in increasing GDP per capita. It is impossible, for example, to read the 'Rural Manifesto' without being convinced of its drafters' genuine sense of moral purpose. Rawlings summarised this in his address to the nation on the occasion of his regime's fifth anniversary in power: 'We are acknowledging the historic debt of the whole nation to the farmer and have thus repudiated the monstrous injustice of a past in which we virtually ran the machinery of the state on the tired backs of rural producers and provided little for their basic needs.'

One cannot, I would suggest, ultimately explain this except as the product of a genuine intellectual conversion on the part of a highly moralistic young man. This should not really be very surprising in view of the influence recently exerted by Batesian economics on many Africanist social scientists. There is obviously a danger that academics who perceive a particular analysis to be logically and empirically persuasive will see no need to explain its adoption by a government leader beyond his having seen the light. But there is a far worse danger of an extremely patronising form of intellectual snobbery according to which genuine intellectual conversion on the part of African political leaders is considered to be extremely improbable. Marxists are likely to be joined by Batesians wearing their 'political rationality' hats in objecting that government leaders' adoption of a particular social analysis and corresponding set of policies can never be understood in a political vacuum, that they can only ever be understood as the product of a particular configuration of class (or group) interests and pressures. In a very loose sense, this is truistically correct. But in any more precise sense, it is either just an ideological assertion, an article of faith; or else simply an heuristic principle which encourages essays in historical and sociological determinism, some of which are very much more persuasive than others. No such essays are likely to be very persuasive in this case because the central fact of Ghana's economic and political experience since 1982, in a sense even since 1979, has been that of Rawlings' personal political domination.

Neither the sources nor the use of this political domination can be explained satisfactorily by the economic dominance of certain classes or by the especial political influence of certain (urban) groups. As of September 1979, Rawlings' charisma – a non-rational though certainly not irrational force – was experienced across a very wide range of urban society but most intensely toward the lower end of the scale. By early 1982, I have suggested, this had developed into a more rationally cautious if at the same time highly supportive attitude. By deciding to back Dr Kwesi Botchwey, the Secretary of Finance, in negotiating an IMF agreement, Rawlings risked alienating the support of those who initially formed the cadres of the PNDC regime, and he did indeed alienate many. Unionised labour became increasingly critical as, in line with the ERP, wage increases were kept below the level of inflation and some 17,000 public sector employees were made redundant by 1985. The drought and bush fires of 1983, though hardly the government's fault, greatly exacerbated workers' desperation and discontent at least temporarily. Most of the very few voices that spoke up for the government at this time belonged to some of the activists in the PDCs and WDCs. Yet Rawlings turned to criticising these organisations and, in December 1984, abolished them.

Why? The PDCs were initially conceived, of course, as forming the base on top of which a pyramidal representative structure would be built, and Rawlings' about-turn has therefore been interpreted by some as indicating his loss of democratising enthusiasm and his increasingly authoritarian temper. There were almost certainly a number of other considerations at work. The operation of the PDCs was highly uneven. Their leaderships were almost always unelected and were often overweening, bullying and favouritistic, hence unpopular.[33] The idealised portrayal of their operation and popular political significance by neo-Marxist exiles in London should not be taken at face value. They were also most active in performing their political functions of representation and ideological education, as distinct from their work for community development in the urban areas. For a government committed to redressing urban–rural bias, it therefore did not make pragmatic sense to enhance the role and power of such organisations. In this sense, the government's policy since 1983 has been the politics of 'economics in command'. In addition, many of the PDCs' leaders at both local and NDC levels were ideologically close and had been personally close to Chris Atim, Akata-Pore and other leftist defectors from the regime. Rawlings probably felt that he could not trust them.

But why, then, has he not put more effort into developing representative (and hopefully supportive) institutions in the rural areas, amongst the agricultural smallholders who are intended to be the most immediate beneficiaries of the ERP? From the perspective of a genuine concern with the development of political representation and accountability, one might respond that this is very difficult to achieve or even to know how to go about, given the character of rural society. Indeed, it is arguably *not for* government to achieve, as distinct from encouraging it, since the history of government intervention or sponsorship in this area (witness the United Ghana Farmers' Council) has been one of the usurpation of control and the twisting of representative functions by government nominees. It of course remains questionable whether we can reliably attribute to Rawlings any such 'genuine concern'. It seems likely, however, judging from the changing tone of his public speeches, that he has remained idealistically alive to this problem but has found it increasingly difficult in practice to refrain from a hectoring and rather schoolmasterly attitude in the face of rural passivity.

In consequence, anyway, the PNDC government now gives the appearance of being suspended in mid-air, lacking any institutionalised social roots. One should be careful here, however, to distinguish the question of the innate desirability of representative institutions from two other considerations. First, the relationship between popular representation and 'good government' is not a simple one. As John Dunn has put it:

> It would be quite unreasonable to anticipate that the cognitive grasp of the dynamics of the world or domestic economy enjoyed by the populace at large will prove systematically superior to that of their past or present African rulers, and correspondingly unreasonable to expect formulations of economic policy in African states to improve merely because of a strengthening of the system of political representation.[34]

Second, there is no simple relationship either between representation and political stability, even if we should prefer to be able to believe otherwise, in the Ghanaian or wider African context. Although his government is not a military government, Rawlings has remained in power to date essentially for military reasons. Here he doubtless owes a great deal to Kojo Tsikata's loyal and masterly supervision of military security and intelligence, but a major reason has also been the continuing high regard in which he has been held by the ranks. This does not mean that his government is currently unpopular with civilians. Reports rather suggest that the popular mood in Accra and elsewhere is one of far greater optimism than there has been for many a year. As his government gains increased instrumental legitimacy from the material benefits it will hopefully soon be producing for many in the urban as well as rural areas, Rawlings may well feel more able to invest popular representative organisations with some real power. Beyond such vague suggestions, however, the future really is very indeterminate. Let me leave the last word to an elderly Ghanaian attending the recent celebrations of thirty years of independence: 'We are like a runner who sets off too quickly, tires, and now he sees he is winning, puts on a spurt.'[35]

7

Liberia

CHRISTOPHER CLAPHAM

The recent history of Liberia may well be reckoned to have followed a course so obvious that it is not only easily explained, but could have been almost equally readily predicted. The Americo-Liberian oligarchy, by which Liberia had been governed since its independence in 1847, had managed to survive the initial explosion of anti-colonial nationalism in the neighbouring territories; but despite its efforts to expand its scope to include elements drawn from the indigenous population, it always provided far too narrow a base for any assimilationist strategy of political integration to have any reasonable chance of success. Sooner or later, the extension of education, migration and the cash economy were bound to foster increasing demands for political participation which such a system could not meet – or not without, at any rate, a rapid and voluntary abandonment by Americo-Liberian politicians to representatives of the indigenous community of key posts, including, notably, the presidency. Otherwise, even though the distinction between immigrants and indigenes had been blurred by intermarriage, and by the growth of a common Liberian political culture based on jobbery and graft, the ability of disgruntled hinterland leaders to appeal to the powerful rhetoric of ethnic exclusion would threaten the dominant coastal minority for long into the future – or until it fell. An economy exceptionally heavily dependent on the export trade in primary commodities would correspondingly be vulnerable to sharp fluctuations in export prices, generated by global conditions well beyond the Liberian government's capacity to control, which could be catastrophic to any regime which relied as heavily as the Liberian one did on the distribution of spoils. If this regime were to fall, moreover, it required no great prescience to surmise that an army already largely composed of hinterlanders would be the immediate source and beneficiary of its collapse; or even that a regime derived from a politically and economically illiterate soldiery would display many of the characteristics of rule by the lumpenmilitariat in other parts of the continent.

All this, allowing for some inevitable simplification, is valid enough. Much of this chapter must accordingly consist in spelling out the details of a process, the basic outlines of which are not in serious doubt. Nonetheless, the

Liberian experience does provide a revealing illustration of the limitations, though also the capabilities, of the West African state. The violent overthrow of a more than century-old oligarchy would seem to have offered the opportunity for a more drastic restructuring of the state and the political system than is likely to follow the ousting of more briefly established post-colonial regimes in other parts of the region. The abandonment of both radical and liberal alternatives, as the new regime was metamorphosed (in a manner all too reminiscent of Orwell's *Animal Farm*) into a bastard descendant of its predecessor, thus suggests the limitations of change within the social and economic structures which the military regime inherited. The constraints imposed by external economic dependence have rarely been more starkly demonstrated; but, in addition, the domestic political structures and modes of operation of the ousted True Whig Party (TWP) maintained a resilience which showed them to be far more deeply rooted than might previously have seemed to be the case. While at one level the Liberian experience has illustrated the incapacity at least of this West African state to change or control its environment, at another it has indicated its ability to survive by filling the niche which that environment prescribed for it.

Survey of events

Small, peculiar, and lacking the links with Western Europe which have followed from colonialism in other countries in the region, Liberia receives little attention either in the European media or in academic discussion, and even Africanists may be forgiven a fairly hazy acquaintance with its recent past. A basic survey of Liberia's recent history may therefore be helpful.[1]

William Tolbert, last True Whig Party president of Liberia, succeeded to office constitutionally on the death of President Tubman in August 1971. Having served as Tubman's vice-president for some two decades, Tolbert was a well-established politician, though (as tends to happen under an American-style vice-presidency) he had been pushed into the background, both by the lack of specific functions attached to his office, and by the awkwardness of his position as the current president's designated successor. Much of his activity had been devoted to the Baptist church, in which he had gained an internationally prominent position. His accession to the presidency marked a change of chief patron, in a system managed largely by patronage, and involved a rapid turnover of individual politicians as Tolbert moved his own men into key positions; all but one of the nine county superintendents, governors of the country's main territorial subdivisions, were for example replaced within a year of Tubman's death. The system itself, however, survived without much change, and even Tolbert's personal supremacy was tempered by the presence of other leading party oligarchs (such as TWP Chairman McKinlay DeShield, or several of the senators from the coastal counties) whose position he could not challenge.

Tolbert differed from his predecessor in personality much more than in policy. Tubman, a man of enormous charm, had governed through the manipulation of personal relationships, while presiding over a rapid economic expansion fuelled by multinational investment (especially in iron ore extraction), which in turn permitted a massive increase in patronage, extending to the hitherto neglected hinterland areas of the country. Tolbert, by contrast, was brusque and insensitive, and had the misfortune to reach power at a time when the boom of the 1960s was giving way to the recession of the 1970s. He had a hectoring manner, illustrated by his habit of descending unexpectedly on government offices and firing officials who were not at their desks, and the turnover of ministers was rapid. His favourite governing device was the slogan or campaign – 'rallytime', 'mats to mattresses', 'the wholesome functioning society' – which he promoted through whirlwind provincial tours, and which his officials obediently echoed in his wake. He continued Tubman's policy of incorporating the hinterland, appointing several bright young men from up-country as ministers – two of whom, Jackson Doe and Edward Kesselly, were to be candidates in the 1985 presidential elections. There was however no channel through which independent interests, organisations or political perspectives, could be incorporated into government.

By the late 1970s, threats were appearing to the long-established True Whig hegemony. Articulate intellectual opposition to the regime crystallised in the Movement for Justice in Africa (MOJA), formed by a small group of radical academics at the university in Monrovia, which used continental issues (notably injustices in southern Africa) as an indirect means of criticising the government at home, and looked eventually to establish a political party in time for the elections due in 1983.[2] It also sought to implement its rural development policies, and to extend its appeal to the most distant parts of the hinterland, by establishing an agricultural cooperative in Grand Gedeh; this was regularly harassed by the authorities.[3] Another opposition grouping, the Progressive Alliance of Liberians (PAL) led by Gabriel Baccus Matthews, was formed among Liberian students in the United States, and transferred its activities to the homeland in the late 1970s. Less radical and more opportunist than MOJA, it likewise aspired to convert itself into a political party, which would mobilise latent opposition to the regime especially among the Monrovia lumpenproletariat, and challenge the TWP at the polls. Both of these movements had a leadership drawn from young Americo-Liberians as well as educated hinterlanders, and both proclaimed policies of national integration rather than explicitly fomenting the settler–hinterland division – though obviously their goals could be achieved only by mobilising an overwhelmingly hinterland following in order to challenge an existing structure dominated by the coastal elite.

Although it was already clear that the TWP supremacy was under challenge, the issue which rapidly propelled these groups from small-scale coteries into national political prominence was Tolbert's attempt to achieve national self-sufficiency in food by increasing the price of rice (the Liberian staple food grain) in order to encourage domestic producers. The classic African conflict between the interests of urban food consumers and those of rural food producers thus precipitated the downfall of the oligarchy. Tolbert's politically disastrous decision to side with the producers may seem paradoxical in a regime based on an urban elite, though it should also be remembered that True Whig politicians had extensive economic interests in the hinterland, and Tolbert himself was rumoured to be in a position to make a financial killing from the proposed price rise. At all events, and even before the threatened increase had been put into effect, its consequences for urban living standards were evident enough to provide the still embryonic opposition groups with the pretext for a march and demonstration at the Executive Mansion (or presidential palace) in Monrovia. Almost inevitably, since neither marchers nor police had the slightest experience in the management of peaceful protest, the demonstration on Easter Saturday 1979 got out of hand; the police fired on the crowd, about seventy people were killed and several hundred injured, and the day ended with the mass looting of shops by both rioters and police.

Like equivalent incidents in the history of colonial Africa, such as the Accra ex-servicemen's march of February 1948, this event dramatically exposed the weaknesses of an unrepresentative but hitherto stable political order. Over the following year the Tolbert regime alternated desperately between concession and repression, while its opponents analogously vacillated between trying to work within the system and hoping to overthrow it. In the immediate aftermath of the riots Guinean troops were brought in to maintain order, duplicating a service which they had already provided in Sierra Leone, but the situation was beyond the scope of a policing operation. The iron ore miners, source of most of the country's export revenue, went on strike. One of the MOJA leaders, Amos Sawyer, announced his intention to stand for election as mayor of Monrovia, confronting the government with a dilemma between letting him fight a fair election (which he would probably have won), and seeking to thwart him with the likely result of fomenting further violence. PAL posed a similar choice by seeking registration as a political party, called the Progressive People's Party, or PPP; this was at first blocked and then permitted, only to be thrown into question once again when its leader Baccus Matthews, apparently carried away by rhetorical exuberance, called on his followers in March 1980 to launch a general strike with the aim of forcing the government's resignation without waiting for the 1983 elections. His inevitable arrest and forthcoming trial in turn prompted the *coup d'état* of 12 April 1980, when a small group of soldiers and NCOs, led by Master-Sergeant Samuel Kanyon Doe, seized the Executive Mansion, killed Tolbert, and established the People's Redemption Council (PRC). Thirteen leading members of the ousted regime were then rounded up, and after the most exiguous of trials, shot amidst a fairground atmosphere on the beach in Monrovia.

The PRC was unique among African military regimes in that ordinary soldiers and non-commissioned officers not only launched the coup itself, but continued to control the government thereafter. The PRC consisted of the original coup group, extended to rectify an ethnic imbalance in favour of Doe's Krahn fellow tribesmen from Grand Gedeh; though several of its members were rapidly promoted to ranks up to major-general, it included no one who had held officer rank prior to the coup.[4] The coup does not seem to have been derived from much more than the resentments of enlisted men at poor living conditions, coupled with an obvious opportunity; there is no evidence of any direct involvement either by PPP or MOJA leaders, or by external powers, and no evidence either of any larger political goals which the coup was intended to realise. Immediately afterwards, the new regime demonstrated both its need for qualified civilians to help run the government, and its complete uncertainty as to the direction which this should take, by appointing a largely civilian council of ministers whose members were drawn from all existing political groupings. Representatives of PAL/PPP and MOJA sat down with three TWP ministers, retained in office from the Tolbert administration, whose leader and colleagues had just been killed under the most gruesome circumstances. The indecent speed with which members of the oligarchy sought to dissociate themselves from the Tolbert regime indicated a dependence of elite groups on the state which has been evident throughout the following years.

Over a period, nonetheless, the improbable coalition put together in the immediate aftermath of the coup was bound to fall apart. At first, this process appeared to go in favour of a progressive radicalisation of the regime. Most of the surviving TWP ministers quietly failed to return from trips abroad, while the MOJA leaders were equipped with the most articulate analyses of the failings of pre-coup Liberia, together with prescriptions for reform. Doe established relations with Libya and visited revolutionary Ethiopia, but this phase proved very short-lived, and Liberia never even attained the radicalism of Rawlings' Ghana, let alone the full-blown Marxism–Leninism of Mengistu's Ethiopia. The reasons for what soon became a comprehensive retreat from any kind of radicalism lie partly in the internal politics of the regime, partly in Liberia's extraordinary level (even by West African standards) of external economic dependence. Doe himself soon proved to have very limited policy ambitions (though extensive personal ones), and was ready to accept the aid and guidance offered by an American government which quickly adapted to the new situation. The radicals tended to gather around Thomas Weh Syen, one of the other two sergeants who with Doe constituted the core leadership of the PRC; the third, Thomas Quiwonkpa, was popular with the troops and remained in charge of the army. The division came to a head in August 1981, over the issue of relations with Libya. Doe won; Weh Syen and four of his supporters in the PRC were executed; and the civilian radicals in the government were dismissed or demoted, or fled abroad.

Subsequent fragmentation, both within the military and among the various civilian political groups, was due not so much to policy differences as to simple competition for state power and the benefits of office, and notably the ambitions of Samuel Doe. The original coup group rapidly fell apart. The execution of Weh Syen and his supporters was followed in October–November 1983 by a split with the remaining strongman, Quiwonkpa. Doe tried to remove him from operational command of the army to a symbolic post as secretary-general of the PRC; Quiwonkpa refused and fled the country, returning in November 1985 at the head of an attempt to overthrow Doe which narrowly failed, with considerable loss of life, including his own. In August 1984, the deputy chairman of the PRC, Nicholas Podier, was arrested in turn, and by the end of 1984 only five of the original coup group of seventeen remained in office. In April 1985 the deputy commander of the Executive Mansion guard supposedly just failed to assassinate Doe; and though there is some doubt as to whether this was a genuine plot, he was rapidly executed.

Civilian support likewise fragmented, although the new regime's all too evident willingness to kill its opponents (in contrast to the less violent methods used by the TWP) helped to cow dissent. At the time of the original coup, only vague assurances were given about any future return to civilian rule, but as the radical option receded, and especially as Liberia became increasingly dependent on American financial assistance and subject to American diplomatic pressure, some kind of Western-style multi-party democracy emerged as the only viable possibility. A Constitutional Commission was set up on the first anniversary of the coup in April 1981, under the chairmanship of the respected MOJA academic Amos Sawyer; he kept going after most of his MOJA colleagues had resigned or fled, and reported in January 1983 with a draft constitution which closely resembled that in force from 1847 to 1980, which itself was based on the US constitution, though without its federal provisions. This was referred to a Constitutional Advisory Assembly chaired by Edward Kesselly, a former Tolbert minister from Lofa county, and promulgated after a referendum in July 1984. The key question involved in the return to civilian rule, however, was whether it would serve as a mechanism for electoral competition between rival civilian parties, as in Ghana and Nigeria in 1979, or whether it would merely provide a means by which the incumbent military ruler could assume a civilian presidency. Sawyer's original draft explicitly excluded members of the armed forces and police from the right to belong to political parties, or even vote in elections, while the thirty-five-year age qualification for the presidency would have prevented Doe from standing. In the event, Doe induced the advisory assembly to change the first of these provisions, and circumvented the second by adding two years to his previously announced age.

Doe's intention to benefit from any eventual civilian constitution had already been signalled in April 1983, when officials intending to run for elective office following the return to civilian rule, save only Doe himself, were required to resign their government posts; this flushed out a number of PPP activists, including Baccus Matthews. Doe announced his candidature after the formal lifting of the ban on political activity in July 1984. The prospective parties formed by the old groupings – the Liberian People's Party (LPP) led by Sawyer for MOJA, and the United People's Party (UPP) led by Matthews for PPP – were refused recognition, and for a long time the only party to satisfy the stringent conditions laid down by the Special Electoral Commission (Secom) was the National Democratic Party of Liberia (NDPL), led by Doe himself. Very much a party of government, this largely attracted placemen from the True Whigs, with quite a number of Americo-Liberians (including Secom chairman Emmett Harmon and foreign minister Ernest Eastman), as well as some hinterlanders such as party chairman Kekura Kpoto, a businessman from Lofa county. Even the True Whigs, however, did not all come across, the most notable absentees being young hinterlanders raised to high office by Tolbert, who fancied their own chances. These included former education minister Jackson Doe from Nimba, who led the Liberian Action Party (LAP), and Edward Kesselly with the Unity Party (UP); a previously unknown schoolteacher, Gabriel Kpolleh, formed the Liberian Unification Party (LUP).

The popular support which the PRC regime initially attracted had by this time disappeared. The army had a justified reputation for bullying and extortion, stretching back to its origins as the Liberia Frontier Force, which was in no way weakened by a coup which gave enlisted men control over the government. Soldiers appropriated the houses and cars of imprisoned or executed TWP bosses, extorted money from civilians, and at the same time awarded themselves a substantial pay increase. The rapid decline in the Liberian economy was not solely the result of the coup, but was certainly exacerbated by it, and easily blamed on it. The harassment of critical journalists and banning of strikes soon heralded the emergence of a regime which was more brutal and authoritarian (if only because it felt much less secure) than the one it had displaced. As often happens, university students were the first to articulate misgivings which were widely shared. In 1982, five student leaders were sentenced to death after 'seeking to clarify' a PRC decree, and only reprieved at the last minute following domestic and international outcry. Thereafter the university was the centre of tacit and at times open opposition to the regime, its recalcitrance symbolised by its failure to award Doe an honorary doctorate, such as he had already received from the University of Seoul. In August 1984, following protests at the arrest of Amos Sawyer on a treason charge, the army invaded the campus, pillaging buildings and beating up students and staff; though definite evidence is surprisingly elusive, several students were probably killed.

That elections took place at all, let alone that opposition parties were allowed to contest them, was due far more to American pressure than to any search for domestic legitimation. The LPP and UPP remained banned, but the LAP, LUP and UP were allowed to present candidates for the elections eventually held in October 1985. The results are only of passing interest, as it is universally agreed, save by those who have a strong interest in claiming otherwise, that these were flagrantly rigged. That Doe was able, even then, to claim only 50.9 per cent of the popular vote indicates the weakness of his support. Of the remaining votes, 26.4 per cent were ascribed to Jackson Doe, who was generally regarded as the rightful winner, 11.5 per cent to Kpolleh and 11.1 per cent to Kesselly. Jackson Doe was reported as heading the poll in Nimba county, Kpolleh in Margibi, and Kesselly in Cape Mount, with Samuel Doe taking the other ten counties. Doe's NDPL also gained 21 of the 26 Senate seats, and 51 of the 64 seats in the House of Representatives. The main object of the exercise was achieved when these results were accepted by the US government, but they did not lead to any consolidation of the regime's position inside the country. Quiwonkpa's abortive invasion, shortly after the elections, was greeted with enthusiasm when it appeared to be succeeding. The LAP and LUP refused to accept the results or take up their congressional seats, and few of the opposition figures nominated to posts in the new administration agreed to serve. The opposition leaders, who united into a coalition shortly after the elections, were subject to continued harassment and arrest. At the time of writing, Doe remains in power.

Discussion

During the past decade, Liberia has belatedly passed through an experience analogous in some respects to the transfer of power to the nationalist movements elsewhere in West Africa during the late 1950s and early 1960s. A long-established political structure, which allowed participation only within the constraints imposed by an elitist form of government, has been swept away and replaced by one which formally represents the mass of the population. The comparison, however, should not be pushed too far. The long-predicted overthrow of the True Whig oligarchy has not been accompanied even by the short-lived explosion of popular participation which came with the nationalist movements. Nor has the ousting of the old regime done anything to relieve the international economic penetration and dependence which the True Whigs from Tubman onwards had encouraged. It has, rather, made dependence increasingly obvious and decreasingly profitable, as the decline in business confidence has coincided with global recession in Liberia's three main external revenue sources, iron ore, rubber, and shipping.

The failure of post-coup Liberia to develop either a populist socialist (or for that matter Marxist) or a genuine liberal multi-party system of government is sometimes ascribed by both foreign and Liberian scholars to the personal ambition, cupidity and penchant for violence of the military regime.[5] In this, there is certainly some justice. The Liberian army, as already noted, was an ill-disciplined agency of internal repression, lacking the commitment even to the ideals of personal honesty and national unity which have often characterised other African military regimes, at least in the immediate aftermath of their seizure of power. It must also be recognised that the educational level of those who have come up through the ranks of African armies is generally very limited indeed – and in the Liberian army probably more limited than most. Many of those who have risen from such a background to the leadership of African states – Amin, Ankrah, Bokassa, Ironsi – have had some difficulty in coping with the intellectual requirements of their position, and all of these had pre-coup experience not merely of officer rank but of high command. Doe is the sole non-officer to enjoy any substantial tenure as an African head of state. A case can, I think, be made that following a consistent and ideologically directed political course requires at least a basic level of education, and that leaders who lack this are liable to drift towards authoritarian self-gratification.

At a different level, however, one can also point to the nature of Liberian political society, and to the absence of a constituency on which either a single-party socialist or a multi-party capitalist system could be based. Certainly, those (notably in MOJA) who aspired to a transformation of the Liberian political and economic order were caught unprepared by the coup, and had not had the chance either to articulate a full range of policies, or to build an effective countrywide political organisation. But at all events they failed to raise any major issue, such as land reform provided in Ethiopia, which could be mobilised to provide a mass base for a new kind of regime, while economic dependence on the export economy would have severely restricted their freedom of action. The prospects for a reasonably liberal multi-party system seemed more promising. Liberia has a very long record of constitutionalism, and throughout the TWP period enormous care was taken to preserve the forms of democratic rule, even though its substance was missing. Both before and after the coup, individual Liberians (among whom that irrepressible champion of a free press, Albert Porte, deserves a place of honour) were prepared to make great personal sacrifices, and stand much danger, in order to achieve the free and democratic Liberia which national rhetoric had always claimed. Nonetheless, the venality of the TWP regime, and its unabashed use of state power as a mechanism for personal enrichment, had been no mere preserve of an Americo-Liberian oligarchy, but were much more widely spread. An economy heavily based on the extraction of minerals and rubber through multinational companies inevitably turned the state, as the agency through which the domestic profits of these enterprises were channelled, into a centralised source of benefits which easily outweighed any rewards that could be achieved through genuinely private economic activity – though many leading Liberians actually gained access to this treasure through private companies which were parasitic, in one way or another, on the control of political power. The objective of the new regime, having seized power, was thus to redirect its benefits towards a new set of beneficiaries, while the old beneficiaries likewise saw the need to ingratiate themselves with the new rulers, in order to preserve what they could. Again, the immediate aftermath of the coup is symptomatic, as the PRC instantly increased civil service and especially army pay, while the surviving TWP leaders desperately sought to exculpate themselves by blaming every possible fault on the dead Tolbert. Most strikingly of all, Doe was rapidly metamorphosed from a gaunt and hungry-looking sergeant in ill-fitting battle fatigues, into a plump, immaculately suited figure with a fashionable Afro haircut.

At the same time, the external element is far too important to be left out of a discussion even of domestic politics. External dependence is indeed domesticated in Liberia, through the use of ordinary greenbacked US dollar notes, along with locally minted coins, as internal currency. This has the effect, among other things, that a decline in business confidence leads to the straightforward removal of money from the country. Between March 1980 and December 1981, in consequence, private sector liquidity fell from $175.5 million to $102.6 million, with devastating effects on government revenue collection and domestic economic deflation. The government tried to remedy the situation by printing $20 million in local coins, but this led to the emergence of a dual currency, with US notes trading at a premium against coins, and the classic operation of Gresham's law in driving notes out of circulation; the difference in value between 'real' US dollars, and the widely despised 'Doe dollars' served as a measure of post-coup economic deterioration. More generally, dependence on foreign companies, and the export of primary products through vertically integrated multinational structures of extraction, processing and end use, limited the level of control that any government could exercise over the economy. Global recession, domestic mismanagement and lack of external confidence led to a steady decline in GDP from $461.4 million in 1979 to $321.6 million in 1983. Government indebtedness increased sharply, and despite American political support, Liberia was barred in 1986 from further borrowing from the IMF. In these circumstances, the United States (which has no major economic interests in the country, but which has important telecommunications installations which would be difficult to move) had little difficulty in buying the regime's allegiance, with a large increase in aid from about $10 million a year before the coup, to over $80 million after it; much of this aid was devised to appeal to the lower ranks of the armed forces, notably by building better barracks. There were numerous allegations of its illicit diversion, confirmed by the US General Accounting Office, which led in 1987 to the appointment of seventeen American 'operational experts' who were to oversee Liberian government revenue collection, disbursement and accounting. The Liberian government has thus been forced into a peculiarly direct and humiliating subservience to its major aid donor. The problems which this relationship has caused the United States have lain not in Liberia's diplomatic obedience, which has been virtually complete, but in the tacit implication of the United States in domestic political issues, over which it has nonetheless had very little control. While the US government was able to lean on Doe to moderate actions which would have caused an outcry in the United States, it could not get rid of Doe himself, and found itself drawn into unwilling complicity with an increasingly unpopular regime. Reports that the United States gave secret encouragement to the Quiwonkpa invasion in November 1985, though unproved, are not altogether implausible.

But while the Liberian state is thus exceptionally dependent, it should also be noted that the state itself has scarcely been threatened, and may indeed be reckoned to have come through a traumatic period surprisingly unscathed. The instant rallying to the new regime, not only of the opposition forces but also of many of Tolbert's own appointees, reflected a recognition of the state as a source of power and wealth in which a very broad coalition of forces had an interest. The Liberian state could no longer, by 1980, be regarded as the exclusively Americo-Liberian preserve which it had once been – any more, indeed, than the colonial state elsewhere in West Africa could be regarded by the time of independence as simply the creature of its alien founders. The rapid expansion of state employment under Tubman and Tolbert, including notably its extension to large numbers of hinterlanders, helped to preserve it when the crisis came. Furthermore, though the threat of secession would be ludicrous in a territory so lilliputian as Liberia, the crisis has been survived without any evident danger of state collapse. Ethnic conflict has intensified, but in the form more of increased rivalries between hinterland people than the mobilisation of the difference between settlers and indigenes. One thing that has obviously changed is the Americo-Liberian monopoly of senior political office. All of the candidates in the 1985 presidential elections were hinterlanders, and their only serious rival from the coastal elite in post-coup Liberia has paradoxically been the most radical of would-be contenders for the presidency in 1985, the MOJA leader Amos Sawyer. But the reaction against the Americo-Liberian community did not last for long after the coup, and their advantages in education and experience have helped them to maintain their position in the state apparatus and professions, in much the same way as their Creole counterparts were able to do in Sierra Leone. In mid-1987, Doe's ministers of finance, planning, rural development, labour, commerce and justice all had Americo-Liberian names – though this is no guarantee that they were all actually of settler descent. On the other hand, Doe's Krahn group, well represented in the army and especially (as one might expect) in the new ruler's personal bodyguard and security service, have gained an unenviable reputation as the guardians and bullyboys of the current political order, and may well be subject to retaliation should the regime be overthrown. Nimba county, home of Thomas Quiwonkpa and the thwarted presidential candidate Jackson Doe, is correspondingly often seen as the main source of ethnic/regional opposition to the new regime, and has been subject to heavy-handed government repression. Lofa county, another important area for army recruitment and the home base of Edward Kesselly, appears to have been surprisingly quiescent; nor has any overt attempt been made to capitalise on the ethnic identity of Liberia's largest single tribal grouping, the Kpelle of Bong county, though Kpelle support may account for Gabriel Kpolleh's unexpectedly strong showing in the 1985 elections. Whether the Liberian state can actually *do* anything, in a developmental sense, remains an open question, since under the new regime, like the old, it has scarcely tried. It also has chronic and increasing problems in paying its employees – and especially those, like country schoolteachers, who are far from the centre of power. But unlike Chad or Uganda, central upheaval has not led to state collapse.

At a formal level, the most important political change in Second Republic Liberia has been the replacement of a single party oligarchy by a multi-party system in which, for the first time, the presidency has been overtly competed for in nationwide elections. In practice, the opposition parties are only kept in being by American pressure, and in some respects the openness and accountability of the regime might be reckoned to have declined. The old True Whig oligarchy, in much the same manner as a Leninist vanguard party (however much it differed from one in other ways) provided a mechanism through which the diligent and ambitious could be incorporated into a national structure of patronage. It was accountable, not in any effective electoral fashion, but at least in the attenuated sense that local political activity was generally required in order to gain the party nomination for congressional seats, while local legislators were expected to spend much of their time in the constituencies; even major national politicians, such as presidents Tubman and Tolbert, had up-country 'farms' or estates which served, not just as sources of income or weekend retreats, but also as centres for the creation of a local political clientele, and thus as a slight counterweight to the pull of the national capital. It scarcely needs to be said that the True Whig machine was in many ways thoroughly inadequate. Such opportunities as it provided to hinterland politicians were subject to the supervision, and to a large extent at the pleasure, of bosses drawn from the coastal elite; while even in the hinterland, advancement was largely restricted to those who combined wealth, education or status in the local community with a willingness to subordinate themselves to coastal control. It is nonetheless striking how, in the post-coup period, political leadership and organisation have been overwhelmingly derived from the individuals and networks which had already been established under Tolbert. The sole new major national level politician to have risen to prominence since 1980 has been Doe himself, along with his former colleagues, Weh Syen and Quiwonkpa, who failed to survive the settling of accounts among the original coup leaders. The others all derive from the Tolbert era, including both those who worked within the True Whig system, such as Jackson Doe and Edward Kesselly, and those who sought to challenge it, such as Amos Sawyer and Baccus Matthews. With the banning of both Sawyer and Matthews in the 1985 elections, moreover, at least three of the four competing parties, including notably Doe's own NDPL, could be seen as the lineal descendants of one or another grouping within the old TWP; Kpolleh's LUP also included some former TWP elements. What the new party structure lacked was the central coherence which had enabled the True Whig leadership to hold these elements together. Doe was not able to establish himself as an acceptable national patron in Tolbert's place, nor did he have the same social framework (not merely of Americo-Liberian ethnicity, but of church, lodge, economic privilege, and political habit) to back him up. In post-coup Liberia, the different sections of the former True Whig Party have wriggled off, like the severed segments of a worm, in their own separate directions.

This fragmentation in turn accounts for the post-coup increase in the level of political violence. There has been little conflict over basic political goals, because there has been little to conflict about. Even the more radical parties, such as Sawyer's LPP, have been able to present no coherent alternative to dependence on an international economy dominated by the United States, and have offered only a radicalised version of the 'national unity and development' platform which has been shared with the other parties. There have been no commanding heights of the economy for any would-be socialist government to seize. Political conflict in Liberia has thus been almost solely about access to state resources, and has been of interest to little more than that section of the population which could plausibly compete for them. The difference made by the coup has been to replace a familiar and hitherto stable (though, even so, increasingly contested) system for allocating these resources, by a free-for-all in which demands increased, while the resources themselves diminished, and the acceptance (it would be too much to call it legitimacy) conferred on the political structure by longevity disappeared. A reasonably effective and peaceful system of dependent clientelism has, in short, been replaced by a much less effective and more violent one.

8

Nigeria: power for profit – class, corporatism, and factionalism in the military

SHEHU OTHMAN

The 'new morality' which has emerged from the military era is such that there is general acceptance among most members of the power elite that power is for profit rather than for responsible exercise of its privileges or for service. This philosophy has resulted...in the privileges of power being used for pillage. The 'new morality' encourages and protects chaos because members of the new elite have vested interest in chaos despite its long term danger to social stability and their real or permanent interests.

Report of the Presidential Transition Committee, unpublished, Lagos, September 1983, p. 30.

No other official commentary on Nigerian public life captures with such brutal frankness and insight the logic behind political competition in contemporary Nigeria. Even the soldiers who overthrew President Shehu Shagari in December 1983 did not hesitate to adopt as the reform charter of their regime[1] the recommendations of the Transition Report which Shagari himself was avowedly following. The absence of fundamental cleavages amongst Nigeria's political class means that struggle for power is always less concerned with radically competing policies or ideals, than it is with who secures power itself and who controls the disposition of its spoils. Political contest is therefore a form of musical chairs, 'a negative condition that does not rule out political...violence, but merely ensures that such conflict mostly destroys only individuals and not structures...'[2] Writing in a similar vein, Joseph aptly described Nigeria's experience since formal independence from Britain in October 1960 as one of a 'debilitating cycle of political renewal and decay'.[3]

By December 1985 there had been seven military *coups d'état*, two of them abortive, and also an appalling civil war lasting two and a half years, provoked by Biafra's secession. A considerable expansion in oil production and revenues in the 1970s was accompanied by a vast increase in economic activities and state bureaucracies, civil and military. But since 1981, the economy has been afflicted by a severe oil crisis, induced by the sharp fall in the world price of oil and made worse by economic bungling. Debts,

113

domestic and foreign, have expanded to elephantine proportions, and a large measure of Nigeria's economic planning has been forcibly surrendered to International Monetary Fund and World Bank advisers. For all its enormous natural resources, Nigeria is still a poor country, economically backward, and fatally dependent on Western capitalist economies for even such basic needs as cooking oil. Corruption, predatory privatisation of public resources, misuse of office, and abuse of the laws, is pandemic and has reached unprecedented heights.

Military rule, then civil war, and the oil rents which flow to the Federal government, have facilitated the centralisation of authority; and this in turn has generated pervasive state intervention in the economy. There exists, both inside and outside the formal apparatus of the state and the public corporations, a comprador yet assertive bourgeoisie whose expansion has depended very heavily upon state favours and on collaboration with multinational capital, but whose hegemony remains shaky, and liable to periodic assault by one armed group or another. The state itself remains the major vortex of political conflict precisely because it presides over the allocation of strategic resources and opportunities for profit making. Struggle for control of state power has therefore often been fierce, vicious, and devastating in its effects, the rules of the political game being weakly defined, and defying universally acceptable definition. Political contest in Nigeria after all involves every means – fair or foul.[4]

The dynamics of the struggle for spoils within, and by, the Nigerian military as a proprietary class since the 1970s is a direct product of the corporate interests of the armed forces and of the factional divisions within them. It is a struggle from which military officers as individuals stand to gain both professionally and materially. It is these corporate, factional and personal interests which best explain the cycle of coups and counter-coups, and the relative stability or frailty of particular Nigerian regimes.[5] Both the internal solidarity of factions and the external rivalries of military factions[6] were as prominent under Gowon as they remained in the Mohammed-Obasanjo, Buhari, and Babangida regimes.

In the heat of acrimonious dispute over his 1979 election victory, President Shagari observed tartly to his adversaries that there were in the ultimate analysis two political parties in Nigeria: the civilians and the military.[7] While the divide between military and civilian elites has become increasingly blurred since the military forfeited its political virginity in the mid-1960s, military officers retain their own corporate interests and values which may or may not be coterminous with those of the civilian elites. Coups and army rule or even the threat of these expedients provide effective means (though in no sense the only ones) of satisfying their corporate expectations, or guarding and advancing their corporate interests. These interests have been articulated through and are clearly reflected in their political attitudes, their perception of themselves and their place in society, their sense of corporate exclusiveness, the types of social institutions they favour, the macro-economic strategies they pursue, the share of national budgets they claim, and not least in their priorities for public spending.

But the corporate solidarity and factionalism of the military have coexisted comfortably, and at times even merged, with the interests of the privileged social strata. For, in the last instance, the military simply forms a part of the bureaucratic bourgeoisie, a proprietary class which not only exercises *de jure* and *de facto* control over public capital and enterprises, but is also intimately (if often covertly) related to private capital through the unofficial incomes and benefits which it draws and through the purchase which it offers to private capital over the administration of state capital.[8] To see these dynamics correctly and to assess their contribution to the continuing political crisis of the Nigerian state requires a historical approach to the development of Nigeria's economy and to the role of the state in articulating and mediating structural conflicts of interests within this.

State, oil, and public economy

Since the colonial period, the state has played an important extractive role in the economy. A key institution in shaping this role was the series of produce marketing boards established in the immediate aftermath of the Second World War. These state buying agencies served to appropriate part of the surplus value from the peasantry and deploy it initially to serve British national interests, and latterly, to finance the expansion of the pre- and post-colonial Nigerian state. 'By 1954', notes Rimmer, 'the Boards had accumulated £120 millions, of which trading surpluses in the seven years since 1947 amounted to £100 millions, or two-thirds as much as the aggregate yield of import and export duties in the same period. A further £30 millions were accumulated in the seven years from 1954 to 1961.'[9] Proceeds from these agencies enabled the local bureaucratic-political elite, along with the traditional nobility, to finance further bureaucratic expansion, invest in industrial projects, accumulate money capital, and via misappropriation and abuse of fiscal procedures, to line their pockets and finance party political activities.[10] This control over state power has been of decisive significance not only for the expansion of the state sector itself, but for the development of local capitalism as a whole.

Sustained economic expansion in the forties and fifties stimulated further developments in local manufacturing, enabling foreign capital to withdraw partly from such activities as distributive trades in order to concede greater scope to local business aspirations, and also to extend its control over more strategic and complex areas of capitalist production. As a result of concessions to nationalist aspirations in the period up to independence, more commercial, bureaucratic, and political opportunities were opened up to Nigerians. But at the same time the Nigerian state also expanded its own role in public enterprises ranging from trading, housing, infra-structural services, manufacturing, insurance, to banking. From independence onwards, accordingly, it was always in a position to control to a large extent the allocation of profitable opportunities, and to create protected niches for its clients, local and foreign.[11] 'By the 1960s nearly all businessmen were necessarily in politics, because the state had become the main source of both finance and contracts; and nearly all politicians were in business.[12]

Impersonal rules no longer governed competition in business or in politics. Nor was there room for appeal to broader values of equity and legitimacy. As Williams has written with graphic clarity: 'The ethics of business penetrated politics, the ethics of politics penetrated business; the ethics of the gangster penetrated both.'[13] Politics was thus a battlefield where the key prize was control over the state apparatus. Throughout this period, the armed forces which at independence had numbered a modest 15,000, remained something of a 'shadow elite'.[14] Although control of the armed forces by the British War Office was ceded formally in 1958, they continued until 1963 to take directives from the British Army Council; and full Nigerianisation was not accomplished until 1965. By 1966–7 annual defence expenditure was still only N25,100,262 or 5.6 per cent of total national budget. A fair index of the military's then fiscal innocence was the fact that General A. Ironsi, its first Nigerian General Officer Commanding, and later head of state, died a poor man with a bank debt of £18,500![15]

The period of military rule, particularly during the early 1970s, coincided with vast economic expansion as GDP expanded dramatically. Public expenditure increased rapidly, reaching N14,417.6 million in 1980, in real terms equivalent to about 5.2 times the 1964 GDP. Foreign reserves stood at N372.7 million in 1960, and by October 1980 they had risen to N5.65 billion (Table 8.1). Oil production, which began on a modest scale in 1958, reached an average of 540,300 barrels a day (b/d) in 1969, then skyrocketed to 2.25 million b/d in 1974 and to 2.3 million b/d in 1979. Subsequently, however (except in 1980 itself when output stood at an average 2 million b/d) Nigeria's production has fallen to well below the already low levels of 1975 and 1978 respectively (Table 8.2).

With the defeat of Biafran claims to oilfields, and the dependence of the oil-producing states on Federal power for protection, the Federal state came to appropriate and preside over the allocation of oil revenues to the various tiers of government. These revenues provided the fiscal base for its direction of public affairs.[16] Civil and military bureaucracies expanded. Seven additional states were created in 1976, bringing the total to nineteen. Together with these increased revenues, came massive state involvement in the economy in alliance with international capital. The state was at pains to develop comfortable niches for its budding bourgeoisie from the early 1970s onwards, notably through the indigenisation decrees of 1972 and 1977. These decrees reserved the oil, iron and steel industries to the state, required majority Nigerian share-holding in certain economic activities, and excluded foreigners from others. Collaboration between the state, foreign firms and

Table 8.1. *GDP, Government revenues, public expenditures, and external assets, 1970–85 (Naira million)*

Year	GDP[a] (Annual % change)	Govt. revenues	Public expenditure	External assets
1970	29,826	633.2	1,130.1	180.4
1971	35,352 (18.38%)	1,169.0	1,092.4	302.7
1972	37,929 (7.29%)	1,404.8	1,400.6	273.3
1973	36,904 (−2.70%)	1,695.3	1,778.8	438.6
1974	41,379 (12.13%)	4,537.0	4,260.3	3,478.7
1975	40,132 (−3.01%)	5,514.7	8,258.3	3,702.6
1976	44,505 (10.90%)	6,765.9	9,701.5	3,082.7
1977	47,766 (7.32%)	8,042.4	11,695.4	2,765.4
1978	43,993 (−7.90%)	7,469.4	12,891.2	1,179.0
1979	45,728 (3.94%)	10,912.7	13,260.5	3,166.8
1980	47,041 (2.87%)	15,234.0	14,417.6	5,655.0
1981	45,667 (−2.92%)	11,978.9	10,774.4	2,592.6
1982	45,668 (.002%)	10,143.9	11,923.2	1,084.3
1983	41,775 (−8.52%)	10,508.7	11,525.4	828.7
1984	39,477 (−5.50%)	11,193.8	9,927.6[b]	1,422.1
1985	n.a.	15,041.8	12,079.0[b]	1,816.8[b]

Notes: [a] GDP at 1980 Factor Cost and data are for fiscal years. [b] Provisional
Sources: IMF, International Financial Statistics Yearbook, 1986; Central Bank of Nigeria, Annual Report and Statement of Accounts, several issues; and Federal Office of Statistics, Lagos, Annual Abstract of Statistics, several issues.

banks financed the acquisition of shares and properties by local managers, businessmen, bureaucrats, and military and police commanders.[17]

The Federal government became the major arena of conflict between private interests as cliques of bureaucratic insiders, backed by military licence, determined public policy and resource allocation in collaboration with their business associates, local and foreign. With the oil boom, struggle for control of the state intensified. Under Gowon, military officers, politicians, intellectuals, and businessmen excluded from key decision-making and opportunities became acutely resentful and the state rapidly lost internal coherence and political efficacy. Except under General Babangida, whose structural reform policies must await later scrutiny, every Nigerian government since 1975 has failed to implement what Allison Ayida, the high priest of Gowon's economic planning, called the 'institutional reforms'[18] necessary for the development and strengthening of capitalist production in Nigeria, or to provide a stable framework for regulating conflicts either between domestic and foreign capital, or amongst local capitalists, or between the indigenous classes which make up Nigerian society. Amid the resulting political instability, continued access to the imported technology of

117

Table 8.2. Oil sector statistics, 1969–85

	1969	1970	1971	1972	1973	1974	1975	1976	1977
Oil output (m/bd)	0.54	1.08	1.53	1.82	2.05	2.25	1.78	2.07	2.08
Oil export (m/bd)	0.54	1.05	1.49	1.76	1.98	2.18	1.71	2.01	2.03
As % of total exports	41.2	57.5	73.7	82.0	83.1	92.6	94.0	91.8	92.7
Oil export value (US$ bn)	0.37	0.71	1.34	1.79	2.88	8.51	7.52	9.89	1L.00
Govt. oil rev (N m)	68	166	510	732	1,016	4,184	4,272	5,484	6,081
As % of total revenue	15.6	26.3	43.6	52.7	59.9	61.2	77.5	77.8	75.7
Average off. sale price ($/b)[a]	2.10	2.35	3.14	3.36	5.02	13.07	13.60	13.80	15.00

	1978	1979	1980	1981	1982	1983	1984	1985
Oil output (m/bd)	1.90	2.30	2.06	1.44	1.29	1.23	1.39	1.49
Oil export (m/bd)	1.83	2.21	1.96	1.23	1.00	0.93	1.09	1.23
As % of total exports	89.6	93.4	96.1	96.9	97.5	96.0	97.3	97.1
Oil export value (US$ bn)	8.93	16.07	24.93	17.30	11.89	9.94	11.53	12.19
Govt. oil rev (N m)	4,809	8,881	13,210	9,710	8,533	7,026	9,099	10,915[b]
As % of total revenue	67.2	89.4	83.6	77.8	75.3	68.7	77.1	72.6[b]
Average off. sale price ($/b)[a]	14.81	21.37	35.29	36.38	34.80	29.25	27.63	28.24

Notes: [a] For all types of crude oil and 1969–78 data refer to posted or tax reference prices. [b] Provisional
Sources: OPEC Annual Statistical Bulletin 1985; CEM Statistical Annex 1985; CBN, Annual Report, several issues; FOS, Annual Abstract of Statistics, several issues.

violence has remained of ever growing significance in enabling those who control the state to impose themselves on the rest of society whenever they so choose.

Barrack and region: camaraderie versus primordialism

'The mutual dependence on one another for survival in war', wrote General Obasanjo, 'helps to promote a sense of camaraderie if not brotherhood, among military officers of about the same seniority and age, more than is possibly true of other professions.'[19] Even in the dark days of the 1960s the Nigerian army retained a distinct corporate solidarity. In the course of their service, military officers tend to be decidedly more cohesive than any other section of the Nigerian elite. But Obasanjo's statement neglects the cleavages within the armed forces that can also arise from the unifying bonds of mess life, course-mate, and peer-grouping. The coups of 1966 both display the deeply ambiguous effects of peer-grouping in bonding and dividing the Nigerian officer corps.[20]

One is also on a treacherous terrain when assessing the tensions between professional loyalties and primordial identities among military officers. The strength of both forms of loyalty can readily be exaggerated, either in normal military life or in situations of conflict. By primordialism here we mean either:

> the assertion of common identity based on ties of race, blood, religion, region and the like or the articulation of a posture – be it one of aggression or alliance – towards other groups on their supposedly shared characteristics, whether of race, tribe, religion, area or some other index...One might talk of primordialism of identity for the former and primordialism of projection for the latter.[21]

The conduct of Nigerian military elites, like that of their civilian counterparts, has arguably often been animated by primordial affinities or loyalties. But these values only prompt specific actions in response to particular goals of power or wealth. Williams's and Turner's argument is compelling:

> The competition for access to resources in Nigeria has taken place predominantly between ethnically-defined constituencies. These constituencies were not simply given, but redefined in the process of political competition. Ethnic identities do not present themselves ready-made, determining in advance the lines of political conflict. They are socially constructed in relation to the exigencies of specific historical situations. Differences and similarities of language, custom, religion and historical experience are used selectively to define and legitimate particular claims to solidarity and exclusion... These criteria are themselves ambiguous and may cut across one another. The definition of appropriate solidarities and choice of political alliances is made according to calculations of relative advantage and political judgement.[22]

The crises of the 1960s certainly demonstrated the presence of ethnic and sectional rifts within the Nigerian military. This was particularly apparent after the Majors' coup of January 1966 when soldiers from different ethnic groups or regions viewed each other with vivid distrust, and sought guarantees of their security within ethnically defined frameworks. The decision to post soldiers to their regions of origin after the July 1966 coup was one such attempt, based on genuine fears of mutual annihilation.[23] Senior military officers of all regions identified with, and lent support to, the claims of their regional civilian Leaders of Thought, themselves groups of ex-politicians which the military regime formed to help resolve Nigeria's political crises. In October 1966, for example, Colonel R. A. Adebayo, then Western regional governor, and other senior Yoruba officers put into motion an elaborate plan for the mass desertion of Yoruba soldiers from the North following fears about their safety. This was at the instigation of Western region Leaders of Thought, but the plan collapsed largely because the officer requested to direct it refused to operate.[24] In both Eastern and Northern regions, the role of particular military officers was of crucial importance both in advocating and in preparing for the war which ensued.

The decision to go to war had important consequences for the shape of subsequent military factionalism outside the Eastern region. The reassertion of unified military command promptly checked overtly aggressive ethnic factionalism. But the new armed forces leadership was clearly the creation of the July coup-makers, notably Lieutenant-Colonel Murtala Mohammed. So whilst Northern solidarity within the armed forces remained largely intact, overt Yoruba military factionalism was decisively neutralised. The slaughter of many Igbo officers in the July 1966 coup, the defeat of the Biafran army, and subsequent reabsorption of few of its middle-ranking officers into Nigeria's armed forces (all without their service seniority)[25] weakened Igbo representation in the upper reaches of the military hierarchy, and sharply restricted the promotion of Igbo officers. Between 1970 and 1985 there was no Igbo officer of the rank of major-general or equivalent in any of the services, or in any strategic federal post.

Control of the armed forces since the July 1966 coup has remained firmly in the hands of Northern officers who are linked by ties of history, region, language, and schooling. These officers do not, however, form a monolithic group despite the seemingly high degree of cohesion among them. A broad and rough distinction could be drawn between officers from the emirate north, mainly *Hausa*-speaking, and those from the Middle Belt, the predominantly non-Muslim areas inhabited by northern ethnic minorities.[26] While both share an interest in articulating a pan-northern posture, the latter also want greater socio-cultural autonomy for their peoples as well as equal access on their own behalf to the spoils of power that accrue from northern solidarity. Eighty per cent of the army's other ranks in the 1960s were northerners, but nine out of ten of these were in fact Middle Belters.[27] Gowon was thus well able to count on the support of Middle Belt army officers (hitherto defenders of 'One North, One People') when he split

Nigeria's four regions into twelve states in 1967 in an attempt to regulate political conflict and to satisfy the aspirations of ethnic minorities.[28] But by September 1974 when it had become clear that Gowon had totally forfeited the loyalty of a number of influential officers from the emirate north, it was Middle Belt officers who instigated the joint northern conspiracy that led to his overthrow.[29]

The main opposition to Gowon centred on the person of Murtala Mohammed with whom Gowon had barely been on speaking terms between late 1966 and 1972.[30] Until late in 1974 when Mohammed was appointed Federal Commissioner for Communications, Gowon had given him no official position even though it was Mohammed who had masterminded Gowon's ascent to power. Several times, Mohammed offered to resign his commission from the army, and in a variety of military and academic settings he sharply criticised Gowon's handling of national affairs.[31] Other war-time commanders also came to resent their exclusion from government and from control over strategic allocation of public resources. Like the public at large, they were especially provoked by the scandalous venality of the state governors, whom Gowon failed to reassign despite repeated demands both from inside and outside the armed forces. Plausible accusations of gross misdemeanours by the late J. S. Tarka, a Federal Commissioner (over which Gowon maintained a curious silence), and the late J. D. Gomwalk, then Benue-Plateau State governor (whom Gowon exonerated without a public inquiry), as well as the detention without trial of their accusers, symbolised even to a largely illiterate public all that was fatally wrong with the Gowon regime. Ten of the twelve governors were later found guilty of corruption on an immense scale.[32] The enormous powers and the massive private accumulation of a number of leading civil servants also raised widespread concern. As a Government White Paper subsequently observed: 'in almost every case considered, there [was] a startling departure from the accepted rules and ethics of behaviour expected of public officers...[And] this pattern of behaviour had almost become the normal practice in the recent past.'[33]

Nor did the war-time commanders have much professional respect for those of their superiors who remained close to Gowon. In their view, the latter were 'sycophants and self-appointed Intelligence Officers spying on honest and loyal officers'. Gowon, they believed, suspected them of disloyalty; and they found their mails tampered with and their telephones tapped. 'Such suspicions', as General Oluleye observed, 'became a rallying point'.[34] A further major source of provocation was the rehabilitation and reorganization of the army itself – demobilisation, control of troops, redeployment of military units, and retraining and redeployment of officers, none of which were carried through in a convincing manner. Defence expenditure had also reached embarrassing proportions, made worse by pervasive corruption within the military itself.[35] There were also the unresolved issues of the controversial 1973 census, of the creation of more states, and of the repudiation of Gowon's promise to return to civil rule, all of which were attributed to his vacillation or obtuseness to the advice of his military colleagues. 'All these things', wrote General Oluleye, 'helped the strengthening of communication between the military and the politicians even if meetings were informal and discussions off-record.'[36] The impact of such issues on the image of the armed forces formed, in the eyes of these officers, a fitting justification for Gowon's removal, though there is now evidence that Gowon's procrastination over demobilisation and military withdrawal was prompted by deference in the first case to northern military opinion, and in the second to the army high command.[37]

Turner has shown admirably how factional rivalries between administrators and technocrats in oil administration gave the final impetus to the coup that ousted Gowon. Alleged collusion between administrators and oil companies offended the oil technocrats whose struggle for a more rational oil policy had brought to the fore a number of issues which became crucial to Gowon's overthrow. Gowon's choice of I.G.T. Ordor as general manager of Nigeria's oil corporation was overwhelmingly rejected at a stormy Cabinet meeting which ended in a clash between Gowon and the man who toppled him twenty-five days later – Brigadier Murtala Mohammed.[38]

Turner's approach is less than sensitive, however, to both historical and geopolitical perspectives. The coup was about the control of state power and the allocation of its spoils: and its antecedents go back directly to the political crises of the 1960s, and the hectic conflicts of interest and personality which had emerged from these. Mr Ordor's appointment, for instance, evoked memories of his Biafran activities and threatened to obstruct northern access to oil-related opportunities. Turner's analysis also fails notably to do justice to the role of extra-military networks such as the so-called 'Kaduna Mafia'.

The military and the 'Kaduna Mafia'[39]

Named after the prosperous garden city of Kaduna,[40] its historical and operational base, the Kaduna Mafia comprises an amalgam of northern politicians and intellectuals, leading bureaucrats, professionals, managers, investors, gentlemen farmers, and military and police commanders inside and outside the state apparatus. As the most sophisticated segment of the northern bourgeois establishment and as gate-keepers of the Nigerian north, they have provided powerful support for federal power, and had great influence on critical issues of national politics.[41] They share a passionate concern for the ethics of the nation, good government, the north, and its traditional values, from which they draw their own assumed legitimacy. Self-styled as the 'Committee of Concerned Citizens', their purpose is ostensibly the defence and advancement of northern interests – politically, economically, socially, and even religiously. In this, they have been more successful than their opposite number in the defunct western region – the Ikenne Mafia,[42] itself the cradle of the Yoruba bourgeoisie and the dominant

122

political force in Yoruba country but as yet never rooted in, or in control of, the Federal state.

The Kaduna Mafia originated from a coterie of seven middle-ranking bureaucrats drawn largely from the office of Sir Ahmadu Bello, the *Sardauna of Sokoto* and northern premier assassinated in the January 1966 coup. Young, talented, and politically conscious, imbued also with the ideals of good and efficient administration combined with fierce 'northernism' associated with the *Sardauna*, and with a clear professional stake in the advancement of northern interests, they set about restoring coherence to the disarrayed leadership of the north.[43] In concert with their peers in the army, the police, and amongst northern university students, they furtively masterminded militant public opposition to Ironsi's policies, and laid the intellectual foundations for northern positions and strategies in the abortive constitutional discussions which preceded the civil war. Meetings between northern civil servants and military officers were regularly held at Lugard Hall in Kaduna, in much the same way as eastern Igbo intellectuals were meeting at the University of Ibadan in mid-1966 to map out secessionist strategies.[44] Thus, the link between the Mafia and the military was born.[45]

In the early stages of the civil war, the Mafia – then known as the 'War Council' – not only provided a measure of finance for the war, but organised the training of senior Kaduna officials in weapon handling, the production of local ammunition and the purchase of French arms, and decisively influenced the prosecution of the war itself from Kaduna.[46] As General Obasanjo points out:

> Delivery of normal arms and equipment on order for the Army in 1966 was hastened. Other than the stock in hand there were no special provisions available for mobilisation. Soon, however, a few trusted officials both in Lagos and Kaduna were saddled, in addition to their normal duties, with responsibility for obtaining arms, ammunition and equipment for the conduct of a war...
> In planning and concept the war was intended to be fought by the troops located in the North and they were to be supplied mainly from Kaduna. To a certain extent, therefore, Kaduna shared pride of place with Lagos as the political and operational headquarters at the early stage of the war.[47]

With the creation of new states, the centralisation of administration, the oil boom, the enhanced fiscal base of the Federal state, and the arrival of an influential corps of Federal bureaucrats at the centre of national decision-making, the Mafia's influence gradually ebbed. Coming to power in his early thirties, inexperienced, single, and lonely, alienated from the officers who had installed him in power but also surrounded by officers he did not particularly trust, Gowon increasingly gravitated towards Federal permanent secretaries for advice on policy and its execution. Dazzled by their 'profound analysis of policy issues',[48] Gowon relied on them to formulate and implement public policy. As Mr C. O. Lawson, then Secretary to the Federal Government, was bold enough to instruct the Lagos Chambers of

123

Commerce: 'The civil servant is the dog that wags its tail in the governmental machinery, signalling to the whole ministry including the minister the direction in which he thinks the ministry should move.'[49]

Permanent Secretaries not only attended Cabinet meetings, but exercised considerable sway over the agenda. They wrangled frequently with commissioners over the submission of memoranda to the Cabinet, and often clashed with them in Cabinet itself. Cliques of military and bureaucratic insiders determined major policies and controlled the strategic allocation of public resources and opportunities. Gowon's closest bureaucratic allies spearheaded a series of socio-political reforms, and superintended the penetration of public capital into economic activities such as oil production, iron and steel manufacture, vehicle assembly, banking, insurance, agriculture, commerce, construction, and communications, in alliance with foreign enterprises. The unfettered rule of the 'Super Permsecs' – as the most prominent of the permanent secretaries were known – had arrived. The Kaduna Mafia resented their virtual exclusion from the determination of public policy and the allocation of public resources. To them, Gowon's rule no longer served the interests of the north; and he seemed indifferent to the ravages of the 1973 Sahelian drought in the northern areas of the Federation. A 'national movement' under his own civilian leadership as advocated by some of his civil servant advisers[50] threatened to perpetuate the control of public resources by military and bureaucratic elements who were predominantly 'southern' and 'Christian'. Having failed in 1973 to convince Gowon to check the influence of his civil servant intimates, the Mafia set themselves to mobilise the northern civil and military support which would in due course bring him down.[51]

Reformers and rebels: friends and foes of change, Mohammed and Obasanjo

In Nigeria, unlike a number of African countries exposed to especially brutal colonial or monarchical rule, like Mozambique or Ethiopia, ideological politics has never had much appeal and has remained steadfastly absent from most agendas. Despite several changes of regimes, Nigeria's goals in terms of economic development, of external relations, and of political and social stability have differed only marginally from those proclaimed at independence. Mohammed's regime came to power in 1975 committed to reformist and populist policies, liberally spiced with nationalism. It intended to strengthen and diversify Nigeria's economic linkages both with the West and elsewhere; to expand the economic role of the state alongside and in alliance with multinational capital; to stimulate private Nigerian capital through state intervention; and to provide a central government able to determine and implement public policy in the national interest.[52]

Intractable issues, like the 1973 census, the creation of new states, a new federal capital, return to civil rule, and the divisive effects of pan-regional bodies like the Interim Common Services Agency (ICSA) and the Eastern

States Interim Assets and Liabilities Agency (ESIALA) all demanded creative and decisive action. Public policy was to be decided on rational and pragmatic criteria, designed to regulate conflicts between interests, to maintain the authority of the state, and to ensure the stability of society. All these, the regime realised, required a strong, central, hierarchical, and efficient military state with technocratic reformers genuinely committed to national ideals as its proxy vanguard.

One of the regime's first actions was to change the composition, organization, and command structure of decision-making bodies. Gowon, his service chiefs, the state governors, and all officers above the rank of brigadier were pensioned off. The Supreme Military Council (SMC) was reconstituted. Its most influential members included Mohammed himself, Brigadier Obasanjo, Chief of Staff, Supreme Headquarters (SHQ), Brigadier T. Y. Danjuma, Chief of Army Staff, the other service chiefs, the three General Officers Commanding (GOCs), and a number of assertive middle-ranking officers, four of whom were given ministerial portfolios. Placed between the SMC and a new Federal Executive Council (FEC), was the National Council of States (NCS) consisting of twelve (later nineteen) state governors and made answerable to Obasanjo.

Strategic military and political posts went to officers who had brought Gowon to power, fought in the civil war, were Mohammed's *protégés*, and also organised Gowon's removal.[53] Like Mohammed, most of the regime's key figures had spent their formative professional years in the ambience of fierce pan-northern nationalism or were well connected to the northern political establishment. General Mohammed, Lieutenant-Cols. Shehu Yar'adua, the coup's anchorman, and Muhammadu Buhari, the north-east governor, for example, were all scions of the northern aristocracy, and had close links with its intelligentsia.[54] They were also nationalists of reformist and corrective bent. In common with members of the Kaduna Mafia, they shared a passionate concern about the ethics of the nation, and with good and effective government. Some had taken part in the annual conferences organised by the Institute of Administration, Zaria – a veiled Mafia academic forum whose 1970s reformist consensus on Nigeria's socio-economic development strategies shared the priorities of Mohammed's regime.[55] All these varied influences, particularly the asseveration of a unitary professional ethos and *esprit de corps*, and the predominance of the military stratum over other ruling social strata combined to give government a new aspect. Permanent Secretaries were banned from the FEC unless specifically invited. This was intended to confine them to their executive function, and regulate their relationship with commissioners.[56] Bureaucrats, the regime believed, could not be relied upon to formulate and direct its reform programmes, but could be used to implement them.

But while the regime was aware of the importance of, and the need to rely on, civil servants, it saw the task of reforms as one for specialist analysis within and outside mainstream government administration. The government

Shehu Othman

appointed a series of committees of eminent Nigerians from outside the public service to examine and report on a number of unresolved public issues. As a result, ICSA and ESIALA were disbanded, seven additional states were created, a new federal capital at Abuja was decided upon, local government reforms were undertaken, reform of the marketing boards was accomplished, the indigenisation decree was strengthened, a land use decree was promulgated, and the làbour unions were brought under stricter controls. New bodies, such as the Public Complaints Bureau (an Ombudsman), the National Security Organization (NSO), and the Corrupt Practices Investigation Bureau were also established to check widespread infractions. Probes into the public conduct of officials of the late regime were also instituted, resulting in exposures of massive corruption and confiscation of venally acquired wealth and properties. 'Operation Deadwoods', a maelstrom of purges the scale of which was unprecedented in Africa, swept aside some 10,000 public employees, either with or without retirement benefits. Among these were some 100 police and 216 military officers.[57]

Simultaneously, the regime assembled a battery of highly educated, intelligent, self-confident, and innovative young men in the Cabinet Office Political Department to coordinate and advise on the making and implementation of major policies. Among these *avant-garde* technocrats were: Yaya Abubakar, Babagana Kingibe, Gidado Idris, Tunji Olagunju, Olu Otunla, Dr P. D. Cole, and B. Kolawale. Except for the last three, all had firm links with the Mafia and three of them had been regular Zaria conferees. As Yahaya also notes: 'It was inconceivable for anybody who did not accept [the Mafia's] eminent status to be given any important assignment or appointment during the Obasanjo era.'[58]

What mainly differentiated these technocratic reformers (and their like-minded military superiors) from the generality of top-level bureaucrats was their age, their close links with academic life, their radical nationalism, reforming zeal, and sharply distinct conceptions of how the necessary reforms should be implemented. Whilst organisationally and structurally part of the higher bureaucracy, and in fact, subordinate to it, they enjoyed unrestricted access to the regime's highest decision-makers. Under this close working relationship, they reanalysed the political advice of their bureaucratic superiors, and provided the focal point for analysis of overall direction of government programmes. An important feature of this phase was the close consultation which developed between them and other academics and the regime's top decision-makers. The extent to which Obasanjo was influenced by these reformers could clearly be seen from his famous radical nationalist 'Jaji Declaration', or his 'FESTAC Colloquium' address – a veiled but essentially Marxist critique of Africa's comprador role in the global political economy.[59]

Under Mohammed, the SMC determined both the broad framework of national policy and the treatment of a number of issues of critical national importance. But because the SMC met only infrequently, Mohammed could

126

take decisions on urgent matters provided that he sought the SMC's approval afterwards. Day-to-day decision-making was exercised by a triumvirate of Mohammed, an impetuous but pragmatic man with enormous drive and energy and the doyen of young officers, Obasanjo, the cautious and cunning intellectual pillar of the trio, and the effective but notoriously ruthless Brigadier Danjuma. On most issues which went to the SMC, though, prior agreement was usually reached at a 'Kitchen Cabinet' comprising the troika, Commodore Michael Adelanwa and Colonel J. Y. Doko (the naval and air force chiefs respectively), M. D. Yusuf (the Police Inspector-General), Lieutenant-Colonel Yar'adua, and Colonel Ibrahim Babangida. General Oluleye, himself an SMC member, wrote of decisions being reached by 'consensus either in Council or the consensus reached by another Supreme Council operating behind the actual scene.'[60]

Yar'adua and Babangida represented the link between the senior officers and a cohesive group of influential middle ranking officers who had brought the regime to power, and through whom the regime's thinking and policies were informally marketed to the wider officer corps. Drawn largely from the Nigerian north, and known by leading civil servants as the 'Young Turks',[61] most were effective and outstanding soldiers with celebrated war-time records, and shared a fierce commitment to a military ethos and reforming zeal within and outside the military.[62] Collaboration between these cliques of military insiders made for easier consensus, and for incisive decisions. But it also generated resentment and disaffection among SMC's leading war-time commanders, one of whom allegedly inspired the abortive coup of February 1976 which killed General Mohammed, amongst others. Mohammed's elevation of himself to General and of his two deputies to Lieutenant-General in January 1976, without consulting with the war-time commanders (whom he also promoted to Major-Generals) had prompted charges of personal ambition and running a closed government. The war-time commanders were especially incensed by the advancement of Danjuma, who had hitherto been their junior. For Major-General Iliya Bissalla, the Defence Minister and alleged architect of the coup, the promotions were even more galling: he had been superseded not only by his course-mates (Mohammed and Obasanjo), but also by the one-time Staff Officer of his erstwhile Command at the 1st Infantry Division – Danjuma. Besides his curt treatment by Mohammed whenever he raised the issue at the SMC, Bissalla had also disagreed sharply with Mohammed over Nigeria's recognition of Angola's Marxist MPLA government.[63]

It also emerged from documents[64] reportedly seized from Bissalla's co-conspirators that they too were opposed to the generals' elevation, which they saw as prompted solely by the desire to enrich themselves. Not only was the new leadership corrupt, it was also going 'Communist' and lacked the moral authority to superintend the mass purges which it had undertaken, while General Mohammed, a scion of the Kano aristocracy, was seen as scheming to install as his civilian successor the veteran and highly articulate

127

Kano politician – Alhaji Maitama Sule. As it turned out, almost all of the forty-three sentenced to death and those imprisoned for participation or complicity in the putsch came from Gowon's own ethnic group, although Gowon himself strenuously denied the new regime's allegation of his involvement. Mostly field-commissioned junior and middle ranking officers from the Biafran war, they were troubled by fears over 'individual career prospects, inspired by the "conversion" exercise; and the threat of demobilisation; [and] by antipathy to the aggressively "professional" approach of the new army commanders, which was translated into hostility to the so-called promotions exercise...'[65] Their aim was to reverse the reforms initiated by Mohammed, to reintroduce the House of Chiefs, to reinstate a number of sacked bureaucrats in their former power, and to inject junior officers into government at state and federal levels.

Except for minor shifts in personnel – notably Obasanjo's advent as leader and Yar'adua's as Chief of Staff – the 1976 putsch altered neither the insiders' preeminent status nor the direction of overall policy. Aided by the institutional reforms undertaken under Mohammed, drawing on the militant nationalism of his Cabinet Office reformers, and assisted vigorously by Yar'adua and Danjuma, Obasanjo effectively superintended the conduct of day-to-day administration from his residence in Dodan Barracks. He introduced sweeping changes in the security establishment, followed by determined army reorganisation, the construction of additional barracks, the retraining of junior officers at home and abroad, and of senior officers at the newly established and prestigious Jaji Staff Command College, an accelerated but generous demobilisation programme which by 1979 trimmed the army's size by over 50,000 to 173,000 (Table 8.3), and above all the tightening of military discipline in the court martial or cashiering of hundreds of officers and men for a variety of misdemeanours. In the face of this zeal and severity even senior officers like Major-General Oluleye could find himself court-martialled for politely cautioning against the regime's reforming zealotry. Group Captain Usman Jibrin, then Kaduna State governor, was sacked in 1977 for daring to voice northern displeasure at the restriction of Radio Kaduna and other erstwhile regional stations from broadcasting on short wave.

The regime's attempts to impose a comparable discipline on the civil service, for all their vigour, had only the most superficial and transitory of impacts. With the exception of Ayida, the SFMG, whose robust interventions and insistence on unfettered bureaucratic direction of agreed policies helped to avert several blunders, hardly any top civil servant outside Dodan Barracks and the Cabinet Office felt confident enough to speak frankly, let alone to dissuade the regime from its corrective policies. Few Cabinet ministers were prepared to risk censure by pressing their departmental views when these conflicted with the thinking in Dodan Barracks. The isolation of senior bureaucrats from strategic decision-making and their resulting loss of confidence created anxiety and disillusionment. Administration slowed to a

Table 8.3. *Total armed forces personnel (selected years)*

Year	Army	Airforce	Navy	Total
1970–71	180,000	3,000	2,000	185,000
1972–73	262,000	7,000	5,000	274,000
1975–76	200,000	5,000	3,000	208,000
	10,000[a]		2,000[a]	12,000[a]
1976–77	221,000	5,500	3,500	230,000
	10,000[a]		2,000[a]	12,000[a]
1979–80	160,000	7,000	6,000	173,000
			2,000[a]	2,000[a]
1981–82	140,000	10,000	6,000	156,000
			2,000[a]	2,000[a]
1983–84	120,000	9,000	4,000	133,000
1985–86	80,000	9,000	5,000	94,000
1986–87	80,000	9,000	5,000	94,000

Note: [a] Reserves
Sources: The International Institute for Strategic Studies, The Military Balance, various years.

crawl, in some cases, to quote Obasanjo, 'to the point of paralysis'.[66] The constant references, in public and private, to corruption, indiscipline, and inefficiency made civil servants increasingly edgy.[67] To protect themselves against accusations of error, they dodged responsibility and ceded the initiative. A memo in October 1977 expressed Obasanjo's 'gravest concern' at 'growing indiscipline' and 'abject laxity noticeable throughout the Public Service...'[68]

The consequences were grave. The larger the spoils involved, the fiercer the intrigues, and the more devastating their consequences. As a secret Cabinet-level inquiry into Nigeria Airways in 1978 noted with graphic and brutal clarity: 'Short-circuiting of the chain of command is common. Routine decisions are taken to the highest level in an effort to "get things moving". [Conversely], vital decisions are passed to operating units without the knowledge of intermediate managers.'[69] As with most lucrative deals, 'the purchase of every aircraft was..."a battle royal"' between the airline and the Civil Aviation Ministry.[70] Even the airline's chief internal auditor confessed his bemusement in the face of the prevailing corruption: 'The sources and causes of fraud and malpractices are as varied as the colours of a butterfly and the more you explore them, the more shades of the same colour you identify.'[71] In this way, the committee reported: 'Nigeria Airways became the epitome of all that is evil in our society: corruption, gross inefficiency, callousness and the like.'[72] The Aviation Ministry cynically proposed a draconic remedy: 'Put bluntly, the airline requires a "Mad Man" who will do to the airline what the "Great Fire" did to London in the seventeenth century.'[73] Their differences were not so much over policy or principle as over who decides and who gets the largest slice of the racket.

Shagari to Buhari and Babangida: consensus, cleavage, and conflict

The overthrow of President Shagari's elected government in 1983 and the subsequent dismissal of General Buhari in 1985 served only to accentuate both the persistence and instability of northern hegemony and the tensions between the northern military class and other elements in the armed forces. In neither case did the conflict arise from fundamental disagreement over the status of the armed forces hierarchy relative to other managers of state power, or over the place of the Nigerian north in national affairs. The fractional struggles mainly stemmed from differing calculations of relative advantage and particular claims, real or potential outcomes in the distribution of state power and its spoils, redefinitions of appropriate solidarities and methods rather than the goal of erecting an effective bourgeois class rule.

Both the Buhari and Babangida coups were mainly carried out by northern officers who reaffirmed their commitment to the professional integrity and *esprit de corps* of the army, and their ambition of reviving Nigeria's tottering economy within the framework of 'free enterprise' in a

130

'mixed economy'. Under Babangida's stern monetarist crusade a gradual, if uncertain, process of rolling back the frontiers of the state has begun; but there has so far been no clear change in the relationship of the ruling group to the people at large, or of the state to citizen: still less any marked shift in the overall distribution of advantages between the various strata of Nigerian society.[74]

Similarly, if there has been no real alteration in the preeminent status and relative economic well-being of the armed forces, it is partly because its command, promotion, and remuneration structures have remained jealously guarded. Each new Nigerian military regime has hastened to promote its senior military members, with other and more junior beneficiaries following in their wake, and all drawing further rewards – official and unofficial, in cash and other media. Soon after General Buhari came to power, his deputy, Brigadier T. Idiagbon, and thirteen other officers were promoted to general and along with all other army personnel acquired an array of new uniforms. A review of armed forces' pay was later followed by major purchases of sophisticated military hardware despite a moratorium on public sector employment, promotions or pay increases in the civil service, new public expenditure, and the completion of a number of unfinished projects.[75] Most conspicuous among the military acquisitions were eight of the eighteen Jaguar fighter aircraft which the Shagari government had ordered from British Aerospace at a cost of £300 million (including spares, hangars, and training), and from which unnamed Nigerian middlemen received £22 million in kickbacks, otherwise known as 'the sugar'. Curiously, the Buhari regime, despite its well publicised earlier insistence that the pay-out must be excluded from the contract cost, later capitulated, claiming that some 'adjustment in kind', regarding training costs, had in fact been made.[76] Not even Nigeria's current economic adversities have slowed promotion within the officer caste, most notably of some sixteen generals by the Babangida regime, and subsequently, of other service chiefs and Babangida himself.[77]

What divergences there were between Shagari and the military hierarchy concerned not the objectives of defence policy but some real and potential erosions of the military's claims and professional prerogatives: its corporate material interests, prestige, operational freedom, aspirations, and military professional self-assertion.[78] For Shagari and his defence chiefs (including those who eventually overthrew him) were firmly agreed on common defence policy objectives,[79] the ultimate goal of which, according to Professor Iya Abubakar, then Defence Minister, was the building of a powerful military machine designed to lend credibility to Nigeria's continental ambitions, and based upon a strong and sophisticated local armaments industry.[80] Shagari had in fact begun to supply the armed forces with new, sophisticated, and costly equipment when the sharp decline in oil revenues (Table 8.2), made worse by the pressures of distributive and electoral politics, predatory privatisation of public resources, the expansion of state employment, deficiencies in fiscal direction and discipline, and not least, political incompetence, forced a sharp cut in military expenditures.[81] These cuts, along with the dubious priorities in such defence spending as survived (particularly in comparison with internal security) severely disrupted the corporate morale of the armed forces.

Shagari's annual defence capital spending (from which the largest private benefits from massive contracts arise), declined markedly between 1981 and 1982 but rose again in 1983 (Table 8.4). This decrease was all the starker in comparison with the corresponding figures under General Obasanjo whose lowest annual figure of 9.1 per cent (1977) was bigger than Shagari's largest of 8.6 per cent (1980). Except for the 1980 figure, annual defence capital spending, both in absolute terms and in relation to total capital expenditures, was largest under Obasanjo. Recurrent annual defence expenditures under Shagari (about 80 per cent of which go into payment of salaries, allowances, etc.), however, moved in a markedly different pattern, reflecting an understandable concern with the immediate and personal needs of military personnel. The largest expenditure ever, both in absolute terms and as a proportion of total recurrent expenditures (except in 1979 and 1981), came in 1980 – a year marked by both high oil revenues and external reserves (Tables 8.1 and 8.2). The sudden and massive increase in expenditure between 1978 and 1979 (from 8.7 per cent to 21.1 per cent) may have been due to the military reorganisation and rehabilitation undertaken by Obasanjo, and made possible by improved oil production and sales (Table 8.2). The decline from 1982 to 1983 reflects both the fall in oil production and revenues and the wider failure of the economy.

In contrast to the fall in defence spending, Shagari's capital expenditure on internal security, mainly on the police, had steadily increased between 1980 and 1983, its ratio to defence allocations rising from 10.5 per cent in 1980 to 36.2 per cent in 1983. While this may have reflected concern with improving the conditions and efficiency of the police (given the 1978 ratio of internal security allocation to defence of 5.6 per cent under General Obasanjo), it was certainly true that under Shagari the police had come to play a highly visible and critical role vis-à-vis party political activities and elections, and one which even the wider public saw as favouring Shagari's own National Party of Nigeria (NPN). Recurrent internal security expenditure grew steadily between 1980 and 1983, and at a rate higher than capital expenditure. Although official data do not distinguish recurrent defence and internal security expenditure between 1973–7, the tendency of internal security spending between 1978 and 1983 suggests that there had been a continuous increase (Table 8.4).

Material disadvantages apart, there were other tart experiences as well. Between 1980 and 1983, the *amour propre* of black Africa's most powerful army suffered a number of humiliating bruises at the hands of weaker regional powers. First came its precipitous withdrawal from Chad in 1980 after a disastrous peace-keeping operation, followed by comparably ineffectual return forays under Western prompting and with some Western

132

Table 8.4. *Capital and recurrent expenditure on defence and internal security, 1973–83 (Naira million)*

	1973[a]	1974[a]	1975[a]	1976[a]	1977[a]	1978	1979	1980	1981[b]	1982[c]	1983[d]
Capital Expenditure											
Defence	77	176.5	354	419	495	709	564	723	479	464	555
% of total	13.6	11.4	10.1	9.9	9.1	12.6	11.7	8.6	8.4	5.8	8.2
Int. sec.						0.40	n.a.	76	87	84	201
% of total						0.6	n.a.	0.9	1.5	1.0	2.9
& ratio of def./int. sec.						5.6	n.a.	10.5	18.2	18.1	36.2
Recurrent expenditure											
Defence	329.7	396.4	774	690	765	596	672	1035	1015	661	535
% of total	27.2	14.6	16.4	12.6	12.2	8.7	21.1	17.2	20.0	13.6	10.1
Internal sec.						130	n.a.	275	397	400	410
% of total						1.9	n.a.	4.5	7.8	8.2	7.8
% Ratio of cap/rec (defence)	23.4	44.5	45.7	60.7	64.7	119	83.9	69.9	48.9	70.2	103.7
Total defence exp. index	36.0	50.8	100	98.3	111.7	157	109.5	155.8	132.4	99.7	99.6
Total int. sec: exp. index			100			100	n.a.	206.5	284	284	359

Notes: [a] Separate defence and international security expenditures for 1973–7 available. [b] Provisional estimates. [c][d] Approved budget estimates
Sources: CBN, Annual Report and Statement of Account, several issues, and Economic and Financial Review, several issues.

financing in 1981 and 1982. Inadequate Nigerian financing of these operations, partly caused by the oil-induced cash-flow crisis, provoked discomfiture within military circles. Further national humiliation was inflicted by the May 1981 border incident with Cameroon in which a Nigerian commissioned officer and four soldiers were killed and three others seriously injured. Then came additional skirmishes with Cameroon and Chad during 1983, the latter resulting in nine Nigerian fatalities and the capture of twenty other Nigerian soldiers.

Characteristically, President Shagari consistently resisted pressures both from inside and outside the military for tough reprisals, arguing that Nigeria's leadership role 'precluded any hasty recourse by us to military response...until all diplomatic persuasions had failed'.[82] Some military commanders were unimpressed. They deplored Shagari's cautious foreign policy, and his pragmatic collaboration with the Reagan administration over the Chad question; and they seethed with anger at their own losses, and at the public suspicion that they were impotent in the face of the purported menace of Libyan expansionism. Their resentment at political constraints was dramatically exemplified when Major-General Buhari, intent on inflicting a crushing defeat on the Chadian army for the capture of some Nigerian soldiers in late 1983, for some days disregarded his orders from Lagos to cease hostilities.[83] The same attitudes are evident in Major-General Babangida's complaint:

> if you see the input that the top hierarchy of the military provided to the last administration all in an effort to assist them, you will be amazed... Look at a simple thing like the whole damn policy, concerning Chad. It was dictated to them by some people outside this country. We would provide the expert advice but nobody would listen.[84]

Nor did President Shagari heed the military's counsel on some of the vexing vestiges of the Biafran war. Genuinely concerned to remedy grievances felt by the Igbo, he revoked the loss of seniority suffered by Igbo returnees into the military and public bureaucracies under General Gowon. And following the revoking in 1981 of the 'wanted notice' placed on Gowon himself for alleged complicity in the abortive coup of 1976, Shagari granted an amnesty in May 1982 to Emeka Ojukwu, the former Biafran leader. Although Shagari had indeed been under considerable pressure from political associates and adversaries alike, the move – when it came – appeared blatantly partisan in motivation. For Ojukwu returned home in June to a heroic welcome, and afterwards, to a prominent position in Shagari's own NPN as well as a senatorial candidacy in the 1983 elections. In the opinion of the public and of many serving and retired military commanders, most of them veterans of the Biafran war, all these were remarkable gestures to the man whom they saw as the moving spirit of the Nigerian tragedy. Furthermore, the equipment of the police with armoured personnel carriers, reinforced suspicions that the NPN was not merely

134

manoeuvring to sustain its political ascendancy, but was also preparing to bully its way through the elections, while furnishing itself with alternative defences in the event of a direct conflict with the armed forces.[85]

Grave economic failures sharpened social and religious conflicts. Oil prices had tumbled while production slumped; industrial activity slowed down to a crawl; stagflation, unemployment, and violent crime persisted; health, educational, and infra-structural services deteriorated; agriculture stagnated; foreign capital inflow remained lethargic; domestic and foreign debts swelled; economic policy-making, implementation, and regulation weakened, as did executive power and state authority. Corruption, within and outside the political class, was pervasive and blatant. Under Shagari's NPN, a class of millionaire hucksters rose to political preeminence at the expense of the poor and the possessors of academic, technocratic, corporate or managerial skills. The wealthy clients of the party spent lavishly on party activities, often funding candidates of their own, or becoming prominent party or state functionaries themselves. Their prosperity derived not from production or corporate business, but from commerce, contracts, speculative concerns, state patronage and favours, and activities as middlemen; and this in turn accentuated their preoccupation with personal linkages to the holders of state power.[86]

The ascendancy of this *nouveau riche* grouping directly menaced the political, corporate, and managerial interests of their erstwhile technocratic associates in the Kaduna Mafia, built and developed over several years of previous military rule. The Mafia was disturbed enough to canvass northern support for Chief Obafemi Awolowo's 1983 presidential bid — after an unsuccessful attempt to suborn the predominantly northern Peoples Redemption Party, a radical petit bourgeois grouping with a populist appeal. Awolowo, however, lost the election, while his Unity Party of Nigeria conceded two states to the NPN and gained one from them. The scale of NPN's electoral victory stunned the Mafia as it did everyone else; but it did nothing to reconcile them to the prospect of a further four years of increasingly incoherent rule. Like their military allies, they wanted northern power preserved; but they demanded, along with it, order and discipline throughout the economy, polity, and society.[87]

Friendship, fraternity, and fragmentation

The Buhari junta which replaced Shagari was predominantly northern in composition and conservative in outlook and direction. Most of the northern officers who belonged to it were course-mates, and had developed close personal friendships for over two decades. They were part of the generation of northerners encouraged by northern civilian ministers in the 1960s to join the army straight from school, in order to make up the northern quota in the officer corps of the armed forces. Only eight of the regime's twenty SMC members came from the south, though four of these held important military,

135

police, judicial, and bureaucratic posts. Numerically, Cabinet and gubernatorial appointments were spread far more equitably amongst ethnic and regional groups. Eleven of the eighteen Cabinet ministers, including the Kaduna Mafia's leading ideologue, were either civilian academics, professionals, or technocrats. Strategic portfolios such as Petroleum, Finance, and Justice were held by non-northerners.[88]

The Buhari regime affirmed its faith in 'free market' philosophy within a 'mixed economy'. Agriculture was to receive the 'highest priority'; and the junta pledged itself to reduce Nigeria's dependence on oil and imported armament, to improve its defence system, to revive industry, to discipline labour, while improving its conditions, to expedite the expansion of Abuja, Nigeria's new northern capital, to restore financial discipline, probity, and executive authority, to pursue affirmative action in public sector jobs and school admissions based on state of origin, to encourage religious education, and to enforce strictly the ban on the importation, sale or display of pornographic material.[89] It was particularly concerned to win the confidence of major trading partners, in order to elicit further credits. The soldiers who overthrew Shagari's second government thus had little, if any, dispute with its own avowed policies: a convergence explained by an affinity of primordial and ideological formation, the soldiers' own lack of distinct economic strategy, and the pilfering of Shagari's own policy document. Their bitter opposition to their civilian predecessors was prompted by the latters' disastrous socio-economic record, monstrous venality, the vastly unequal shares of power and resources which accrued to competing ruling groups, and, above all, by anxiety at the threat which these failings posed to the stability of the entire system of ownership and distribution of resources in which both ruling coalitions held a common stake. As General Buhari, in a parody of nationalist rhetoric, declared when he assumed power: 'This generation of Nigerians, and indeed future generations, have no other country than Nigeria. We shall remain here and salvage it together.'[90]

The Buhari regime's overall economic strategy was deflationary. It cut some categories of imports, reduced state expenditure, subsidies, and public sector jobs, passed a number of protectionist measures, raised taxes, froze wages, and banned strikes inside and outside industry. Foreign exchange management was rationalised, with priority attached to external debt servicing, and then to imports of industrial raw material. Despite some relative success, though, import licence allocation remained highly contentious, as were a series of counter-trade deals entered into with individual countries and foreign firms. There was also a measure of visible revival in executive authority, fiscal control, and cohesion and firmness in policy-making, inspired both by General Buhari's own apparent asceticism and by the regime's draconian measures. A state governor was dismissed for pecuniary malfeasance; and in spite of its intimacy with the traditional nobility, the junta penalised two of their leading figures whose private visit to Jerusalem had compromised Nigeria's boycott of Israel.

There was, too, a renewed sense of urgency about the country's predicament; and a positive but ephemeral spasm of patriotic fervour spurred by the regime's authoritarian 'War Against Indiscipline'. This crusade assailed all forms of social entropy, degeneracy, and dishonourable conduct, and apotheosised the virtues of honesty, patriotism, hard work, sanitation, queueing, family life, and the good society.[91] Most people apparently sanctioned the stern measures, including the death penalty, reserved for a range of economic, violent, and anti-social crimes. But when convicted drug peddlers were executed, this provoked hostility and veiled charges of official onslaughts on the Nigerian south. Further executions seem to have been averted only after a senior police commander, related to General Buhari himself, was implicated in a drug scandal. Various attempts to keep militant labour, students, and professional groups in check served only to fuel popular disquiet and antipathy, as did the infamous Decree No. 4 which made it an offence to publish or broadcast anything 'which is false in any material particular' or which embarrassed the state or its officials.[92]

Hundreds of functionaries of the *ancien régime*, together with their business associates, were hurled into detention, and trials by military tribunals handed out long prison sentences. But here, too, there was widespread resentment of the pace, manner, and outcomes of the process, which was widely perceived as discriminatory in favour of northern states and the NPN. Southern opinion was critical not only of the failure to try former President Shagari (an aristocrat from the Sokoto Caliphate of blessed memory) and his deputy, Dr Alex Ekwueme (an Igbo millionaire and parvenu politician), but of the decision which kept Shagari under house arrest while Ekwueme was held in prison.[93] More generally, there was pervasive resentment of the now defunct Nigerian Security Organization (NSO), seen increasingly as acting at the behest of a Buharite military faction, and disturbing even senior military commanders by its excesses. The arrogance with which this clique exercised power, and its relentless attempts to suppress a campaign of surreptitious opposition in the press alienated it from most groups. Among journalists who were detained for between eight and twenty months without charge or trial were Rufai Ibrahim, Haroun Adamu, and Tai Solarin – all of them able and serious critics of the Shagari years.

Suspicion of the regime's apparent sensitivity to northern concerns, aggravated by an upsurge of pan-northern revivalism coordinated by the northern governors, heightened ethnic, sectional and religious tensions.[94] These damaged the overall unity of the armed forces, prompting renewed confederate demands from retired Yoruba Generals; and provoking the startling observation by Hassan Usman Katsina, a northern prince and retired General, that soldiers were not 'fit to rule'. The regime made nervous attempts to muffle all political discourse.[95] But in a barbed retort, General Obasanjo criticised the regime's apparent partiality towards the north, insisting that access to resources and opportunities 'must be fairly even and unobstructed'. He condemned the regime's affirmative policies as 'seemingly undue favour', and the attitude of its greatest beneficiaries as 'arrogant, disrespectful, overbearing, immodest and unco-operative'. Echoing a sense of grievance by now widespread amongst the Yoruba, he insisted that 'The feeling persists in some quarters that there is a grand design to perpetually exclude some group from political leadership because the group to be so excluded has economic ascendancy.'[96]

In themselves, all these divisive issues undermined the credibility and stability of the regime. More fatally, they intensified the strains within the ruling junta. Two factions became increasingly evident in the SMC. One was the group centred on Buhari himself, epitomised by his Chief of Staff Idiagbon, the most hated symbol of the regime, and backed by the NSO machine. The other was personified by the convivial but cunning Chief of Army Staff Babangida, himself the army's quintessential high-flier and hero of many field commanders and young officers. It was Babangida who, after encircling a rebel-held enclave with tanks during the February 1976 putsch, went in alone and unarmed to lure the rebels to a crushing defeat.

There were areas of agreement between the two camps, both on military and on other affairs. General Buhari had proceeded with all previously planned major defence expenditure projects: notably the upgrading of the Nigerian Defence Academy to university status, the building of an Air Force and Naval academy, the establishment of the N30 million armoured personnel carrier plant in Bauchi, and a number of military reequipment and modernisation programmes. Indeed local military production and capability had been strengthened under his government. The hitherto somnolent Defence Industries Corporation began to produce military explosives and arms; a Research and Development cell was established within the Defence Ministry; an Army Bank was planned; and several retired or serving military commanders received prominent appointments at home or as diplomatic representatives abroad.

The initial strains within the SMC seem to have arisen from the question of political detainees. The Buhari faction saw the choice as one between applying rough and ready justice or risking public outrage by letting off many of those whom the regime could not hope to prosecute successfully, a possibility which threatened to increase the instability of the regime. Hence, much of the stalling and bungling not to talk of other inequities that were real enough but never redressed. By contrast, the Babangida camp took the simple and more liberal view (perhaps with equally good grounds) that the detainees should either be charged and put on trial, or conditionally released. Past misdeeds, they argued, ought not be corrected by methods which might well foster further rancour. The issue was debated 'almost daily, either in [the SMC] or out of it'; but the views of Babangida's grouping were ignored.[97] Collective decision-making thus gradually broke down, while the balance of power shifted decisively to the supporters of Buhari.

Mutual distrust intensified, as even members of the SMC itself came under apparent surveillance by the NSO, command over which had recently been denied to a *protégé* of Babangida.[98] In addition to a number of alleged incursions into his official preserve, Babangida himself was frequently suspected of plotting to overthrow his close friend General Buhari, a man whom he had personally requested to head the new regime. Suspicions were also rife of 'glaring fraud associated with the countertrade...[and] the issuance of import licence' as well as the perpetration of 'injustice...with impunity'.[99] There were further sharp dissensions, too, over issues of economic and defence policy, sometimes with clear ideological overtones. Whereas the Buhari camp pursued a deflationary economic strategy and rejected any deal with the IMF, the Babangida faction insisted that austerity measures without structural adjustment of the kind advocated by the IMF were unlikely to alleviate Nigeria's economic predicament. They attributed the loss of Nigeria's regular crude oil customers to counter-trade policy, and disagreed with the priority which Buhari attached to external debt servicing, for which 44 per cent of Nigeria's annual external earnings were now earmarked.

The immediate occasion for the split went far beyond the issue of immediate defence spending. The Buhari regime's deflationary policies and its reordering of spending priorities meant cut-backs in most areas except debt servicing and agriculture – which formed the thrust of its development strategy. Thus total annual defence allocations in 1984 (N928.2 million) and 1985 (N975 million) were all below the lowest of Shagari's expenditure of N1,090 million for 1983. This budgetary trend and the shift towards agriculture directly menaced Babangida's very different vision, one which concerned the very nature of society and the mission of the military within it. At the very time that Buhari was touring army formations in February 1985, telling soldiers that austerity measures applied to them as they did to everyone else, Babangida launched extravagant proposals for increase in military spending at a well-publicised lecture in Lagos. He urged that Nigeria's entire industrial base should be developed around a defence-orientated economy. Drawing on Brazilian experience, he advocated the building of an 'arms city' in the hinterland, arguing that the relevant technology 'could be obtained by borrowing, stealing, direct purchase and licence-buying for the purpose of investigation and development'. This project was feasible within a timespan of twenty-five years; and the strategic industries, like iron and steel, which it required should be developed 'as a deliberate policy to produce locally defence-related goods'. The lecture as a whole constituted a public challenge to his rivals within the SMC and in government: 'those who advocate less spending on defence cannot win'.[100]

As the army's leading strategic planner between 1979–83, Babangida had convinced the civilians to develop a number of defence-related industries. Buhari's energetic retrenchment thus threatened his whole conception of the country's future, along with his own personal future and that of his allies. On

27 August, accordingly Babangida overthrew General Buhari and his closest associates, citing a number of grounds for his action:

> The principle of discussions, consultation and cooperation which should have guided the decision-making process...were disregarded [sic] soon after the government settled down in 1984...Maj.-Gen. Buhari was too rigid and uncompromising in his attitude to issues of national significance. Efforts to make him understand that a diverse polity like Nigeria required recognition and appreciation of differences in both cultural and individual conceptions only served to aggravate this attitude.
>
> Maj.-Gen. Tunde Idiagbon was similarly inclined in that respect. As the Chief of Staff, Supreme Headquarters, he failed to exhibit the appropriate dispositions demanded by his position. He arrogated to himself absolute knowledge of problems and solutions and acted in accordance with what was convenient to him, using the machinery of government as his tool...The situation was made worse by a number of other government functionaries and organisations, chief amongst which is the Nigerian Security Organisation.[101]

After Buhari: the prophet of the market

President Babangida affirmed his regime's resolve to unite the country, and immediately fulfilled many of the pledges made in his maiden presidential broadcast. The twenty-eight member Armed Forces Ruling Council (AFRC) which replaced the defunct SMC reflected a variety of ethnic, sectional and military interests, as did the Cabinet and the NCS. Only Buhari and his closest military allies were made to retire; but personnel changes or subsequent retirements brought many of Babangida's intimates into key positions, most notably some hot-headed Majors who carried out the coup. These particularly affected military personnel from the core of the north, prompting a particularly vitriolic attack on Babangida for having only two Hausa-Fulani in the AFRC, and not a single Muslim GOC.[102]

The regime released many political detainees conditionally; subsequent trials were based on the recommendations of quasi-judicial review committees. Some of those already convicted had their sentences reduced. The notorious Decree No. 4 was quashed while other harsh decrees were subjected to benign neglect. Such measures, together with the regime's initial commitment to human rights, considerably eased the choking climate of Buhari–Idiagbon's authoritarianism. Joseph thus commented: 'staunch critics of the abuses of power by previous Nigerian governments found themselves in the unaccustomed role of praising the actions of the military government'.[103] The percentage of Nigeria's annual external earnings earmarked for debt-servicing was also slashed, and a grandiose scheme for rural improvement has been initiated. The public has at times been consulted on major national issues, and the regime has launched an agenda of institutional reforms and issued a schedule for a return to democracy.

It is in the sphere of economic reforms, which the regime made its top priority, that the most striking changes have come. Intent on implementing the IMF-inspired policies over which its two predecessors equivocated for fear of popular revolt, the regime sponsored a nation-wide debate on whether to accept the controversial US$2.5 billion IMF loan and its conditionalities. Predictably, the public and even the mass of the soldiery spurned the proposal. But in a virtuoso orchestration of public opinion, the government claimed this outcome as a mandate for an alternative home-grown strategy, and proceeded to impose monetarist policies which were far more radical than those required by the IMF itself, and with the discreet assistance of both the IMF and World Bank. Much of Nigerian industry is thus being gradually deregulated, and the Nigerian naira floated in a volatile inside market. The result has been some of the highest and most damaging interest rates ever, and a drastically devalued currency. The import licensing system, hitherto a notorious instrument of accumulation for state managers, has been dismantled, along with the commodity marketing regimes. Drastic cuts in state subsidies, notably on petroleum, have been imposed, and the process of privatising a number of public enterprises has begun. Market criteria now provide the template for the conduct of the great bulk of public business.

Although the Babangida regime has superintended the struggle for preeminence between Nigeria's major economically contending social strata, his regime's policies, whatever their other merits or hazards, have not resolved the question of order and cohesion within the ruling stratum itself. Political aggrandisement has an inner logic of its own. Only four months after it ascended to power, the regime announced the discovery of a coup plot by senior and middle-ranking officers, ten of whom were executed and five others jailed, while several more were cashiered in March 1986.[104] Amongst those executed, were Major-General Mamman Vatsa, an AFRC member and course-mate of Babangida himself, eight middle-ranking officers, and one Major. All but one of these came from ethnic minorities, notably from Benue State. But all, more significantly, held demanding positions, and in comparison with other officers might fairly be considered 'intellectuals', both in their professional qualities and their wider interests.

Major-General Vatsa, a minister and member of both the Buhari and the Babangida juntas, was a prolific poet who moved freely and regularly in Nigerian literary circles. Lieutenant-Colonel M. Iyorshe, once a celebrated cadet, belonged to the army's *crème de la crème*, and like Major D. Bamidele, held a training appointment at the prestigious Jaji Staff Command College before his arrest. Both Lieutenant-Colonel C. Oche and Lieutenant-Colonel M. Bitiyong had undertaken serious academic study: the former as a doctoral candidate at Georgetown University, Washington before he was recalled to co-ordinate intelligence matters at Buhari's Supreme Head-quarters, and the latter – then the Army's Director of Logistics – in the form of research into the Nigerian armed services. Of the four airforce officers, two were seasoned pilots attached to the presidential fleet, while the others each commanded a key airforce formation. Commander A. Ogwuji, the only naval officer among them, was commanding officer of the naval vessel, *NNS*

Olokun, beside being in the Lagos State Cabinet. All were allegedly dismayed by the regime's *volte-face* over the IMF issue, its commitment to human rights, and the presence in government of some of Buhari's ministers and governors, along with other middle and junior-ranking officers brought in by Babangida.[105]

All this is a little too pat. Digging further, one might hazard a more plausible and more charitable explanation, both of the plotters' motives and the official presentation of those motives. The latter in all probability stemmed simply from the desire to appeal to public patriotism (in the face of the carefully orchestrated pro-government rallies) and to the *esprit de corps* of the armed forces themselves, particularly among the middle and junior ranks of the officer corps. On their part, the executed officers may have wanted to restore the kind of order and discipline associated with the Buhari regime, as well as to redistribute political power amongst the members of the armed forces. They shared a suspicion of the Babangida regime's more forgiving attitude to past misdemeanours; and, above all, they not only resented their own exclusion from strategic political appointments, but saw themselves as intelligent and competent enough to participate directly in Nigeria's governance.[106] It was, in fact, the latter grievance which prompted President Babangida, two months before the alleged coup plot was smashed, to appeal to disaffected officers not to split the armed forces. It was not feasible, he pleaded, to oblige every officer with a political office, and 'political appointments do not necessarily imply any indication of superior capacity or lack of it'.[107]

Despite fresh rounds of political appointments, disaffection among the middle and junior officer ranks remains evident. For all the force of his words, it is easy to detect the discomfort in President Babangida's words to the graduating class of the Jaji Staff College in July 1987:

> This administration is determined that the good old days of mutual trust must return into our barracks; the Mess life must be reawakened; the cohesion of our military as an institution must be retrieved with military despatch and precision; the hierarchy of Command must be respected in the context of fairness and justice to all; and discipline in our services must be restored.[108]

Still, no previous Nigerian leader has established a firmer grip over the military hierarchy and indeed the country than Babangida has done. By consummate skill and disarming personal charm, he has dictated the composition, tone, and thrust of his regime. Consequently, Babangida's regime has 'a much more personalised power structure than the oligarchy which preceded it'. Following a reshuffle of a number of state governors in July 1988, President Babangida lectured them as follows: 'I shall not hesitate to remove from office any of you found wanting on grounds of incompetence, impropriety and *disloyalty* to me in any *capacity*' (emphasis added).[109]

There have, of course, been serious disagreements and compromises over a number of major policies between Babangida and his military subordinates. But there has so far been no clear alternative power centre, no single military commander or minister of independent political means. For Babangida relishes, indeed glories in, his personal contribution to recent Nigerian history. Despite his apparent personal modesty he sees this contribution as a key ingredient in the politics of his time and country. Without him, it is reasonable to suggest that the contours of the unfolding economic changes might have been different and, perhaps, with a chance of permanence. His economic ideas doubtless derive from elsewhere, and his rhetoric is written for him: but he has elevated determination to an art form, and erected fearlessness into the acid test of political calibre.

Three years of his rule have enhanced both the power of the presidency and his own personal grip over the armed forces, although it is plainly too early to judge their long-term consequences. After halting fresh purchases of military hardware and reducing the salaries of officers, he also persuaded the mass of the soldiery to accept a pay cut and then imposed a corresponding cut upon civil servants. He has not hesitated to dismiss ministerial or gubernatorial appointees who have stepped out of line, including his own deputy, Commodore Ebitu Ukiwe.

The initial emphasis on human rights, on debate, and on the pursuit of consensus which the Babangida regime made its hallmarks has sadly given way to Machiavellian and authoritarian methods of social control. Manipulation of the media has become pervasive, as have the arbitary arrests of trade union, academic, and student activists, and proscriptions of trade unions. The regime has acquired a reputation for 'government by proscription'.[110] There are equally ghosts of suspicions about immense official corruption which, as is usual in the Nigerian circumstances, are only verifiable after a forcible change of regime. Once, the president was accordingly booed at close quarters by young Muslim radicals in the northern town of Kaduna; while his wife, whose public prominence is widely resented, was allegedly 'rubbed up' by students in Sokoto state.

Hundreds of officers have been pensioned off or prudently reposted to military or political positions at home and abroad. As Lieutenant-General T. Y. Danjuma lamented: 'From December 1983 till today, the wastage rate in the officer-corps of the Nigerian Army is easily of war-time proportion.' The army, in particular, has become thoroughly subordinated to Babangida's will.[111] From being the redoubt of the northern political establishment, it has become the vanguard of his governmental crusade. And certainly, if the measure of his support or success in this regard is to be found in the behaviour of other military officers, then their abject surrender to his assumptions is proof enough of his convincing preeminence. Witness Lieutenant-Colonel Abubakar Umar, then Governor of Kaduna State: 'The President's decision on the IMF loan issue is a very democratic move. And, due to the present democratic nature, some of us say we can follow him into battle blindfolded.'[112] But, then, that antinomy merely reflects the paradox of the professional military ethos; its fantasy and its esotericism.

Conclusion: reformers, romantics, and radicals

Soldiers who seize power often march 'out on a straight path towards their vision of a good society'.[113] But the analyst need not share either their confidence about the appropriate route or their heavy burden of responsibility. There has been vigorous recent debate within the Nigerian left about the potential contribution of military interventionism to radical social renewal in Nigeria.[114] But nothing in the historical record thus far suggests that any fraction of the Nigerian armed forces (let alone these forces as a whole) is well placed to serve as an agency of radical social change.

Through all the changes of regimes the ideological and policy concerns of the military have strayed only marginally from those of the late colonial ideal. Coups, as we have seen, have merely provided a means of creating further opportunities for soldiers and their civilian associates alike. But the sustained failure of the economy and the increasing instability which this has generated now demand the bolder remedies which the Babangida government is attempting to provide. It is too early, as yet, to judge how effective these remedies are likely to prove. The deep privations of the proletariat, peasantry, urban and rural poor, combined with the latent disaffection of the *petite bourgeoisie* and the salaried employees in the state bureaucracies, parastatals, universities, and even the armed forces themselves, remains a source of social ferment. This may provoke among a minority of the latter 'a kind of radical nationalism' and a genuine rejection of the existing order.[115]

Yet it remains deeply unclear which elements in Nigeria's complex and poorly demarcated class structure really have the capacity to furnish the requisite political dynamism. As with earlier 'fits of messianism and indulgence in myth making'[116] from Nigerian commentators of both left and right, part of the new left-wing focus on the transformative potential of military radicals is open to the gravest doubt. It exaggerates the prospective contribution of youth, energy and the social confidence to be drawn from relative privilege and severely underestimates the conservative influence of the military ethos itself. More importantly it wholly neglects the constraints imposed by the underlying relations of production which form the very basis of power and the order of domination, and serve to reproduce the power of private capital and to reward its more or less diligent servants. It also greatly overestimates the ability of even the most militant of army officers to rise above the importunities of ethnic and sectional factionalism, or to elude the close links between the formal command structure and effective status hierarchy of the armed services and the glittering prizes of private wealth which Nigeria's political economy since Independence has held open to the lucky few who retain a privileged link to the summit of state power.

144

9

Senegal

CHRISTIAN COULON AND DONAL B. CRUISE
O'BRIEN

On the eve of President Leopold Senghor's retirement, the Senegalese state appeared to be 'a quite remarkable success story'.[1] This success was attributed to the emergence of an authentic national political culture, to relatively viable linkages between the communities (local, religious or ethnic) and the state. The success was manifest in the capacity of the governmental party as an effective political machine. The quality of political leadership made the Senegalese state a 'uniquely effective political apparatus',[2] and an instrument of stability although still unable to initiate an effective development policy. The state in Senegal at least was not a political 'artifact' working in a void, without effective links with society at large.

Today the problem is to know if the success continues, in a new context of political transformation, with a very precarious economic and social situation. Can the 'democratisation' initiated by Senghor, and pursued with still more determination by his successor Abdou Diouf, respond to the rise of a militant Islam, to the development of a regionalist movement in the Casamance, to the discontent provoked by austerity measures under the guidance of the International Monetary Fund?

Starting from these questions, we must first examine the mechanics of the democratic renewal, and then look to the changes that have occurred in the relation between the state and society, the changing forms of hegemony. In a third section we deal with the very serious problems that the state must confront. Finally, we attempt to explain why the crisis in Senegal has not overwhelmed the regime (even if the outlook is not reassuring). In order to grasp the impact of the recent democratisation, one must place it in the broader context of the transformation of the state.

Democracy in Senegal

Leopold Senghor's retirement from the Senegalese presidency at the end of 1980, entailing the succession of Abdou Diouf (prime minister since 1971), has introduced a further constitutional liberalisation in Senegal. Where three political parties had been constitutionally allowed since 1976, with their stipulated ideological positions to left and right, President Diouf was to oversee a measure allowing the legalisation of 'all' political parties, without ideological stipulation or restriction. The principal significance of this measure (April 1981) has been its allowance for the emergence to legality of the numerous clandestine parties (the *groupuscules*) of the more or less extreme left in Dakar. Thus fourteen political parties had been legally recognised by 1983, including five of the far left. Communist-style opposition (three of the Third International, two of the Fourth)[3] could apparently be greeted with some equanimity by the government, although constitutional restriction was still applied in other areas. Thus it was stipulated that the parties in applying for legal status must reject affiliation to 'race, ethnic group, sex, religion, sect, language or region'. The politically most significant categories in this list are three; religion, region and language; and the 'liberalisation' of April 1981 is to be understood in the light of these exclusions. These items are apparently not negotiable: the initiative of April 1981 demanded of the new political parties that they swear to respect the constitution, while the new president spoke of this liberalisation as 'L'ouverture, mais dans la fermeté' ('An opening up, but with firmness').[4] Political parties based on religion, region, or language will still be firmly banned, while parties based on Western ideology will be openly welcomed. Marxism in particular appears to be greeted as politically innocuous, a harmless distraction for the over-educated young.

The general elections of 1983, for the legislature and the presidency, were the first electoral test of the Diouf regime and of the new constitutional openness.[5] The eight parties contesting the parliamentary election were indeed allowed a substantial freedom in campaigning. The press was largely unrestricted, as were public meetings of the various parties: only money and organisational means placed limits on the public expression of party views. On the state-run media of radio and television, the arrangement was to allow the governing Parti Socialiste 'equal' time with the totality of the opposition. The opposition understandably complained that this division gave unfair advantage to the governing party, seven times as much media exposure as any of the campaigning opposition parties (excluding the ordinary news items, which gave even more single-minded attention to the government candidates). But with other West African comparisons in mind, one is perhaps more impressed with the allowance of *any* official time to parties of opposition. The campaign was more seriously distorted by electoral regulations which ruled out coalitions of parties, either for legislative or presidential elections: thus the opposition went into battle in dispersed order against the might of the government machine. And the preponderant patronage resources of government were demonstrated during the campaign in the declarations of electoral support from the leaders of the Sufi Muslim brotherhoods: given the fulsome terms of Sufi allegiance to a spiritual guide, these maraboutic declarations for the president and the government party may have guaranteed the delivery of hundreds of thousands of votes –

enough apparently to put the election in the bank for Abdou Diouf and the Parti Socialiste.

But if the government held most of the cards, the conduct of the 1983 elections certainly did not suggest Socialist over-confidence. The Supreme Court ruled some days before the election that the secret ballot would be 'optional': this was to mean that a booth would be available (perhaps at the far end of a hall) for those who expressed a wish to vote secretly, while others would vote openly using the coloured slip of their candidate. Anyone voting for the government would wish to vote openly, in the hope perhaps of some future reward, and only a very few opposition supporters thus voted 'secretly'. The Supreme Court, overseer for the elections, also ruled that an identity card (bearing a photo) would not be required at the polling station, only a polling card (no photo). The result of this latter dispensation, together with a ruling that transport facilities were to be unrestricted within each of the country's eight regions, brings to mind the injunction of early machine politics in the United States – 'Vote early and often'. Opposition party observers were on occasion expelled from the polling stations, and there were rumours of ballot stuffing – this latter a traditional feature of elections in Senegal. These irregularities may furthermore seem redundant when one remembers that it is the government which counts all the votes, in Dakar and behind closed doors: no question of opposition party observers in the central counting house. Those who counted the votes have been civil servants, and it is remarkable that the opposition parties have not made this a major public issue, although the partisan neutrality of the state bureaucracy is the thinnest of legal fictions. President Diouf states the matter bluntly: 'The government is indissolubly linked to the Socialist Party, to which it owes everything.'[6]

The declared result of the 1983 elections was an even more overwhelming triumph for the governing party than that of the previous general elections (1978): Parti Socialiste, 111; Parti Démocratique Sénégalais 8; and Rassemblement National Démocratique, 1 (1978 result: PS 82 seats, PDS 18). Voting had been by proportional representation, on a single national list, for one half of the parliamentary seats; by majority vote in separate constituencies for the other half of the seats. The opposition won none of the constituencies, and was represented in the national assembly thanks to the element of national proportional representation. The national counting house could declare parliamentary results for the opposition which would be virtually impossible to test. The simultaneously held presidential election gave the expected approbation for Abdou Diouf (82 per cent). But where such a presidential result had been expected by most commentators and probably by all politicians other than the defeated candidate, Abdoulaye Wade, the scale of the Socialist Party's victory was greeted with howls of protest from the opposition: 'fraud', 'electoral masquerade'. Where Diouf's election could be seen as understandable acclaim for a young, dynamic and reputedly honest candidate with some important recent initiatives to his credit, the Socialist Party's victory was seen as containing an important element of sharp electoral practice.

Fraud there very probably had been, but the opposition was to fail signally in its attempts to mobilise popular protest against these declared results: the opposition protest began well, with the formation of a Front du Refus by eleven political parties, with an agreed statement in March calling for new elections. But these new elections failed to materialise, and the Front slowly disintegrated (down to eight parties in April, to six parties in May 1983, as the Senegalese political logic of splitting and factionalism took hold). The protesters were almost exclusively city people and their protests appear to have aroused little interest outside the cities: perhaps one may see in this urban/rural political division some continuity from the historical division between the coastal communes and the hinterland (*la brousse*). An attempt was made in 1985 to revive the opposition forces, as the Parti Démocratique Sénégalais joined with five other parties in the new Alliance Démocratique Sénégalaise. These allies were soon in confrontation with the law, involved in a banned anti-apartheid demonstration (August 1985), as a result of which the leaders (Abdoulaye Wade and Abdoulaye Bathily) were to spend several days in jail. But Wade's new alliances, with parties of the far left, were to cost him in desertions from his own PDS as a further three of his parliamentary contingent left the party (down to nine in 1987).

The general elections of 28 February 1988 then conformed to the 1983 precedent in most respects (optional secret ballot, polling card with no photograph, notably) but the verdict of the Dakar crowd on the declared result was of an unprecedented violence. The official result gave Abdou Diouf 73.7 per cent of the presidential vote, against 25.8 per cent for Abdoulaye Wade; in the legislative election 103 seats went to the Parti Socialiste, 17 seats to the Parti Démocratique Sénégalais.[7] The serious rioting in Dakar which followed the declaration included the burning of cars and buildings by young PDS supporters. Abdoulaye Wade and some associates were then to spend some time in jail during a state of emergency. A notable feature of the result was that the PDS did well in the Casamance (winning both seats for example in Bignona) thus providing some outlet for regional political frustration. Electoral malpractices were apparently particularly flagrant (or more closely observed) in the capital city: Dakar thus remains the centre of Senegalese disaffection as well as of government.

Multi-party politics in Senegal, with the openings created by the Diouf regime in April 1981, has thus not resulted in any dramatic realignment of political forces. The governing party continues to hold its monopoly in the dispensation of patronage, continues to operate through a network of urban and rural influentials. In the countryside the only opposition party with an effective presence remains Abdoulaye Wade's Parti Démocratique Sénégalais (which did relatively well for example in the heartlands of the Mouride brotherhood in the 1983 elections).[8] The numerous other parties have failed to reach beyond an urban constituency. The leftist *groupuscules* have thus made a poor adjustment to the open air of competition, Senegalese style.

Democracy in Senegal may perhaps be sought rather in the unedifying operation of the single party dominant under various names since independence. The Parti Socialiste is not only internally democratic in its own odd way, it would even (although one is unlikely ever to know) probably win in an undoctored version of a free national election. Where internal democracy is concerned, the Socialists have been described as being in a permanent electoral campaign.[9] Party cards are sold in an annual membership drive, each aspirant local politician seeking to maximise sales to clients and supporters; elections are held every two years for the party offices at *section* and *département* level. It is from these officials, the winners of the Socialist Party's internal elections, that the great majority of Socialist parliamentary candidates will be chosen: and since the Socialist parliamentary candidate is most unlikely to lose thereafter, one can see that the stakes in the party's internal elections are high. The Socialist Party's internal elections are keenly fought, with charges of corruption, occasional violence, and much intricate factional manoeuvre: an excellent subject for future Africanist political study.[10]

Central power does of course intervene in the factional politics of the ruling party. Senegal's president is also the Secretary General of the Parti Socialiste, and he can always speak for a national majority. But as Robert Fatton remarks in a recent study of Senegalese democracy, 'The diffuse and clientelistic nature of the Parti Socialiste [imposes] certain limitations on his decision-making power.'[11] Abdou Diouf has dispensed with some elderly and well-established figures within the party hierarchy, including old associates of Leopold Senghor, those who have been known as the party's barons, but he must then encourage the rise of the barons of the future. Such is the logic of Senegalese clan politics, in which Diouf is seen as an innovator in encouraging the emergence of a new and better educated generation of 'technocrats'. This is an intricate enough game, playing off one ambition against another, and always bearing in mind the amount of support which any given party notable can mobilise, the amount of trouble he could cause. One need not then be surprised that Abdou Diouf has 'expressed the ironic sentiment that being General Secretary of the Parti Socialiste [is] more complicated and difficult than being President'.[12]

Electoral politics in Senegal is thus a partial reality. Where elections between parties are concerned, one might compare the Senegalese situation with that observed by Graham Greene in Liberia (*Journey Without Maps*, 1936) where Liberian politics are described as 'A crap game played with loaded dice ...', 'The curious thing about a Liberian election campaign is that although the result is always a foregone conclusion, everyone behaves as if the votes and the speeches and the pamphlets matter. The Government prints the ballot papers ... the Government polices the polling booths, yet no one assumes beforehand that the Government will win ... A curious fiction is kept up even among the foreign representatives.' Liberia provides a caricature, perhaps, but in one respect, that of the possible change of government through election, Liberia appears to have outdone Senegal, 'There was a kind of unwritten law that the President could take two terms of office, and then he had to let another man in to pick the spoils.'[13] No such unwritten provision exists in Senegal, where the opposition has never yet won a single election, and where the incumbent president may move aside only after twenty years.

Given the way that multi-party democracy has operated in Senegal, one has been perhaps a little perplexed by the tenacity of opposition politicians in engaging in battles which they seem bound to lose. And it is not surprising to hear reports of a rising 'cynicism' of late among the opposition, which Professor Fred Hayward has compared with a similar development in Sierra Leone before the military intervention.[14] But the Senegalese opposition might perhaps be unwise to push their cynicism too far, for there are real freedoms in Senegal (of the press, of association, of speech) which it would be a pity to lose. And the considered judgement of Robert Fatton, that one is better with a flawed democracy and a chance at least to influence the government agenda, than with the 'specialists of coercion' at work under Africa's authoritarian regimes, seems entirely appropriate.[15] But on the other hand one has no advance right to surprise if the parties of opposition seek extra-constitutional recourse.

A new state

Numerous studies of Senegal have emphasised the patrimonial and clientelist character of its politics.[16] One may bear in mind the general point that these clientelist networks, resting on the power of local bosses, politicians, or *marabouts*, have allowed the political system a certain social base. The structures or institutions meant to promote development may not have provided the expected economic results, corrupted as these institutions were by a clientelist logic (notably in the case of the Office de commercialisation de l'arachide [Groundnut Marketing Board]).[17] The institutions of 'development' however have provided some communication between the 'centre' and the 'periphery'; the spoils that they offered, in terms of power and resources, constituted the stakes for the bosses and their clienteles.

The intervention of the Senegalese state in society, in spite of its bureaucratic and developmentalist discourse, was promoted through local groups and communities equipped with their own leaders. These bosses acted as brokers between the state and society. Reliance on such intermediaries results in what Professor J. S. Barker has called 'the paradox of development':[18] the government is torn between the need for political support that requires it to respond to the demands of the local community, and the need to carry out a policy of development that drives it to transform the community. But while the logic of political support at first prevailed, recent developments have worked in the sense of a more direct mode of incorporating society into the state, with a redefinition of the role of the party and the ruling class in the political system.

A more direct incorporation

The evolution of the Senegalese state tends to more direct intervention in society, moving from a feeble state to a 'complete' state. The incorporation of society into the space of state control is at the expense of the groups and 'hegemonic apparatus' that traditionally provided communication between the state on the one hand and the communities on the other. A quasi-indirect mode of administration (very close to that favoured by colonial rule, notably in the rural areas) gives way to a state of a more clearly Jacobin type. Without overtly seeking to eliminate intermediaries, this new state seeks to develop its own instruments of domination and to create a more homogeneous and malleable political and economic space, which is to be more closely controlled.[19]

A few qualifications are required to complete this overall analysis. First, this tendency does not simply mean that the patrimonial and clientelist state has disappeared. The Jacobin logic is a project which can be discerned, but which tends to remain unrealised because the state does not have the necessary means, and because it meets with resistance or diversionary tactics which limit the impact of its initiatives. The state must act prudently, and despite its proclaimed intentions it is also still impregnated with patrimonial and clientelist practices.

This new mode of incorporation is thus rather less than a full state control. It can be reconciled with democratisation of political life and a liberalisation of the economy, as paradoxically has occurred in Senegal. The return to a multi-party system thus denotes a concern to legitimise and channel political initiatives which otherwise might escape the government's control or act against it. The liberalisation of the economy can also be seen to indicate an official intent to create a space in which the old modes of production (associated with the Islamic brotherhoods and local communities) give way to an economic order inspired by capitalist and 'modernising' rationality. The official project thus works in the direction of breaking up the old, particular modes of organisation and constructing a more coherent and uniform framework.

This tendency, which we have termed 'Jacobin', is not however new in Senegal, even if it is now more pronounced. Since the 1960s, and especially in the 1970s, a whole arsenal of ambitious judicial reforms has set up the rules for the penetration of the 'periphery' by the 'centre'. The law on the national domain (1964) thus unified land legislation and enabled the state to intervene in a particularly sensitive sphere, even if the management of these lands was entrusted to rural communities which have been described by one observer as 'simple play things in the hands of the *préfet* and the *Trésor* (Exchequer), virtually non-existent'.[20] The same logic was also at work through the new

151

Family Code (1972), which provoked the opposition of many Muslim leaders, and which endowed the state with a direct arm of intervention in what had been hitherto the concern of 'custom'.[21]

In the urban milieu, the policy of '*déguerpissement*' (chasing away) and the battle against those who in administrative vocabulary are referred to as 'human congestion', beggars, street-hawkers, the handicapped, the mentally ill, has been the subject of an impressive judicial pronouncement that can be seen as indicative of an official intent to the control, segregation, and locking up of hitherto uncontrollable 'marginal' or 'abnormal' people.[22]

Another manifestation of this new hegemonic policy can be seen in the government's major economic projects. Henceforth, the state and the multinationals are to act jointly to develop the country. In this perspective the groundnut basin, with its *marabouts* and its particular modes of production, is no longer the priority. 'The state', writes J. Copans, 'will thus only have a declining need for its "groundnut industry clientele".'[23] These changes are most apparent in the Casamance and now especially in the Senegal River region. The development of the Senegal River Valley involves a direct training of peasants without working through the intermediary structures and groups on which the groundnut industry depends. This type of development has been confided notably to SAED (Société d'aménagement et d'exploitation des terres du delta du fleuve Sénégal or Company for the Administration and Exploitation of the Senegal River Delta Lands), with a technological sophistication that is resisted by the local peasantry. The latter mark their independence by creating very active village associations and groups.[24]

This new political and economic order tends to the erosion and marginalisation of local networks of authority, and in the end creates an increased dependence of peasants and city-dwellers upon the state. Despite the difficulty that the state experiences in the management of its programme, its effects do make themselves felt.[25] The changing relations between the Senegalese state and society are then to be seen in terms of several factors. There is the logic or rather the ideology of the nation–state; especially that of the French tradition working to 'civilise' society. This logic and ideology are also sustained by particular situations. In Senegal, the peasant *malaise* at the end of the 1960s and the beginning of the 1970s (drought, poor peanut price) revealed the limits of clientelism and offered the state a chance to intervene in new ways, the more so since this crisis sapped the resources of the local bosses (*marabouts* excepted) or transformed patrimonial practices into corruption scandals, as was the case with ONCAD. The dislocation of the urban milieu under the impact of the rural exodus engendered a more interventionist urban policy. Finally, there has been the arrival of a new generation of leaders or 'managers' in the public or para-public sectors, more 'technocrats' than politicians: these new leaders tend to be hostile to machine politics, in their preference for the organisational machine of bureaucracy. The rise of Abdou Diouf to supreme power is the symbol of this movement.

The reformism of Abdou Diouf

As we have already indicated, two opposing tendencies may be distinguished in the ruling elite. The first originated in the patrimonial and clientelist state, which it virtually controlled; Barker properly labels this as the 'adaptive-manipulative tendency'.[26] The other tendency is that of the technocrats and entrepreneurs, who wish to embark upon the modernisation of the state.

Young technocrats, with responsibility in government or in managing state companies before they entered politics, have enjoyed a growing influence over the years. They were already numerous in government during the 1970s.[27] Diouf is both the symbol and the champion of this new political generation, and by becoming the head of state (1981) he gave this generation a remarkable impetus, even if he did have to humour the old political bosses ('barons').

President Diouf's policy of renewal consists of appealing to the energies of the country, of extolling 'transparency' in political and administrative action, and democratising the Parti Socialiste. In this policy, the priority is to finish with the clientelist networks and practices which had penetrated the party and even the institutions and organisms of the state; to the point (as happened with ONCAD) that the national leaders no longer even had control of these structures.[28]

This policy of renewal was thus a scarcely veiled attack on the 'old guard'. 'Democratic openness', 'national consensus', 'total multi-partyism', these are some of the themes and slogans which were intended to shake up the party, to invite it to go beyond factional quarrels in order to become a *parti animateur* or a party with a driving force, and to give the initiative to a technically competent *cadre*.

This will to renewal gave the new president a positive image in Senegalese public opinion. His policy of rigour and openness earned him wide support, at least at the level of grand principles, for at the level of immediate local reality this Dioufist political generation lacks a very solid social base.

> As technocrats spending most of their time running the state bureaucracy, they had few close ties with the party faithful at the grassroots levels. The lack of contact with the less educated and more traditionalist rank and file members of the party was largely due to the fact that Diouf and the relatively young, well-educated, cosmopolitan group around him defined themselves as members of a national intellectual elite rather than the representative of local, regional, and ethnic constituencies.[29]

If one bears in mind the strength of the local bosses and the shortcomings of the technocrats, one can understand why Diouf has still not gained control over his own party;[30] and this situation does not seem to have improved over the years for Diouf and his supporters. The government party has never been in such a state of confusion and division. Diouf has certainly succeeded in eliminating some senior officials of the party and the state: old hands from the Senghor era like Adrien Senghor or L. Alexandrenne, political stars in decline; but other strong men of the regime, like the ex-prime minister Habib Thiam or the ex-foreign minister Moustapha Niasse, suffered the same fate. Far from being strengthened, Diouf's team has become more isolated by these moves, and Diouf himself is more and more dependent upon his advisors, particularly Jean Collin, Secretary General at the presidency and *éminence grise* of the regime. The influence of these 'modernist technocrats' appears to be preponderant in the government and in the ruling circles of the Parti Socialiste, but it is much weaker in the party machine where men like Clédor Sall, Alioune Badara M'Bengue, or Amadou Cissé Dia, well-informed politicians, keep their ascendancy; it is thus outside party structures, through personalised committees of support, that Diouf and Collin mobilise their partisans.[31]

The new state thus lacks the social basis and the local entrenchment of the patrimonial and clientelist state, which has assured the stability of the country; the regime now is confronted with serious challenges, which accentuate its isolation; the state lacks the resources which might allow it to resolve these challenges or escape from its isolation.

The state under stress

Problems have accumulated over these last few years. Abdou Diouf, without being quite discredited, is now threatened on several fronts: an economic and social crisis, with the readjustment that this involves; the rise of a militant Islam; the development of a regionalist movement in the Casamance; the urban crisis.

The crisis

Senegal like many African countries is in a state of economic crisis bringing it under the control of the International Monetary Fund, while the prospect of recovery remains distant. The economic predicament of the country is highly alarming; if one is to believe recent statistics from the World Bank, real per capita GNP has decreased 0.5 per cent between 1965 and 1984; the balance of payments deficit has increased from $16 million in 1970 to $274 million in 1984, and the foreign debt which was $131 million in 1970 increased to $1,565 million in 1984.[32]

Senegalese agriculture is in a state of near collapse. Groundnuts, which remain the basic product of the agricultural sector and which are crucial to budgetary and external revenue, no longer 'nourish' either the peasant or the state. Due to drought and/or farmer disaffection, production is chronically irregular: 1,450,000 tons of groundnuts in 1975; 508,000 in 1978; 521,000 in 1980; 1,145,000 in 1982; 559,000 in 1983; 700,000 in 1984; 590,000 in 1985.[33]

A very considerable portion of this harvest furthermore escapes the official marketing network, and is smuggled (in the direction of the Gambia), or transformed by the peasants themselves for their personal consumption or for sale on the informal market. Of an estimated harvest of 700,000 tons in 1984, only 150,000 appears to have been sold through the official network.[34] The low prices paid to the producer, as well as the ponderousness, inefficiency, and corruption of the state marketing board, explain these peasant strategies of evasion. But one should also note that neither the dissolution of ONCAD nor a rise in the groundnut buying price to the producer have modified this behaviour. The peasants have learned to do without the state, and the oil pressing factories work at 25 per cent of their capacity. The decline in state revenue is considerable.

Rice production on the other hand has regularly increased, but with consumption having almost doubled in twenty years (rice is the staple food in the towns and is tending to become a staple in some rural areas), Senegal must import more of it every year. Major government agricultural projects, intended to give a decisive impetus to the country's economy, are not yet operational and are in any case controversial. The failure of SAED in the Senegal River Valley, which did not succeed either in mobilising the peasants or in balancing its own books, does not augur well for the future of these initiatives.

Major industrial projects, such as the Dakar *zone libre* or Dakar-Marine (ship repair), have turned out to be costly failures. The production of phosphates is stagnant. Only fishing and tourism are promising sectors, although in the latter case the foreign firms involved repatriate an important part of the profits. Public finance is thus in a worrying state of deficit. State revenue has suffered the ups and downs of the production and marketing of groundnuts, whereas public spending has steadily increased due to a public sector of 70,000 bureaucrats (1985).

Faced with this situation, an economic and financial adjustment plan was launched in 1981, supported by special drawing rights accorded by the IMF and by financial aid from France and the USA. The Senegalese government declared its commitment to a policy of market prices and a limit on wages. But the financial imbalance was accentuated anew in 1985 (a deficit of close to 100 billion CFA francs), showing the difficulty of efforts to bring things under control. The 'New Agricultural Policy' has not yet proved itself, with its plan for a relaxation of official supervision, making the peasant responsible as well as in profit (particularly in the case of groundnuts). The 'New Industrial Policy' to reduce customs protection and barriers, to relaunch private initiative (privatisation of a portion of the public sector), and to oversee salaries, has yet to be effective. Rigour and economic and financial stabilisation mean that times are hard for many Senegalese: within the pro-government union, the CNTS (Confédération nationale des travailleurs sénégalais or National Confederation of Senegalese Workers), revolt is brewing: factions openly opposed to IMF policy (notably the 'union renewal' tendency of Secretary General Madia Diop) have been organised and a more docile union, the UDTS (Union des travailleurs sénégalais or Union of Senegalese Workers), has made its apearance.[35] The risks of a social explosion are real, especially if the privatisation and liquidation of thirty or so firms are carried out as anticipated.

The university crisis of February 1987 is another sign. It was not just a simple student insurrection but also underlined the preoccupations of a generation of intellectuals of whom only a small minority will find a job. More recently (April 1987) the protest movement and strike of the police, starting from a banal incident in a police station, shook the machinery of the state itself.

The 'renewal' promised by Abdou Diouf is thus in difficulty; the more so as corruption still reigns in the highest spheres of the regime, as was apparent in 1984 during the scandals of the Banque centrale des Etats de l'Afrique de l'ouest (BCEAO), and the Union Sénégalaise de Banque (USB), when considerable financial deficits were noticed; and in 1986, with a corruption scandal involving a well-known Mouride transporter, Lobat Fall. Recovery is thus not in prospect and the government does not seem to be in control of the situation. One need not thus be surprised at the emergence of new disputes, such as those linked with the rise of militant Islam.

A resident Islamic peril?

President Abdou Diouf has said repeatedly that there is no Muslim fundamentalist offensive in Senegal; but to stay just a few days in Dakar is to realise that the tranquil and moderate Islam which has long prevailed in this country is now in question. One finds in Senegal the atmosphere of Islamic agitation which marked the early years of colonial rule, a period when the economic, social, and political upheavals introduced by the European presence produced large scale religious movements such as gave birth, for example, to the Mouridism of Amadu Bamba.

The relations between *marabouts* and the colonial government improved over time. The celebrated *marabouts de l'arachide* were more concerned for their plantations and their businesses than for 'Islamic revolution'. First the colonial administration and then the Senegalese government itself supported their agricultural activities and set up these religious notables as local bosses and political intermediaries. Clientelism prevailed and services were mutually rendered. The *marabouts* exercised a sort of indirect administration over an entire section of the population and favoured the development of groundnut cultivation. The politicians acknowledged the heads of the brotherhoods as 'chiefs of the hinterland (*la brousse*)' and linked themselves to them in order to recruit followers and voters. Everything seemed to be for the best in the Islamic and patrimonial worlds.

But for the last ten years or so, and especially since the accession of Abdou Diouf as head of state, Islam seems to be a more and more autonomous force. The Islamic awakening is apparent in all social strata and manifests itself in a variety of ways. The increase in the number of Islamic associations of all kinds is one sign of this renewal, whether they be traditional *dā'iras* grouping the disciples of a single *marabout* or modernist groups with social, political, and cultural goals influenced by reformist ideas. Another sign is the success and continuing growth of pilgrimages to brotherhood centres or to the sacred places of the Islamic world. 'Intellectuals' themselves, who were once attracted to Parisian ideologies rather than to Islam, now show a remarkable religious zeal. Many among them see Islam as the only counter-culture capable of confronting Western hegemony.

Islamic fundamentalism appeals only to a minority, but a growing one, with its concern for the struggle against secularism. It also denounces the 'degradation' of morals and the pernicious and secret influence of French Freemasonry in ruling circles. Journals like *Djamra, Wal Fadjri,* or *Etudes Islamiques* represent an Islamic protest which seeks to lay the basis for a new moral, social, and even political order: one should also mention the abortive and picturesque attempt by Ahmed Niasse, no doubt with outside inspiration, to found an Islamic political party (*Hizboulahi* or Party of God).

The brotherhoods are not really committed to this militant Islam, although their leaders sometimes support certain aspects of the combat of the 'radicals', in particular their campaign against French Freemasonry. But on the whole, *marabouts* apply themselves instead to containing these initiatives and gaining what profit they can from them, confident of their own popular support. They use this situation to renegotiate their alliance with the government and the Parti Socialiste on a new and still more advantageous basis. Certain brotherhood leaders, Mourides in particular, regularly adopt anti-establishment tones without however following in the footsteps of the regime's opponents. The Khalife of the Mourides, Abdou Lahat M'Backé, has thus become a master in the art of the 'remonstrance'; as at the time of the 'radio incident' when he succeeded in getting the director of the National Radio dismissed, for refusing to allow a *communiqué* from the brotherhood on the air. This demonstration of anger however did not stop him from publicly condemning the Federation of Young Mourides in January 1986, for being too close to the Parti Démocratique Sénégalais (PDS). He also instructed people to vote for Abdou Diouf and the Parti Socialiste during the elections of 1983 and 1988.[36] Vigilance, however, prevails among the Mourides, who suspect Abdou Diouf of countering the growing influence of their brotherhood around the country by favouring the activities (and businesses) of the rival Tijaniyya brotherhood (to which the president belongs) and also favouring the reformist movements. Trust between *marabouts* and politicians no longer reigns as once it did.

The rise of Islam is closely linked to the problems of day-to-day existence. Islam provides a moral and social identity for those who are excluded or marginalised from 'modernisation', as indicated by the success of the Arabic or Franco-Arabic schools that abound in the towns. These 'alternative' scholastic establishments recruit extensively among students who have not

157

succeeded in Western-type schools. The risks of the development of a frustrated intellectual elite are thus considerable, unless the state attends to its own Islamic cultural arrangements. Brotherhood Islam is also a structure of aid and support, mostly material, for destitute peasants, urban dwellers in distress, and even merchants or businessmen who can no longer count upon the assistance of the patrimonial and clientelist state of yesteryear.

The Islamic renaissance is linked to the transformation and also to the powerlessness of the state. In seeking to do without intermediaries, the state creates a void from which Islamic forces profit in order to create an autonomous space for themselves. This process has not however reached its conclusion (perhaps never will): in many ways the *marabouts* thus still remain the guarantors of the established order. Democratisation has furthermore not succeeded in creating a new, legitimate political order. The low rate of electoral participation is evidence of this. The dynamics of social and political life thus operate on an extra-legal basis, whether along religious or political paths. Regionalism likewise operates outside the legitimate political field determined by the state.[37]

The Casamance revolts, the country against the state

Casamance 'regionalism' is a sizeable challenge for the Senegalese state. It attacks state control in its most sacred aspect, that of national unity. And the Jacobin state is very poorly placed to respond on this terrain, muzzled as it is by a centralist logic that reduces regional and ethnic differences. The Casamance problem is not of course a new one. The French colonisers had already faced the same difficulty there, notably when they wanted to endow this region with 'chieftaincies' that had no equivalent in the traditional political organisation of the Diola in particular.[38] Casamance particularism was already apparent in relation to state authority. But over time this resistance seemed to soften or to be expressed in prophetic movements. The realism of the colonial administration, then the flexibility of the Senegalese state machinery, seemed to have succeeded in accommodating the Casamance. These last few years have however shown that the compromise was precarious, and that any move in the direction of further integration into the state could touch off an explosion.

Since 1981 the Diola people of the Casamance have been in a state of rebellion: the revolt of the *lycée* students (1981), then the following year the more important demonstration in front of the governor's mansion in Ziguinchor during which the Senegalese flag was replaced by the emblem of the Casamance movement; new riots in December 1983 (twenty-five dead and eighty wounded) at the outcome of legal proceedings involving members of the independence movement; new confrontations between demonstrators and the forces of order in November 1986 and January 1987 resulting in around ten deaths. The arrests of some of the leaders, including the priest Diamacoune Augustin Senghor, supposed leader of the movement, have not weakened the determination of the Casamance militants; neither have the

158

relatively moderate verdicts handed down from the courts to imprisoned leaders and demonstrators.

These Diola revolts have a marked traditionalist side: meetings in the sacred wood, the presence of women who have an important social and religious role in animist society, use of rudimentary arms, etc. But this ethnic spontaneity is also structured and organised by the Mouvement des forces démocratiques de Casamance (MFDC or Movement of Casamance Democratic Forces), which has reclaimed the name of a former regional party. The latter joined Leopold Senghor's Bloc Démocratique Sénégalais before independence. The members of the present MFDC are for the most part men of humble origin, strongly attached to their ancestral traditions, whereas the local leaders of the Parti Socialiste are for the most part bureaucrats. The local Catholic clergy does not control the movement, but several Diola priests champion a Christianity adapted to Diola culture and are generally thought of as defenders and spokesmen of the people. The movement has some real support in Guinea-Bissau, where several ethnic groups are culturally close to the Diola, who in turn helped the Guinean groups during their struggle for national liberation.

The Senegalese government has certainly tried to propose reform; by dividing the Casamance into two administrative regions, by setting up a development plan, and by increasing the number of Casamance natives in the state and party leadership (at the moment there are five ministers from the Casamance in the government). But this reform has done nothing to calm spirits. Certain administrative *cadres* from the Casamance have demanded, in a memorandum on the events in Ziguinchor (1984), that a more innovative programme be adopted (nomination of a governor coming from the region, change in land policy, promotion of local languages, development of social services).[39] But nothing so far suggests that the government intends to modify its approach to the problem in any fundamental way.

Casamance particularism is explained by the geographic isolation of the region, the poor quality of its infrastructure, and more generally by the neglect of the region from Dakar. It also stems from the growing presence of merchants and bureaucrats from the 'north' who tend to impose their language and their religion (the Diola remain profoundly animist even when they convert to Catholicism or Islam) as the only legitimate ones. Faced with this 'internal colonialism', a strong sentiment of frustration produces the search for a distinctive identity.

But the heart of the Casamance question is in what D. Darbon has termed 'a general incapacity for communication' between a hierarchical and centralised state, and acephalous and egalitarian societies used to village-level self-rule.[40] This structural difference is enormous, although it can be tempered through intermediary authorities which modulate and adjust these contradictions. Such was indeed the case for a long time: the state did not seek directly to penetrate Diola society, and ethnic and regional entities remained within the government party. But in the Casamance, as elsewhere, 'modernisation' of the state moves in the opposite direction and thus confrontation is inevitable. One example here is the law on the national domain, whose application is felt by the Diola to be an assault. Seeking at all costs to assure its direct social control, the state loses all sense of communication and encourages political adventurism, as we have already noted in the area of Islam and in the urban field.

To live in a Senegalese fashion (vivre sénégalaisement)... without a state

The expression *vivre sénégalaisement* is currently employed to refer to the day to day difficulties inherent in poverty, but also to the ways of getting by, the art of making do without the situation being fundamentally modified. *Vivre sénégalaisement* consists then of 'struggling along' in precarious circumstances. The Senegalese thus have a whole panoply of practices to employ, where they cannot count on the state; they find their own recipes for survival.

The 'informal' economy (in reality much more structured than the so-called 'formal' economy), smuggling, or the switch to subsistence crops (millet, beans, etc.) represent a first type of response, through short-circuiting or ignoring the economic institutions and legislation by which the state defines a space of its own. It is a question of avoiding the state, from which one expects nothing good, or of acting as if it did not exist.

Senegalese peasants have become experts here either by limiting their groundnut production and favouring crops that can feed them (this to the great panic of the state which does not conceive of 'food self-sufficiency' in this way); or by pressing the groundnuts themselves in order to sell the oil on a clandestine basis; or by routing their harvest towards the Gambia or Mauritania and leaving the oil mills of the state groundnut industry without groundnuts. We have seen that these phenomena have grown considerably over the last few years. 'What Has Become of the Seeds?' lamented *Le Soleil* of 9 April 1986, stigmatising the bad faith and low sense of civic duty of certain peasants.

Senegalese smuggling involves more than groundnuts. Sugar, cooking oil, electric batteries, cloth, cans of tomato paste, for example, are traded vigorously across the Senegalo-Gambian frontiers. One must also point out the development of the extraordinary parallel market in Touba, the capital of the Mourides and a veritable clandestine Harrods, Senegalese style, which the state cannot keep under control without angering the heads of the brotherhood. The informal activities are not all illegal, but one of their salient characteristics is that they are in general little in step with the law, and that the merchants who go in for these activities tend to be 'irregulars' pursued by the police. The state and the 'informal' sector rarely make a good couple.[41]

Mutual aid associations and institutions are the social side of these informal initiatives. In many respects they function as a social security system. Without the assistance of the state it is in these relational networks that one can find the necessary resources and support for survival. Relations of personal dependence added to a deeply rooted associative tradition explain the importance and development of these 'assistance' structures during difficult situations, especially in a context of crisis. The aid of *marabouts* to their *talibés* is part of the duties of religious leaders, even if it does maintain inequality. And during periods of drought many peasants set this maraboutic solicitude against the powerlessness or indifference of the state. In the urban milieu the success of maraboutic associations, the *dā'iras*, owes much to the uncertainties of the city and to the need for welcome, protection, and warmth that migrants from the hinterland experience in Dakar.

Savings associations or *tontines* are also support groups as well as having some 'informal' commercial aspects. The *nāt* for example are groups of women of the same profession, for mutual aid. The *tekk* are groups organised around a social event (baptism, death) in order to help those who have to pay for it.[42] The informal sector operates in teaching by the opening of unofficial Arabic schools, with students who have failed in the official educational system. On this point as on so many others, Islam offers recourse and an alternative solution.

Islamic ambiguity

The Islamic dynamics that we have described do not necessarily transform the political scene. The Islamic breakthrough does bear upon the state, and even obliges it to redefine or renegotiate its relations with Islamic actors who have become more demanding and audacious. But Islamic mobilisation also has political limits that we must briefly explain. Social reconstruction in this Islamic movement firstly fills a void and tempers the risks of anomie and explosion to which the state might be victim. In this way in the towns the social control assured by the brotherhoods ultimately constitutes an important element of stability, and thus tends to avoid the riots that have occurred in some Islamic countries in crisis situations. For if state urban policy (or the shortcomings thereof) neglect the social (re)organisation of the most powerless groups, the development of Muslim sociability, thanks to the actions of the brotherhoods, compensates for these deficiencies and, to a certain extent, allows people to ward off the dangers of the city.

The Tijaniyya brotherhood already had a solid urban tradition and also a faithful clientele amongst the elites and merchants. It has continued this movement. On the other hand, the Mourides were originally a typically rural organisation, but they also have followed the roads to the city, accompanying the peasant exodus. Quite at ease in the culture of 'ordinary' people, and tightly grouped around its *marabouts*, the Mouride brotherhood offers a training and solidarity system well-adapted to situations of change and crisis. At the beginning of this century the Muridiyya had such a role in social reconstruction for Wolof peasants faced with the upheavals brought about

161

by colonial penetration and the slave trade economy. It has the same function today with the urban crisis. The miraculous appearance of Amadu Bamba in a store on one of Dakar's grand avenues symbolises the brotherhood's migration to the city.[43] The state may be jealous of the social control the brotherhoods exercise in the city, but it knows that maraboutic order is better for it than revolt and anarchy.

This new Islamic order can also set itself up as a parallel culture, or even a counter-culture, and in this way become a threat to the political system. The development of an Islamic discourse against secularism signals the rise of a radical questioning of the post-colonial state. These Islamist ideologies are however not certain to generate a genuine social movement. Beyond the claims, emblematic more than programmatic, for the establishment of an Islamic state, one wonders about 'the alternatives that they can set against the criticised order, which hardly occupy a central place in their intellectual production and practice', as B. Badie observes of Islamic protests in general.[44] The Senegalese Islamist discourse, like so many others, is made up of moral protests and criticisms of Western modernity which hardly lead to the formation of a political project to unify civil society.[45] As for the brotherhoods, they sometimes play the Islamist card but without seeking to win. They make use of it, like a sword of Damocles, in their pressure group strategies before the state. But no one is duped, and it is difficult to envision our elegant and perfumed *marabouts* as puritan *mollahs* or even as *ulama*. The Islamic wave would have to be very powerful for them to change their manners and their strategies, and they still prefer to remain a parallel power and a lobby.

It is nevertheless a fact that the *marabouts* can undermine the action of a government, but the divisions between brotherhoods obstruct the creation of a maraboutic front as a political alternative. The *marabouts* prefer to have their own men to support their affairs, in ruling circles. The government furthermore does not hesitate to exploit these brotherhood cleavages and rivalries or to favour particular interests, including those of this or that religious head. They understand that these men will not militate for a 'union of Muslim forces'. The government does try to coordinate the activities of the numerous groups which take their inspiration from Islam through the Fédération des Associations Islamiques du Sénégal (FAIS). Maraboutic associations (*dāʾira*) are however outside the fold of this federation: while the state cannot substitute itself for the brotherhoods, it can try to endow itself with Islamic legitimacy. Abdou Diouf's government, much more clearly than its predecessor, has made some steps in this direction, for example by active participation at the Organisation of Islamic Conference (OIC) and by encouragement for the teaching of Arabic. However, it cannot go very far on this terrain, attached as it is to its secular label. The state however does apply itself to showing its good faith and thus to limiting the impact of criticisms from the Islamic militants. An Islamic window-dressing also attracts aid given in the name of international Muslim solidarity, and Senegal has done quite well here.

International support

Senegal looks after its external image, and despite its problems and deficiencies has managed to attract a considerable amount of international aid: as a 'moderate', 'stable', and 'democratic' country, it has sympathy in the Western camp; as a country of Muslim tradition, it has support from the Arab states.

Leopold Senghor, a man of culture of international renown, the father of the Negritude and Francophonie movements, had a global reputation from which his country profited: Abdou Diouf, as his boss's disciple and successor, has benefited from a favourable prejudice on the international scene. But he has also equipped himself with appropriate assets: a pious Muslim, head of state of a Pan-African stature (he was president of the OAU in 1985–6), initiator of a new social and political dialogue, he renewed and refreshed the vision of his country abroad. All this explains the abundance of foreign credit that Senegal has been able to obtain. One must also add here the strategic interest that it represents.

As an essential mechanism of the 'French connection', in political, cultural and military terms, Senegal remains the privileged recipient of French aid. The recent visit to Dakar (December 1986) of the French Minister of Cooperation, M. Aurillac, the most Senegalese of French ministers (he was at one time Senghor's advisor), followed by that of J. Chirac, reassured the Senegalese government that its 'socialist friendships' with the former majority in France had been but a momentary cause for concern.

Behind France, the USA plays a substantial role in Senegal. According to the Economist Intelligence Unit, the United States 'also seems to see Senegal as of increasing importance'.[46] Dakar was the first of six stops on the African tour of Secretary of State Schultz. Friction between France and the USA over the financing of development projects has brought suggestions that Senegal may turn to the USA for its wheat imports. Senegal can only profit from this international rivalry.

These two countries tend however to be insistent on the reforms needed to put the Senegalese state and economy back in order. The difficult negotiations between Dakar and the IMF underline the Senegalese dilemma, between the imperative of political stability (which demands that one not take rigour too far), and that of financial rehabilitation. The international lenders are also certainly conscious of this contradiction: but there are differences between experts close to the USA, who are quite 'radical' in their approach, and those linked to France, with a more moderate attitude. Beyond these differences, there remains the fact that Senegal is in a position of increased dependence:

163

Christian Coulon and Donal B. Cruise O'Brien

'Senegal is being kept afloat by Western aid, the IMF and Middle Eastern largesses', noted *Africa Confidential* in 1985. But since then the 'largesses' of the Arab countries have been reduced and those of the West made more conditional. Senegal's external image no doubt permits it to get the support indispensable to its survival: but the weapon is double-edged, for this aid implies reforms which limit the distributive capabilities of the state and thus risk making it the target of every malcontent.

Conclusion

The Senegalese state thus appears more and more dislocated and fragile. Within the state and party apparatus the divisions are sharp and the *malaise* has even reached the forces of order and no doubt the army. Moreover, state relations with society are problematic when they are not actually conflictual. Some sectors of society place themselves on the margins of the state, while others seek to redefine the nature of the state itself (as in the Casamance and certain Muslim *milieux*). Only external aid and what remains of patrimonialism and clientelism appear to allow the state to subsist. However, the powerlessness of the opposition and the ambiguity of the Islamic movement restrict the capacities for change and give the regime a sort of legitimacy by default that assures its durability, at least for the time being. We seem to be far from the 'remarkable success story' of ten years ago; even if in the circumstances that now obtain, the survival of the regime is to be seen as a substantial achievement.

10

Sierra Leone: state consolidation, fragmentation and decay

FRED M. HAYWARD

The development of the state in Sierra Leone[1] during the 1970s and 1980s has been marked by contradiction and crisis. On the one hand, we have witnessed the centralisation of state power, the personalisation of authority, and the extension of state control into most sectors of society. This process has been paralleled by a steady growth in the size of the state, which has become the largest employer in the nation and which has come to be held responsible for the country's economic health. On the other hand, we have observed an overall weakening of state institutions, the development of powerful autonomous political and economic spheres of influence, and the fragmentation of political structures that had guaranteed its hegemony and assured legitimacy in an earlier era. State decline has been intensified by failures in government performance, escalating corruption and the incapacity of the state to generate sufficient revenue to meet its rapidly expanding budgetary requirements.

As competition for power and scarce resources grew more acute during the 1970s and 1980s, the incumbent APC (All People's Congress) political elite tried to limit political competition. The centralisation of power in the hands of President Siaka Stevens also continued unabated. In the process, inequities and public dissatisfaction increased. The response of the ruling elite to demands for accountability was the routinisation of manipulation and coercion. The marked decline in the effectiveness of many state institutions continued, reflected most notably in the deterioration of the road system, tax collection, education, and agricultural services. By 1980 decay had become endemic.

The paradoxical nature of state-society relations during this period is illustrated by growing state manipulation of the electoral process and the development of mass resistance to the state. The last two decades have seen major changes in electoral institutions, the nature of participation, and public response to the process. This period was marked by a substantial weakening of the influence of civil society on the state, with the concentration of wealth in the hands of political elites and their allies, rampant corruption, and growing disillusionment and discontent.

It was in this context that Siaka Stevens decided to step down as president

165

after almost two decades at the helm of Sierra Leone politics. His successor, Major-General Joseph Momoh, was Stevens' personal choice, although formal procedures for succession were followed including a national election on his candidacy. President Momoh inherited a centralised but largely ineffectual government, a divided ruling party, and an economy in crisis. He surprised many people by asserting his own authority and setting his own agenda. He sought to create an active, open presidency which was perceived to be so, and one free of ties to the old order. Momoh asked for commitment and 'discipline' from both state officials and the people, and talked about the need for a 'new order'[2] which would make the state both responsive and responsible to civil society.

In what follows, the tortuous process of change and reformulation will be examined along with the many paradoxes which have arisen along the way.[3] The state in Sierra Leone is neither a monolithic structure nor substantially in control of its own destiny. It is buffeted by a wide variety of internal and external pressures over which it has little influence. While the state has been presented in many guises over the last fifteen years, often playing contradictory roles and operating at cross-purposes, for the most part it has become increasingly repressive, predatory, and rapacious. The changing nature of state-society relations in Sierra Leone suggests the ease with which leaders and/or the regime can appropriate state power and resources for their own ends, under conditions which prevail in much of Africa.

The changing nature of the state in the 1970s and 1980s

Sierra Leone is one of the few independent African states to have experienced a truly open multi-party political process which was both representative and accountable.[4] The citizenry expected their representatives to champion local as well as national needs and voted them out of office if they did not. Opposition parties were free to express their views, to win elections, and to seek control of state power if they did. In 1967, Sierra Leone became one of a handful of African countries in which an opposition party came to power after winning a national election. The governing SLPP (Sierra Leone People's Party) was held accountable in a national election – and found wanting. The leader of the APC, Siaka Stevens, was asked to form a new government. This moment of opposition success was thwarted almost immediately by a military coup which removed Siaka Stevens and brought to an end a long history of competitive politics in Sierra Leone.

The APC was returned to power after a counter-coup in 1968. The restoration of civilian rule seemed to promise a return to a democratic and competitive system in which the state was accountable to civil society. It appeared to indicate a renewal of the close links between the state and representatives of civil society that had existed under Milton Margai. Sierra Leoneans also seem poised to participate in a new populism that had been a hallmark of the APC election campaign. The 1967 elections had, after all,

166

demonstrated that the masses could have a major impact on the state through the electoral process. While there was some initial difficulty in reasserting political control over the military and guaranteeing state security, by 1970 Siaka Stevens and the APC seemed firmly in control. The by-elections of 1969 increased the APC's parliamentary margin over the SLPP from seven to twenty-two seats, progress was being made on the economic front, and the opposition SLPP had become badly divided because of a dispute over party leadership.

Centralisation and personalisation of power under Stevens

Stevens was an astute and shrewd politician. He worked to consolidate power and assure personal control over the state. In part this was a reaction to the challenge posed by the military, in part it reflected Stevens' style of personal contact with the people. It was also his effort to ensure direct control over the apparatus of the state. Those in positions of authority became personally responsible to Stevens. The power and autonomy of the civil service had been broken earlier by prime minister Albert Margai.[5] Stevens perfected what Albert Margai had begun, making major appointments in the civil service himself and using many of the other positions as patronage.

During the 1967 elections Stevens and the APC had campaigned on a populist platform that was characterised by exhaustive campaign sweeps throughout the country. The APC portrayed itself as 'the people's party' in contrast to the SLPP which had a history of working through chiefs and other elites. Stevens saw himself as the people's representative – their patron.[6] Even in office he made himself available to anyone who wanted to see him. And people came from all over the country: farmers, workers, chiefs, the unemployed, office seekers, students. The waiting rooms at State House were always full of petitioners. Most eventually gained audience and, in the early days in particular, usually came away satisfied or content to have been heard. Stevens was generous with his financial and material assistance, and in the process created a loyal network of clients all over the country.

Stevens sought to control the power and autonomy of chiefs by increasing both personal and state involvement in major aspects of chieftaincy politics.[7] The APC in opposition had experienced the repercussion of SLPP links with the chiefs. The party had gained support among the masses by criticising the abuses of power by chiefs. After coming to power, Stevens talked about limiting the authority of the chiefs and altering their tenure:

> There is another school of thought developing now. Since we can't have a government for more than five years, it is hard for some people to understand why we should have a chief for life. People just can't understand that. Now what we might do, we might have chiefs for four years. It is difficult to explain that the government at the top is for five years and that this one at the bottom

167

is for life... If he is satisfactory, if he is fine for the people then he can stay in. If he is not, then just like the national government he goes out. Now if we do this we will get a very different kind of chief.[8]

Plans were made to remove several chiefs who had been especially hostile to the APC in opposition.[9] By acting to remove chiefs who had been vigorous in opposing the APC, Stevens both undercut those chiefs, and made it clear that he wanted to limit the autonomy of chiefs in general. In so doing he weakened some of the major barons[10] and supporters of the previous government and made good on his promise to protect the masses from the abuses of chiefs. Access to the state could be achieved without the chiefs as intermediaries. And Siaka Stevens himself would be in State House to represent the masses. While Stevens did not become involved in chieftaincy affairs on a daily basis, neither the installation nor removal of a chief could take place without his knowledge or approval. He made his position clear: 'No chief can keep his job without the support of the government.'[11]

Stevens' power was reinforced by the patron-client network he built throughout the country.[12] When he needed political support he used this network of clients with great skill. These links enhanced Stevens' control of the state and his ties to the people. In the long run, however, they were ties to the man, not to the institutions of the state. Thus while national authority (in the person of the president) had been strengthened, there were signs that this did not carry over to the state.

Institutional fragmentation

As Stevens worked to bring the reins of state power under his personal control, he fragmented state power and weakened the autonomy of important elements of civil society.[13] Ministers and other officials were increasingly beholden to the president and were expected to work directly through him rather than the party. All major appointments, contracts, or other significant business in the ministries required his approval. This weakened the authority of the civil service, the budgetary controls of the Ministry of Finance, and the political leverage of the governing APC. It also limited the autonomy of the ruling class to seek its ends through a variety of different state institutions and kept most elite conflicts within reach of presidential intervention. Centralising power in his hands allowed Stevens to influence the outcome of conflicts and encourage friction between particular elites where it served his interests.

Many institutions important in representing the interests of civil society were weakened during the 1970s, including unions, agricultural cooperatives, farmers' associations, the universities, business organisations, and professional associations. Some groups, such as the bar association (whose members were often remarkably successful on behalf of the oppressed), remained powerful and largely autonomous. Other institutions, like chieftaincy, were to remain influential in spite of the increased intervention of the state.

The move to a *de facto* one-party state following the election violence of 1973 weakened the power of the governing party as well as the opposition SLPP. Once party competition was effectively eliminated, the role of the APC in the electoral process became a minimal one. As a result the party lost a major source of patronage. In contrast to the single party in Tanzania which was called upon to mobilise mass participation in national development efforts, the APC was not asked to mobilise a populace assumed to be safely within the bosom of the party. The electoral functions which remained were taken over by the president and his staff. Actual decisions about particular candidates were usually made locally, as long as there was no objection from State House. The president believed that this allowed local constituents to identify and remove political liabilities.

The consolidation of power around Siaka Stevens and the development of a system of personal rule played a major role in reducing Parliament to almost total insignificance. It played almost no role in introducing or debating legislation, serving rather as a vehicle for presenting decisions made by the president, vice president and other leaders. What had once been a powerful and influential institution was reduced to near triviality. Unless an MP became a minister, there was little he or she could do for the constituency. In 1982, Parliament sat on only twenty-nine days, proof of its emasculation. MPs fell back on their flags and other symbols of office to assert authority. Almost everyone knew, however, that their power was largely illusory. As a representative body Parliament had no power or resources. Accountability in that context had no meaning.

State security and hegemony

In spite of the popularity of both Stevens and the APC in the post-coup era, there were a number of serious problems which threatened the security of both the regime and the state. The military was still not firmly under political control,[14] as evidenced by several unsuccessful coup attempts.[15] Furthermore, the fragmentation of the state meant that Stevens and the APC did not have as strong a hold on the country as one might have expected given Stevens' personal popularity and the party's electoral mandate.

There were other threats to Stevens' authority in the emergence of disillusionment and alienation within the APC. Several important ministers and supporters grew increasingly critical of both the policy failures of the party and what appeared to be an expanding pattern of greed and corruption. In May 1970, Ibrahim Taqi, Minister of Information, was dismissed for his continued criticism of corruption within the party, and his assertion that the APC was moving away from earlier populist principles in favour of concentration on how much each individual member could benefit.[16] At this time a new political party, NDP (the National Democratic

Party), was formed by a number of ex-APC stalwarts. They hoped to attract support from dissatisfied members of both parties and in particular bring together Mende and Temne opposition elements. Several prominent APC politicians left the APC with Taqi[17] to join with the NDP to form the UDP (United Democratic Party). That effort was short-lived as the UDP was banned by the government in October and its leaders arrested. Both the government's action and the UDP's rapid rise to prominence illustrated the tenuous position of the government. The severity of the government response suggests that the ruling elite recognised their vulnerability to a mobilised public and demands for accountability.

The level of elite insecurity was exacerbated by violence in the north and Freetown by supporters of the UDP and by a series of coup attempts culminating in an effort on 23 March 1971 by the army commander, Brigadier John Bangura. While the attempted coups were eventually put down, they demonstrated the fragility of state security. Shortly thereafter, Stevens acknowledged the inability of the state to ensure its own security by signing a mutual defence pact with Guinea and requesting security assistance. About 200 Guinean troops were sent to Freetown to serve primarily as a presidential guard.

Stevens then moved to re-establish control of the army and police and to consolidate state power. He established a para-military security unit responsible directly to him. Legislation was introduced to make Sierra Leone a republic with an executive president and vice president. This would also bring to an end long-standing colonial links with Great Britain – an action heavy with symbolism and popular appeal. It would also eliminate the potential embarrassment of judicial appeal to the Privy Council in Great Britain. Throughout the process of reorganisation, the Guinean troops were to remain, departing finally in 1973. While the overall security of the state was maintained, the on-going factional struggles, the need to call on foreign troops to protect the state, and periodic military threats, emphasised the tenuous nature of state hegemony.

The state and society: chieftaincy, local politics, and national elections

The changing relationship between state and society in Sierra Leone is exemplified by major changes in the nature of state ties to chieftaincy, local politics, and national elections. From the early 1970s until 1986 the state moved to limit the autonomy of civil society at all levels. In the process the democratic structure of the state was weakened, as was the representation of the diverse elements of civil society and the ability of the populace to hold political elites accountable. That was to have profound consequences for legitimacy as well as for popular resistance to state manipulation and intrusion at the local level.

State intervention in local politics, especially chieftaincy, had its origins very early in the colonial period as a product of colonial hegemony and control. This pattern of intervention continued in the post-independence period.[18] The SLPP, under Albert Margai, tried to incorporate chieftaincy into the apparatus of the state to ensure party control of power. Siaka Stevens initially talked about limiting the power of chiefs (as noted earlier), then moved to coopt them in much the same fashion as his predecessor. Stevens brought the personalisation of chieftaincy politics to new heights: chieftaincy became intimately tied to a personal rule in which political rewards and authority were dependent on the ruler.[19] Chieftaincy, like other offices, was to be achieved only with the blessing of the ruler. As Crawford Young notes, 'public resources at the command of the ruler became a reservoir of benefices and prebend to assure fidelity. Holders of high office, individually, became clients of the ruler...'[20]

The expansion and refinement of state intervention in local politics under both Albert Margai and Siaka Stevens affected local competition and spawned new levels of conflict and intrigue. State manipulation exacerbated both ethnic and regional conflicts, with competing national elites mobilising local support on both sides. In the Stevens era, some of these resulted in very serious ethnic and regional conflicts in which there were few local beneficiaries and a legacy of violence.[21] In most cases, state intervention succeeded. However, there were situations in which manipulation was so blatant that the process was totally discredited, and others in which state intervention failed (as in Jaiama Nimikoro) because local resistance could not be overcome and national leaders acceded to local wishes rather than lose control completely.[22]

The power of the state to manipulate local politics is limited by the effect of divisions within the political elite and by local resistance to state intervention. Even when national political figures attempted to intrude into chieftaincy and other local politics, it was often unclear who was using and who was being used.[23] What is particularly striking about the relationship between the state and traditional authority in Sierra Leone is the effectiveness of the latter in resisting the intrusion of the former. Part of that success was a consequence of the legacy of legitimate chiefly authority during both the colonial and early post-colonial periods, part resulted from the successful manipulation of national politics by traditional elites.

Competitive elections were an integral part of politics in Sierra Leone long before independence. Elections served to link state and society, albeit imperfectly.[24] This process was exemplified in 1967 when the opposition APC defeated the SLPP leading to the appointment of Siaka Stevens as prime minister. Efforts by the Stevens regime to alter the nature of electoral participation during the 1970s and 1980s are revealing. The 1970s saw changes in the electoral process which effectively diminished the scope and openness of popular participation, limited representation, and effectively excluded the highest state offices from electoral accountability.

In 1977, students from Fourah Bay College called for new national elections. The university community in general, and the students in particular, had remained largely autonomous during this period, free to debate and criticise national politics on campus in a context which was remarkably unhampered by government. In many respects students saw themselves as a conscience of civil society. Their demand for elections (in contrast to earlier experience) provoked an invasion of the campus by APC stalwarts and violent attacks on the students. That in turn sparked widespread demonstrations, violence, and indignation throughout the country. Public resentment of the violence was so great that the APC felt compelled to set a date for new elections later that year in order to restore order. Although this election was not free of violence, the SLPP managed to win fifteen seats out of ninety-seven. It also filed a number of election petitions against successful APC MPs alleging violence and corrupt practices. Several of these petitions, including some against prominent party leaders, were very damaging to the APC and seemed likely to succeed in court, giving the SLPP a renewed opportunity in by-elections. The court was never allowed to render judgement because in June 1978 Parliament passed constitutional provisions creating a one-party state. This action was ratified by a referendum.[25] Following the referendum, elected SLPP MPs had twenty-four days to declare for the APC or lose their seats in Parliament.

These constitutional changes produced a consolidation of state power that could not have been achieved through competitive elections – even with the use of violence. Yet in many respects, these actions revealed the profound weakness of the APC's hold on the reins of state power and the tenuousness of their links to Sierra Leone society as a whole. For the APC, the one-party state seemed to ensure control – a goal more important than that of democracy.

Public resistance to electoral manipulation in 1973 and 1977, in spite of violence, demonstrated the willingness of people to try to express their preferences under extremely difficult circumstances. While state manipulation of the electoral process assured control, it robbed the process of its democratic meaning. The political elite seemed to fail to appreciate that fact. Having reduced the links with the people, the elite was shocked when the masses expressed their discontent in demonstrations and violence of their own.

One factor which kept the electoral process alive, in spite of the violence and manipulation during this period, was the widespread public recognition of the potential benefit of a ministerial position for the constituency. That hope increased interest in all seats in the expectation that 'their' MP would become a minister. Those MPs and ministers who also understood this relationship were careful to steer major resources and positions to their constituencies. Those who did not usually paid the price for ignoring their voters, as demonstrated by the election results in 1982 in which more than half the MPs and 44 per cent of the ministers lost their seats; in 1986 the turnover was 35 per cent for incumbent MPs and 56 per cent for ministers (see Table 10.1).[26]

The relationship of the state to the electoral process changed drastically

Table 10.1. *Incumbent success in contested elections: 1982 and 1986 elections*

	1982				1986			
	MPs		Ministers		MPs		Ministers	
	N	%	N	%	N	%	N	%
Won	20	43	5	56	36	65	4	44
Lost	26	57	4	44	19	35	5	56
Totals	46	100	9	100	55	100	9	100

after the inauguration of J. S. Momoh as president. He promised 'free and fair' elections in 1986 with multiple candidates in each constituency. The authority of the state was to be used to ensure that the process conformed to these norms. Candidates who violated the rules were removed, major efforts were made to ensure that there were multiple candidates in each race, and the president studiously refused to intervene on behalf of any candidates. Even those close to the president who violated the 'Code of Conduct' were disqualified. As a consequence, the 1986 elections were the most open and free since 1967. While there were still some problems of violence and irregularities, the contrasts with the elections of 1973, 1977, and 1982 are striking.[27] The level of openness is also reflected both in the substantial increase in the number of candidates running for each seat, and in the significant decrease in the number of uncontested seats when compared to elections earlier in the 1970s and 1980s (Table 10.2). There was, however, a notable drop in electoral turnout[28] which reflected a lingering fear that voting in 1986 would follow the previous patterns of violence and intimidation.

President Momoh hoped that competitive elections would help forge new links between the state and society; links which would serve him well by demonstrating strong support for his efforts to tackle the economy in what he knew would be a difficult and painful process.[29] He knew that he needed his own base of public support and some degree of autonomy from the 'old guard' if he was to remain in power. Neither the mantle of Siaka Stevens nor military support would be enough to ensure success in the long run.

In the 1986 elections, the voters demonstrated their dissatisfaction with a high number of incumbents by voting almost 40 per cent of them out of office. Watching the campaign as an observer, especially in the rural areas, one was struck by how much hope was raised by the president – hope reinforced by the fairness of the electoral process in 1986 and citizens' expectations that they would have a major impact on the state.

The new Parliament began with an energy and determination that seemed to bear out these expectations. MPs insisted on being active participants in the political process. In the budget debate, in March 1987, the back-benchers

Table 10.2. *Uncontested seats: 1973, 1977, 1982, 1986*

Election	No. uncontested	Total seats	Per cent
1973[a]	58	102	56.9
1977	47	97	53.4
1982	31	97	32.2
1986	19	116	16.4

Note: [a] After the SLPP withdrew, the number of uncontested seats rose to 97, bringing the total uncontested to 95.1 per cent.

were extremely critical of the mini-budget and argued that the government's fiscal policies were wrong.[30] Their criticism forced major changes in government policy. It also became clear that the president was looking to Parliament for ideas as well as support.

The political economy

The first ten years of independence produced relatively impressive economic growth in Sierra Leone: the gross domestic product increased nearly 5 per cent a year. Foreign exchange earnings and public revenue were adequate, the consumer price index was stable, and external debt relatively small. From 1972, however, a number of circumstances converged in many ways that had negative effects on the economy. These included a decline in diamond output, the closure of the Marampa iron-ore mining operation (the second largest foreign exchange earner after diamonds), plus the rapid increase in international oil prices which tripled the oil bill between 1973 and 1974.[31] Although the first round of oil price increases was somewhat offset for Sierra Leone by an increase in world prices for diamonds, coffee, and cocoa, the second round of increases in 1979 brought an additional doubling of the oil bill in one year. This further hurt the industrial and mining sectors, which accounted for about 60 per cent of consumption.

There were other economic difficulties. The fall in international diamond prices in 1980 hurt export earnings in spite of an increase in production.[32] The diamond situation was also clouded by the failure of the government to work out an agreement on the financing and development of kimberlite mining, which should have been on line to avoid a major decline in diamond output as the alluvial deposits were exhausted. These problems were compounded by low prices for coffee and cocoa.

By the 1980s the economy was in serious crisis, suffering from the effects of the international economic slowdown, compounded by mismanagement and corruption. The awarding of contracts, import licences, foreign exchange, government subsidies, tax exemptions, credits, and almost any government service, was increasingly dictated by personal contacts, bribes, and private arrangements with senior state officials. Even the state controlled DIMINCO (which generated most of the nation's foreign exchange) could not get the foreign exchange it needed to maintain its equipment in a condition to produce at full capacity, in spite of a very efficient mine operation. In contrast, the stores in Freetown had ample supplies of imported food, appliances, automobiles and other luxury goods which had been purchased with foreign exchange. The elite seemed able to afford an increasingly affluent life style, luxury homes were being built in large numbers in Freetown, and it appeared that many of those at the top were prospering.

The government failed to deal effectively with the economic crisis, almost from the outset choosing instead to meet short-term problems by deficit financing and increasing the money supply. While that produced short-term relief, it compounded the long-term economic difficulties for Sierra Leone. Financial problems were exacerbated by the huge debt created by the decision to host the Organisation of African Unity meeting.[33] The balance of payments situation worsened as did the shortage of foreign exchange. At the same time the government failed to encourage areas of the economy in which progress could be made, such as small-scale industries and agriculture.

The economic failures reflected a number of state policies which were very costly. Expansion of agricultural production was discouraged by state policies designed to keep agricultural prices down to prevent urban protest over food prices, high levels of taxation of the agricultural sector,[34] and by the high profits to be made by those in a position to benefit from state sanctioned monopolies on agricultural and other imports. During this period the economy came to be increasingly controlled by the political elite along with its business allies, many of whom were Lebanese. Under both Albert Margai and Siaka Stevens, many very successful indigenous businessmen and women (including Creoles) were forced out of important areas of the economy to make way for those favoured by the state leadership.

Siaka Stevens understood that political power was tied to the economy. He used state control of import licences, access to foreign currency, loan guarantees, and other state incentives, to reward those loyal to him. In Sierra Leone, the state became the primary instrument of economic accumulation.[35] Stevens knew how important it was to have goods on the shelves and in the markets. He believed that the black market helped ensure that goods were available in the markets.[36] Thus, neither the problem of smuggling nor the parallel market were seriously attacked. As the economy deteriorated, the parallel market continued to grow, and so too did the wealth of those who could benefit from it. For the ordinary citizen, however, there were no such alternatives. Commodities essential to the well-being of the average citizen – such as rice, milk, kerosene, and medical supplies – became increasingly scarce and costly.

By the time President Momoh was inaugurated in 1985, the country faced a crisis of major proportions, including curtailment of credit by the World

Bank, IMF, and other creditors. Negotiations with the IMF and World Bank were undertaken and, in 1986, a wide range of IMF conditionalities were accepted including floating the Leone. At that time the black market rate was about Le 25 = $1. It was hoped that the Leone, officially pegged at Le 6 = $1 would stabilise at about 16:1. However, by March 1987, the rate was at an all time high of 65:1, dropping to 49:1 in April; and a more promising 23:1 in August.

While the economic decline in Sierra Leone in the 1970s and 1980s has had many causes, both external and internal, it was exacerbated by the actions of a small number of officials and businessmen who have profited immensely from their links to state power. For some, it has allowed diversion of state resources (as in the Vouchergate and Squandergate scandals),[37] for others ties to political leaders opened the way for lucrative state contracts or other business opportunities. The political and economic costs to Sierra Leone were substantial. They greatly weakened the capacity of the state to reverse the downward spiral and set a daunting task for President Momoh in the mid-1980s.

Problems of legitimacy

Legitimacy, as Lonsdale notes, 'is the universal aspiration of rulers, their occupational delusion, their search for power'.[38] Among the high points of state legitimacy during the period under review, was that which marked the return of Siaka Stevens and the APC to power after the coup. As leader of the opposition in the 1960s, as the major driving force during the 1967 election campaign, and as a symbol of the people's choice during military rule, Stevens had impressed people with his commitment to, and defence of, the basic values held dear by most citizens.

Siaka Stevens' used his personal popularity and charisma[39] to build a following which propelled him into office. Once in power, he used the resources of the state to establish a powerful and effective network of clients and supporters. His personal charm and persuasiveness also provided a base which helped deter additional military intervention and protected him from his detractors long after the corruption and ineffectiveness of his regime were apparent. Looking back on that earlier period, one is reminded of the excitement engendered by the APC throughout most of the country. People were attracted by the populism, the promises of development, the criticism of elitism, corruption, and nepotism, and they were caught up in the debate over the one-party state, which pitted the APC on the side of freedom and democracy against the SLPP on the side of elitism, greed, and repression.[40]

By 1973 Siaka Stevens and the APC had lost a good deal of this support, and some of their actions had begun to call into question the very legitimacy of the state. The state was increasingly tied to repression, corruption, and institutional breakdown. To some extent the loss of state legitimacy was fostered by the weakening of state institutions as a consequence of the personalisation of authority in the hands of the president. The state became increasingly moulded in Stevens' image and increasingly associated with him personally. The fact that the man and the state had become almost indistinguishable meant that the institution as a whole lost legitimacy when the man lost legitimacy. There was a widespread feeling that the leadership of the APC had discarded the core party values which had animated and mobilised supporters all over Sierra Leone. Party leadership was increasingly equated with personal advancement and wealth. The institutions that had been weakened by the president were now too weak to sustain him when he began to lose his appeal. The economic crises, the corruption, the violence and repression, had in any case gone too far to be overcome by charm, remembrance of past achievements, or fine talk.

By 1985, the state had lost much of its popular legitimacy. It had not, however, entirely lost its authority, although its ability to govern, to coerce, to control were increasingly limited. It was in this context that President Stevens decided to step down, to find a replacement who would be able to guarantee state power and provide the security and peace necessary to allow him to enjoy retirement. The choice of General J. S. Momoh seemed ideal from Stevens' perspective. Momoh was his hand picked head of the army, almost universally liked, an experienced appointed member of Parliament, and someone who had always been open to advice from the president.

Momoh moved quickly to shore up the legitimacy of the state. He campaigned vigorously for his own election as president, even though there was no opponent, and in doing so impressed the people with his sincerity and desire to improve conditions in the country. The success of the national elections in 1986 further enhanced his position. During the first year in power President Momoh carefully distanced himself from the previous government, while giving Siaka Stevens 'his due' as elder statesman and leader of the party. Yet it was clear that President Momoh would not tolerate interference[41] and that Stevens would not be the power behind the throne many expected.[42]

In spite of the reversal of the downward spiral of state legitimacy by President Momoh, his grasp on the reins of power remained tenuous. The economic situation, his inability quickly to mobilise the institutions of the state to solve the pressing economic crisis, and continued political stagnation and corruption, made his position very delicate. The coup plot in March 1987 was but one demonstration of President Momoh's vulnerability.

Conclusion: state and society in Sierra Leone

State–society relations in Sierra Leone have undergone a number of major transformations. In the early independence period the state operated largely as a guardian of civil society, a champion of the common people, and the locus for national development and growth. There followed twenty years in which its dominant mode was extractive, rapacious, and venal, with periods of neglect, indifference, and incompetence. Over the last decade Sierra Leone has moved from a system in which society was represented and relatively autonomous, to one in which major efforts were made to stifle autonomy, limit representation, and prevent elite accountability. During this period the state became almost solely an instrument for the economic accumulation of the state elite, including the party, bureaucracy, police, and military.

The state in Sierra Leone has not been monolithic, but made up of multiple actors and institutions tied to very different networks of power and support. In this sense, it is difficult to speak of the 'interest' of the state,[43] for there were many interests represented – often pulling the state in opposite directions as they sought to use it for private economic gain. Conflicts for power were reflected in growing violence and repression against elements of civil society which the ruling elites increasingly saw as obstacles to the paramountcy of the state.[44]

The preoccupations of those in power during the 1970s and 1980s were state-centric – concentrating more on the well-being of those controlling the state, than on the interests of society. This was a major departure from the experience under Milton Margai, who combined an austere elite paternalism and respect for traditional authority with party competition and openness.[45] While Albert Margai, who succeeded him in 1964, had begun the process of prebendalism, it was Siaka Stevens who perfected and broadened it. Major benefits and privileges did not flow without his patronage and blessing. Yet even at the height of Stevens' power, the state was neither his personal fiefdom nor autonomous from other powerful political and social influences. Within the state structure itself, these included his vice presidents, ministers, the civil service, and to some extent, the security forces. At its zenith, the Stevens regime was not able to eliminate the autonomy of many powerful groups in society, including traditional elites, professionals, and large segments of a surprisingly well informed and mobilised populace. Thus, even when the state was at its most extractive and venal, there was never the sense of powerlessness and hopelessness that has pervaded Zaire or Uganda.

The 1970s marked the beginning of successful efforts to dominate and weaken civil society. The performance of the state during this period flew in the face of deep-seated traditions and attachments to participatory values in Sierra Leone.[46] Yet civil society was fragmented and thus vulnerable to assaults on its autonomy. Siaka Stevens' efforts to enhance state power succeeded, but never completely. As we have seen, the chiefs managed to use Stevens and the apparatus of the state even as he was using them. The professionals pulled back and protected their flanks, but never gave in. The opposition withdrew from the elections in 1973, showed a last gasp of strength in 1977, and were finally felled by the establishment of a one-party state. Yet political opposition continued to exist, much as a kind of two-party system has continued to function for over a quarter of a century in Ghana.[47] In Parliament the Back-Benchers' Association became very powerful. Under Stevens, it was the only effective mechanism of criticism in

Parliament.[48] By 1986 the Back-Benchers' Association had become important to President Momoh as a significant voice of the people – as a measure of the temper of civil society.[49]

There were other voices during the 1970s and 1980s, including the press, which became 'the opposition press', not because it represented a particular group or position (for indeed its supporters and positions ranged widely over the political spectrum), but because it became the voice of criticism and opposition to government policies and programmes.

Even at its height, state power was dispersed among the political elite. As the power of President Stevens declined,[50] competition for the official mantle of authority increased. During this period there were many poles of power, including the various vice presidents: S. I. Koroma, C. Kamara-Taylor, Frances Minah, and Salia Jusu-Sheriff. As state power weakened, other groups in society, which had been biding their time, moved to express various concerns and demands and prepared to join the struggle for control.

The prospects of J. S. Momoh's presidency aroused new hope among the people. During the presidential elections held to confirm Momoh's nomination, people scrambled to demonstrate support. Even at Fourah Bay College, where the nomination of the head of the military as the candidate for the presidency had been greeted with great cynicism, faculty and students were eager to vote so that no one would be under the impression that the College was in opposition.[51] Chiefs came to meet Momoh, during his campaign tour of the country and in Freetown, to pledge their support. Professional associations, trade unions, businesses, even public corporations and ministries voiced their congratulations and support in a flood of newspaper advertisements and letters. While Momoh's ascendancy in 1985–86 seemed to rekindle public support, there remained powerful forces threatening his authority – some with semi-independent authority within the apparatus of the state which enabled them to stall and frustrate state business.[52] Others waited eagerly in the wings for the president to fail so that they could take the reins of office.

Elections in Sierra Leone have represented an important vehicle for the expression of the power of civil society. The successes of the 1986 elections increased the popularity and legitimacy of the Momoh government because they were broadly competitive and the fairest electoral contests in almost two decades. Yet because Momoh chose to remain above the fray, the process did not produce a new group of parliamentarians beholden to the president, nor did it allow him to build up a network of clients of the sort used so effectively by Siaka Stevens.

Soon after President Momoh's installation, another pole of political power developed around former President Siaka Stevens who had quickly discovered that he could not control Momoh as president. By the May 1986 elections, there were severe strains between the former and the new president. Stevens began to talk in a way that suggested he might like to return to power. There appear to have been others who felt that way. A coup plot, announced in March 1987, suggests that a number of people were prepared to assume office even if they had to use violence to do so.

The most notable failures of the state in the 1970s and 1980s concerned government performance. This is especially true in the economic area, both from the point of view of the 'revenue imperative' and in terms of generating economic growth. While the state has been able to cover its revenue needs through borrowing and increases in the money supply, it has been at a very high price, reflected in the dramatic decline in the value of the Leone and in massive dislocations in the economy.

Sierra Leone is in the midst of a major crisis of state power. It is a crisis which has been building since the early 1970s. The costs of past failures have been high. On the other hand, most members of the old order have been removed from power and in their places are some better trained politicians and technocrats who have a perspective on Sierra Leone which is little coloured by colonialism and less tainted by the self-interested patron–client networks established during the Albert Margai and Siaka Stevens eras. As is the case with any other high officials, they have their own interests[53] – both personal and civic. The moves toward greater public involvement, in both politics and the economy, suggest a commitment to civil society that can give it a stake in the future and help maintain legitimacy and accountability. President Momoh expresses a view of state-society relationships which is based on a long history of links between the two, links which are based on indigenous values, yet reflect many of the 'realities' of living in the modern age. It remains to be seen if this new generation of Sierra Leoneans can resolve the crises confronting state and society in Sierra Leone.

11

Conclusion

JOHN DUNN

In interpreting the political history of post-colonial Africa it is helpful to bear in mind three simple contrasts. The first is a contrast in cognitive orientation: between the project of explaining the course of its political history and that of appraising the significance of this political history. (Each of these projects makes its own distinct demands, since the epistemic ideal of the former is a very high degree of detachment, while the latter cannot even be coherently attempted without at least an implicit evaluative commitment on the part of the interpreter.) The second contrast, important both explanatorily and for the appraisal of political significance, lies between the inherent transience (the permanent vulnerability) of all political achievement and the relative potential longevity of political destruction. (This contrast is close to being a universal of human political experience.[1] But it has gained increasing salience from the massive human weight of state power in the modern world.) The third contrast, again bearing uneasily both on explanation and on appraisal, falls between three different conceptions of the nature of the state: between the state as an agency of development, the state as guarantor of the physical security of its citizens or subjects, and the state as an (always potentially chaotic) arena of struggle. Two of these conceptions may well appear somewhat trustingly normative, and the third to be both unmistakably explanatory and irreproachably detached. But it is of the greatest importance for political understanding, as Alasdair MacIntyre has long insisted,[2] that the merits and demerits of human institutions may make (and often do make) a major causal contribution to determining their fate; and it is at least equally important that merits in human institutions are not mere projections of human preference but causal characteristics that can arise and persist if, and only if, the ecological setting and internal arrangements of these institutions permits them to do so.[3]

The politics of West Africa have been studied extensively since well before colonial rule came to an end. Some aspects of them are now reasonably well understood. The principal limitations of our current understanding have resulted mainly from an excessive concentration on the appraisal of significance at the expense of the humbler, simpler, but equally indispensable tasks of historical recovery and explanation. The appraisal of political significance by foreign observers plainly involves the application of what are in some measure alien standards. This is not in itself a weakness: merely a tautology. But it can readily become a source of weakness if it is not constrained and disciplined, in its turn, by an intimate and accurate grasp of what has happened and of why this has happened as it has. A particularly treacherous combination in political understanding is the fusion of analytical models which purport to be both universal and detached with evaluative commitments which are in themselves relatively parochial, applied together to a political history which is in itself as yet incompletely known and far from clearly understood. The initial address of political science to the African continent was exceedingly confident. The source of this confidence (often linked for the individuals concerned with a vivid sympathy with the hopes of the post-colonial future) was above all the sense of being in a position to bring to bear on the experience of a geographical zone, manifestly underequipped to comprehend its own experience with either rapidity or assurance, the privileged understandings of more civilised societies and political projects. The historical impress of this presumption upon Western interpretations of African politics is apparent enough in the successive impacts of modernisation theory, of Marxism, and of the latter's limp Latin American offshoot, the theory of dependency. All of these focused on real and consequential features of Africa's post-colonial political trajectory; and Marxism at least, in the hands of some of its more diligent and sensitive practitioners, has done much to help us to grasp the significance of many indubitably important developments. But all three have also proved massively over-sanguine in their presumption of cognitive mastery: insisting on attempting to soar long before they were in a position even to crawl with much agility. It is instructive that none of the pieces in the present volume – for all their diversity of intellectual style and, in many instances, their enviable intellectual boldness – show much residual trace of this excessive assurance. I take it that this change of mood, in and of itself, represents a step forward: not because modesty is humanly more engaging than arrogance, but simply because immodesty is a real impediment to political understanding.

The single most salient division within the post-colonial history of West Africa is the division between states which have sustained what is essentially the same regime from the date of decolonisation up to the present day (Senegal, the Ivory Coast, to a lesser degree, as Bayart explains,[4] Cameroon) and states in which an initial post-colonial regime has been at some point overthrown by plainly unconstitutional political action and in which its successor or successors have always looked distinctly less secure just because of the disruptive circumstances of their birth. The polar contrast between these two groupings is, of course, somewhat artificial. There is much important change, social, economic and political, in even the most stolidly reproduced regime over two and a half decades, and some degree of political inheritance, through all the vicissitudes,[5] in even the most erratic of constitutional trajectories. But the poles by now are in some ways very far apart. The political history of True Whig Liberia, while it lasted, of Senegal under Senghor and Diouf, of Houphouët-Boigny's Ivory Coast, is above all the history of an effectively managed political arena. The political history of Ghana, of Burkina Faso, of Sierra Leone, with their unsteady oscillations between civilian and military rule and their (at least on the basis of their own productive capabilities) uniformly unimpressive economic performances, in times of feast as well as those of famine within the world commodity cycle, has been more eventful, less coherent and altogether more destructive. It is utterly implausible that the contrast between these two very different trajectories reflects any clear discrepancy in the structures of the societies concerned – either in economic endowments, or in class structure, or in the organisation of class action. But whatever its origins (and French garrisons, an effectively international currency and other colonial residues have plainly in several instances played major parts in securing it), it is evident by now that the successful reproduction of these regimes has been the product of sustained political skill, and that this skill has at least spared their subjects many evils to which other African populations have been exposed through the political failures of their rulers.

The successful reproduction of an existing regime is seldom inspiring in itself. But the preservation of political order in changing societies, as Samuel Huntington emphasised in the heyday of America's postwar hegemony,[6] is far from being the worst of all possible evils. Few would nominate the Republic of Senegal high on the list of modern states as benefactors of the welfare of their subject populations. But, by now, as Donal Cruise O'Brien has long insisted,[7] its contribution to sustaining orderly and civilised domestic relations has become at least as impressive an achievement as its tentative and equivocal flirtations with democratic routines. It is therefore of the greatest importance that each of West Africa's three leading exemplars of regime continuity has seen in the decade since 1978 a severe threat to this continuity, a lurch, restrained to widely varying effect, towards the increasingly unstable West African mean. There are many ways of looking at these discomfitures; and only a very detailed and sensitive political history (sketched helpfully but with necessary brevity in the present volume) could hope to explain why they have taken the particular form that they have done. But even a grosser and more external perspective indicates some obvious precipitants.

One major precipitant, of course, has been the sharp deterioration in terms of trade since 1973 (recently mitigated but far from being reversed) between exporters of oil and exporters of other primary commodities (and especially of the products of tropical agriculture),[8] and the savage burden of state and commercial debt incurred by countries desperate to offset its effect and fecklessly promoted by Western banks awash with petrodollars. It is obvious enough that these two factors together posed a quite new level of threat to the viability of strategies of export-led development and to the fiscal prudence and control of even the most comfortably accommodating post-colonial states. Yves Fauré's thoughtful account of the structural character of the Ivorian crisis acknowledges the causal impact of contingencies of political judgement and even fantasy. But it also stresses compellingly both the structural vulnerability of the Ivorian development strategy itself and the severe political problems of sustaining the apparatus of political patronage and ingratiation required to carry it through.

Fiscal prudence is difficult enough under the pressures of competitive democratic politics. But it is a markedly more demanding governmental ideal where regime support is engineered principally through the careful allocation of material benefits to influential state clients. The profligate state is also the generous state, the sensitive and caring patron of those whom it chooses to treat as its personal clients. The more sanitised and inexpensive state, dear to the hearts of socialist puritans and the International Monetary Fund, is not necessarily perceived at what had previously been its receiving end as dutifully parsimonious so much as mean, niggardly, and heartlessly indifferent. The politics of sustaining regime support necessarily involves also the politics of semblance and meaning, a domain which in the West African cases neither socialist puritans nor officials of the IMF have shown themselves adept at understanding. In Fauré's treatment,[9] more clearly than in any of the other contributions to the present volume, we can begin to grasp more precisely how the muted but protracted crisis of the credit institutions of world capitalism articulates with the most intimate issues of regime management at the heart of a West African state. No general model of the state as merely a largish group of materially motivated men and women can hope to do justice either to the character or to the intensity of the political demands which the last decade and a half have levied upon the state apparatuses of West Africa. Still less can such a model hope to offer realistic guidance on what can be done politically by any form of governmental policy decision, to brace these elaborate but vulnerable institutions for the further sharp disruptions in world economic activity which they are virtually certain, sooner or later, to have to endure.

These considerations bear most directly upon the concept of the state as agency of development and custodian of the material welfare of its subjects. But they carry through in the last instance, at least equally decisively, to each of its other guises, as putative guarantor of the security of its subjects or as always potentially chaotic arena of struggle. Despite the stout efforts of President Reagan and Mrs Thatcher the role of agency of development and custodian of popular welfare is still very much at the centre of the self-understanding of all but the most decrepit or benighted of contemporary state powers. It is equally the shibboleth of international aid agencies and of the commercial and ideological critics of their operations and of the activities of Third World states themselves. As a conception of what a state ought to be (but often fails to become or to remain) it represents a cosmopolitan and firmly teleological standard of unmistakable human relevance. But what it cannot be said to offer is much initial help in understanding why states behave as they (often regrettably) do. (An instructive contrast is offered here, for all the vivid distaste which it conveys, by Christopher Clapham's impressively poised and disabused portrait of Liberia in the aftermath of the True Whig ascendancy and of its roots in the True Whig past.)

In the case of states that prove themselves capable of sustaining their own constitutional legitimacy through time the state's most important contribution to the present and future welfare of its subjects comes in the choice and implementation of governmental economic policies.[10] These themes have been the focus of a large proportion of Africanist scholarship, in political science as much as in economics, over the last fifteen years: some of it of a very high order.[11] Despite the high quality of much of this work, however, it is plainer now even than it was fifteen years ago (and by no means solely in West Africa) that these are exceptionally difficult matters to understand at all clearly and accurately. A governmental economic policy is a set of more or less coherent practical proposals, based upon contingent predictions, advocated by economists or public officials in varying numbers in relation to a particular state and adopted (or rejected) by that state's government for what appear to it to be good reasons. Any economic policy which is in fact implemented plainly has a causally determinate character: a set of potentially identifiable consequences. Any proposed economic policy, if it were to be adopted, would also have determinate causal properties in a particular setting. But it is often one of the most determinate causal properties of a given economic policy in a particular setting that it will not (and in some sense could not) be implemented. Sometimes this is simply because it stands no real chance of being adopted by the existing government. But often it is principally because the state to which it is being commended is not an entity that could in principle execute the particular range of tasks which the policy assigns to it. In any discussion of economic policy it is exceptionally difficult to distinguish clearly between advocacy, prediction, analytical control or cognitive confusion, and more or less systematic self-deception or endeavours to deceive others. Any possible analytical model of the state as a causal reality can hope to capture this extraordinarily intricate and treacherous space only in the boldest caricature. But at the same time any realistic assessment of what is actually going on in modern politics, in West Africa as elsewhere, must recognise that it is in this space above all that a state today most persistently seals and reseals both its own fate and the fates of those over whom it rules.

As agencies of development and promoters of the welfare of their subjects, none of West Africa's states has yet attained a very commanding record; but they vary dramatically in the destructiveness of their impact upon the productive energy, initiative and effectiveness of their denizens. Criticisms of their performance centre for the most part either on the deplorable patterns of distribution that obtain within West Africa's more dynamic economies or upon the economic lassitude or even involution of their less dynamic counterparts. But the most pressing anxiety of all is simply whether even the most dynamic and effective of their economies has yet hit upon a pattern of growth that will not prove self-limiting in the relatively short term. The impossibility for the present of sustaining the Ivory Coast's expansion on the basis of a limited range of agricultural primary products in the face of falling commodity markets and a world glut of cocoa may have been exacerbated by its government's fiscal miscalculations; but it is increasingly likely to prove, as Fauré insists, less a passage of cyclical discomfort than an inherent contradiction within its overall strategy of development.

The most punctilious admirers of Adam Smith[12] and Karl Marx[13] should concur in preferring a dynamically expanding economy in a poor country which distributes its productivity gains with drastic inequity to a torpid or regressive economy that succeeds in imposing a uniform level of misery throughout its domestic population. And all the more so since the latter outcome is virtually certain, short of universal starvation, to be a matter of ideological profession rather than of concrete social experience. But it still takes a certain optimism to applaud a pattern of development which depends upon the continuing extraction of a high level of repatriated profits and local support costs for foreign enterprises and expatriate personnel, and which distributes its gains amongst the indigenous population in a dramatically inegalitarian way. All patterns of economic distribution rest upon the effective reproduction of property rights through the application of political power. And no system of political power that fails over lengthy periods of time to remedy the predicament of a large segment of its worse off subjects can expect much cosmopolitan applause or local affection in the modern world.

This last consideration is likely to come to bear in due course, however unsteadily, on the prospective political stability of an incumbent regime. But, as already noted, success or failure in the reproduction of an incumbent regime also bears, and with greater immediacy, both upon the prospects for pursuing any coherent economic policy at all and upon the opportunities for an entire population to plan and execute its economic projects with any confidence and control. No one has yet shown very convincingly just how to see this delicate structure of mutual dependences in West Africa (or perhaps anywhere else).[14] But it may be helpful to distinguish at least three very different preconditions for pursuing an effective development strategy. The first of these, plainly, is purely material. At one extreme it is simply a matter of comparatively rigid local factor endowments: the productive potential of land, mineral wealth and demography. At the other it is potentially far more plastic, even over relatively short periods of time: the skill levels, health and cooperative responsiveness of a local labour force and local entrepreneurial (or managerial) cadres, the existing stock of plant and set of economic linkages. No West African country is very handsomely endowed from this point of view (not even Nigeria). But none are exactly land-scarce at present, except on an extremely local basis; and many have quite impressive potential comparative advantages that have yet to be exploited at all deftly. No West African country, even in the Sahel zone, is plausibly compelled simply by the niggardliness of nature (or by colonial depredations) to expose its population to recurrent famine or to interminable misery. For all the overwhelming – and often brutally destabilising – buffeting from the rhythms of the world economy and the relative fragility of West Africa's economic potential, it is not simply material factors that have caused its post-colonial history to go so badly in many respects.

To see more clearly just what has caused it to do so it is necessary to consider carefully each of the other two preconditions for pursuing an effective development strategy and to assess just how these interact not only with the state conceived as an agency of development but also with the state conceived as guarantor of the security of its subjects and as a permanent arena of struggle. The first of these preconditions is severely cognitive. Economic policies can be (and very often are) self-contradictory. They can also be predicated upon massive misjudgements of the potential responses of domestic producers or of international price movements, and on the failure to take account of factors the actual impact of which will transform the causal relations that they do attempt to consider. They are also often predicated upon projections for the performance of state institutions which confuse governmental decisions at the summit of a state with the prospective performances of very many agents in its poorly controlled lower reaches. (Public Choice theorists may not have produced very convincing models of how African states make political choices – or indeed of what African states actually are. But they have done a great deal to underline the unfortunate implications of this last confusion.)

There is every reason to doubt the political capacity (perhaps even the purely cognitive capacity) of either the American or the Russian states to pursue economic policies through time in the face of these difficulties. It would be well nigh miraculous if the state apparatuses of West Africa failed to prove still less capable of doing so. But since the capacity to do so is in part purely cognitive it would also be astonishing if that capacity did not vary markedly from state to state. States with large populations of well educated professionals, relatively sophisticated public bureaucracies, effectively operating statistical services and even political leaders (or at least advisers to political leaders) who are of high intelligence and have benefited from at least a domestic university training are better circumstanced to devise and sustain reasonably consistent and well-considered economic policies than states which lack most (or any) of these advantages. The tart comments of Clapham on the disadvantages of bringing the experience of a young army NCO directly to bear upon the determination of state policy are very much to the point in this context. But Richard Jeffries's respectful analysis of the remarkable conversion of Jerry Rawlings's ebulliently populist government to the essentials of the IMF's view of the present predicament of the Ghanaian economy points a different and less distressing moral. The contrast

187

between the qualities of the state apparatus of independent Ghana at the point when this passed unequivocally into the custody of Kwame Nkrumah and its comparative decay and demoralisation at the point of Rawlings's second coming, whatever the eventual fortunes of Rawlings's government, shows that political courage and determination and a capacity for sober economic realism are no prerogative of cultural or educational privilege.

The eventual fate of Rawlings's regime is also likely to prove instructive about the third of these preconditions for the pursuit of an effective development strategy: the purely political capacity to implement an economic policy in practice. One dimension of this, of pressing importance in West Africa and, if Mr Gorbachev and President Reagan are to be believed, by no means trivial even in decidedly wealthier and more powerful states, is the simple ability of a government to cause its orders to be obeyed by its own subordinates and its laws to be obeyed by its own subjects. A second, very attractively treated in this collection by Bayart, Fauré and Otayek, and palpably present in Othman's rich portrayal of the travails of the Nigerian state, is the capacity to sustain its authority as a government in the teeth of the unpopularity that most clear and well-considered policies are likely to incur.

On many analytical models of political processes, the line of least resistance is the very course of action that an institution will be causally necessitated to follow. But the consequences of pursuing an economic policy which genuinely represents the line of least resistance at any one time are seldom likely to be beneficial in the longer term. The capacity to sustain political authority in a relatively weak or poor state is most crucially the capacity to withstand the vivid animosity of those who will suffer directly from the implementation of particular policies. It is dismally much easier for such a state to make real enemies than it is for it to win committed friends. The logic of collective action makes the pursuit of the long-term advantages of large numbers, few of whom will benefit at all rapidly, a very soft political target in the face of the opposition of much smaller groups who stand to lose drastically in the first instance. The political reproduction of a regime is an exercise in the mustering and conservation of support. It is seldom facilitated by stalwart pursuit of policies of real vision, or even of policies which treat the longer term as being as important as the short term. The mustering and conservation of political support is a topic which it requires great ethnographic delicacy to treat at all illuminatingly – and not a little persistence and good fortune even to investigate to much effect. Here Bayart's work in particular has set quite new standards for the understanding of African politics.[15]

In the longer term it is usually the success or otherwise of a modern government's economic policies that does most to affect the life chances of its subjects, whether these are conceived in relatively concrete indices of mortality statistics, nutritional status and health, in crude average figures of GNP per capita, or in the richer and more elusive currency of realised capacities favoured by Amartya Sen.[16] Those at the centre of a state are apt to be the last to lose access not just to arms and ammunition but also to oil and the mobility which this permits, to imported food supplies, and to the more locally indispensable of pharmaceuticals. To subject a population to famine by the pursuit of feckless governmental policies is no doubt less appalling than a practice of deliberate genocide. But it can hardly be said to discharge a government's responsibility to guarantee the physical security of its subjects. In the face of the present price trends of agricultural commodities, of existing levels of indebtedness, and of the vast lurking horror of the AIDS epidemic, any West African state will be doing well if it can prevent the welfare of its citizens from deteriorating over the course of the next decade, let alone succeed in enhancing this at all handsomely. This is unlikely to be a period in which a turn towards autarky will benefit the populace at large. A reversion to head-loading would scarcely represent a welfare improvement over the use of motor transport; and it is improbable that AIDS will prove particularly responsive to ethnomedical approaches. The desire to represent the interests of a peasant majority is an ambition in some sense common to the IMF, Peter Bauer, Lenin (or at any rate Mao) and the late Thomas Sankara. But none of them has hit upon a very convincing political recipe for realising the ambition in practice. It is hardly surprising that African peasantries should have proved so sceptical of the representative pretensions of those who address them in unyielding alien accents, from massive social distance, from beneath a canopy of overwhelming coercive power, often against the grain of their most intimate cultural and social assumptions, and with a very limited interest in how the world does in fact appear to them. Three decades after the end of colonial rule in West Africa, accordingly, the more ingenuous conceptions of how a benevolent government can hope to sustain itself politically and to implement its policies effectively have become correspondingly implausible.

But, as Rathbone and O'Brien point out in their Introduction to this volume, the disappointments of West African state performance when judged by the cosmopolitan and teleological standards of the world's more dynamic economies[17] should not be permitted to distract attention from their more evident contributions to human welfare. Since the suppression of Biafran secession no state of the West African littoral has made full-scale war on a portion of its subject population, as over lengthy periods of time, for one reason or another, the governments of Ethiopia, the Sudan, Uganda, Angola, Zimbabwe and Zaire have had occasion to do. It cannot be said that West Africa's soldiers, policemen or Border Guards have always proved to be punctilious observers of their public duties. But, by relevant comparative standards, they have done a great deal less damage than they might have done – and vastly less than they had the physical power to do. The view that the protection of the physical security of subjects against one another (and more particularly against the more ambitious and powerful amongst their number: Richelieu's *les grands*) was the primary responsibility of a government was the central thesis of the greatest of all theoretical interpreters of politics, Thomas Hobbes.[18] If African states had already proved (or if they prove in the future) weaker than they have done thus far, the single likeliest consequence would certainly be that the lives of their citizens became on average nastier, more brutish and shorter than they have been in the decades since independence.

The view that what a state most fundamentally is is a more or less effective artificial construction for the protection of its subjects is less optimistic than the conception of the state as agency of development. But it is every bit as much a normative view. By contrast, the conception of the state as arena of struggle, the key battlefield for class warfare, for counterposing friend to enemy in modern politics, is plainly intended to explain rather than to commend. Thus far, in relation to West Africa, it has been a somewhat bowdlerised rendering of Lenin's version of this conception that has been applied most assiduously. But in view of the continuing elusiveness of class contours in modern Africa it seems increasingly likely that an application of the starker and more abstract vision of Carl Schmitt might prove every bit as illuminating.[19]

In any case, what is clear is that applying this explanatory approach at all effectively (unlike invoking the normative standards of development or protection) makes purely informational demands that we are as yet very far from being in a position to meet. It is on this point that it seems imperative to close. There is, for example, nothing very elusive about the idea that the material foundation for political support in Africa is principally the perquisites of state office and the disbursing of selective advantages to which such office gives access: any more than there is about the prospective tensions between such a basis for political support and the capacity or inclination of the state to serve as an effective agency of development. But the discriminations which are essential for understanding Africa's modern political history cannot be established just by invoking this exceedingly simple conception: they need to be located, with the utmost precision, within its capacious terms. The perquisites of public office at any one time are comparatively finite. Even the selective advantages to which it gives access cannot be indefinitely expanded. What is crucial for the fate of African regimes is how exactly these facilities are deployed in the construction and maintenance of political coalitions over a wide and highly differentiated terrain. Austerity and profligacy are alike in being strategic choices: and the mustering or squandering of political support is an exercise in the articulation of cultural meanings, sympathies and capacities to trust[20] at least as much as in the crude selection of recipients of largesse. It is precisely the *political* experience of post-colonial Africa – what has happened politically in one country after another since the end of colonial rule and why it has been this sequence and not other and very different sequences that has occurred – which we still have only the shakiest conception of how to explain.

As an activity, politics is an exacting and necessarily heavily improvisatory practical skill, deployed in permanently competitive conditions and on the basis of very limited information. As such, as thinkers from Machiavelli to Michael Oakeshott and Alasdair MacIntyre have forcefully insisted,[21] neither its own precise contours nor the outcomes which it engenders can be predicted except in the haziest and most approximate fashion. Much of politics, therefore, cannot be explained with any real precision except in the classic retrospective idiom of historical narrative. More importantly (since the haziness of political explanation may seem simply a matter of its visual opacity: a contingent fact about our observational opportunities as historical human beings) a large part of what does in fact (in historical retrospect) explain political outcomes is simply political starting points: how political relations stand at the historical point which the explanation takes as given. (All explanation has to start somewhere; so it can hardly be judged a deficiency of political explanation that it should be compelled to take a starting point of some kind as given.)

This feature on its own is sufficient to establish the futility of any attempt to reduce the explanation of politics to non-political categories. What explains the trajectory from political starting point to political outcome is in essence a series of political dynamics. These dynamics are certainly affected from the outside by an immense variety of factors: demographic, social, economic. But what is fundamental is that they are also and very drastically affected from the inside, by factors that are already quite explicitly political: by the concerted agency of very large numbers of human beings, acting in large or small groupings, or even individually, to muster and bring to bear, disrupt or overthrow, the facilities for coercion or reward that exist within a particular society. Politics can be thought of – and thought of illuminatingly, if a little artificially – as a single domain of potential explanation. Seen as such a field, a large proportion of what explains its contours at any point in time is simply the sequence of prior states of the same field: its own earlier mutation through time. What explains present politics is largely past politics. To grasp this is to repudiate categorically the possibility of a non-political (supra-political or infra-political) mode of explanation in the last instance, lurking reassuringly behind the unnerving flurry of political engagement, and to vindicate instead the logical and analytical priority of the categories of humane understanding over all superstitious apings of the magic of the scientific revolution in the attempt to understand politics.

Some implications of this perspective are already common currency today in academic attempts to fathom African politics: notably an insistence on the omnipresence and vigour of manipulative endeavours in the vicinity of African state apparatuses in the quest for rents and protections of a giddy miscellany of kinds. So too in the case of an emphasis, developed with particular richness on the basis of Kenyan materials, on the fluidity of roles and the elaborate complementarities of advantage made possible by straddling, broking or switching between different institutional arenas of village, town and administrative or commercial metropolis.[22] These themes cast little light (except on occasion *negatively*) on the felicity or folly of varieties of African state policy. But their analytical prominence and the elusive array of information which would be needed to apply them at all precisely to any contemporary African society do underline the extent to which we still need to make headway with the simple historical mapping of the growth and mutation of dense, intricate, and very poorly identified fields of political action.

Only this more modest and painstaking approach can really enable us to move decisively beyond the petulant superficiality that has disfigured so much academic analysis of African politics. Even then, we cannot hope to understand everything. It is the epistemic fate of all analysts of politics (historians as much as political scientists) to limp more or less clumsily along in the wake of political agents; and the latter often have the most pressing reason to do their best to cover many of their traces. To understand all in politics would never be to forgive all. But a compelling political history of post-colonial West Africa would at least impose some more realistic constraints on our conceptions of what it makes sense to resent or applaud in its recent political past. More importantly, it would also help (as nothing else could do) to show what it really makes sense to hope for or to fear in its proximate political future.

Notes

1 Introduction

1 H. Weiss, *Political Protest in the Congo* (Princeton: Princeton University Press, 1967), pp. 198, 217.
2 J.-F. Bayart, 'La Revanche des sociétés africaines', *Politique Africaine*, 11, September 1983, translated as 'Civil society in Africa', in P. Chabal (ed.), *Political Domination in Africa* (Cambridge: Cambridge University Press, 1986).
3 See, for example, the introduction to and some of the essays in, D. Crummey (ed.), *Banditry, Rebellion and Social Protest in Africa* (London: James Currey, 1986).
4 See especially G. Kitching, *Class and Economic Change in the Making of an African Petite-Bourgeoisie, 1905–1970* (London: Yale University Press, 1980).
5 K. Arhin *et al.*, *Marketing Boards in Tropical Africa* (London: KPI, 1985).
6 A. Cohen, *The Politics of Elite Culture: explorations in the dramaturgy of power in a modern African society* (London: University of California Press, 1981). Also J. R. Cartwright, *Politics in Sierra Leone. 1947–67* (Toronto: University of Toronto Press, 1970).
7 N. Chazan, 'The anomalies of continuity. Perspectives on Ghanaian elections since independence', in F. Hayward (ed.), *Elections in Independent Africa* (Boulder: Westview Press, 1987).
8 P. Chaigneau, *La Politique militaire de la France en Afrique* (Paris: CHEAM, 1984).
9 J.-F. Bayart, *La Politique africaine de François Mitterrand* (Paris: Karthala, 1984).
10 See Comi M. Tulabor, *Le Togo sous Eyadéma* (Paris: Karthala, 1986), p. 313 and throughout. Also Achille Mbembe, *Les Jeunes et l'ordre politique en Afrique noire* (Paris: L'Harmattan, 1985), pp. 234–5 and throughout, and Mbembe, *Afriques Indociles. Christianisme, pouvoir et état en société postcoloniale* (Paris: Karthala, 1988).

2 Burkina Faso: between feeble state and total state, the swing continues

1 25 November 1980: *coup d'état* by the Comité Militaire pour le Redressement Politique National (CMRPN) presided over by Colonel Saye Zerbo; 7 November 1982: advent of the Conseil de Salut du Peuple (CSP) presided over by Commandant Jean-Baptiste Ouedraogo; 4 August 1983: seizure of power by Captain Thomas Sankara, accession of the Conseil National de la Révolution (CNR); 15 October 1987: end of the CNR and institution of the Front Populaire presided over by Captain Blaise Compaoré.
2 See on this subject R. Otayek, 'Quand le tambour change de rhythme, il est indispensable que les danseurs changent de pas', *Politique africaine*, 28 (December 1987), pp. 116–23, and P. Labazée, 'L'Encombrant heritage du capitaine Sankara', *Le Monde diplomatique* (November 1987), p. 15.
3 C. Savonnet-Guyot, 'Etat et sociétés au Burkina. Essai sur le politique africain', roneo, s.d. p. 1.

4 J. Dunn, *West African States. Failure and Promise* (Cambridge: Cambridge University Press, 1978), p. 16.
5 Bayart, 'Civil society in Africa', in P. Chabal (ed.), *Political Domination in Africa* (Cambridge: Cambridge University Press, 1986).
6 For example, J. F. Médard, in 'La Spécificité des pouvoirs africains', *Pouvoirs*, 25 (1983), p. 99.
7 We prefer, with J. F. Médard, to speak of 'neo-patrimonialism' rather than 'patrimonialism' to the extent that relations which rest upon tradition are transposed into the 'modern' context, in *L'Etat sous-développé en Afrique noire: clientélisme politique ou néo-patrimonialisme?* (Bordeaux, CEAN, 1982, T and D), p. 36.
8 R. Otayek, 'Avant-propos', *Politique africaine* (le Burkina Faso), 20 (December 1985), p. 9.
9 Savonnet-Guyot, *Etat et sociétés au Burkina*, pp. 3–4.
10 For a detailed study of these different systems, cf. C. Savonnet-Guyot, *Etat et sociétés au Burkina. Essai sur le politique africain* (Paris: Karthala, 1986), p. 227.
11 On the Mossi Empire, see E. P. Skinner, *The Mossi of Upper Volta* (Stanford: Stanford University Press, 1964), and M. Izard, *Introduction à l'histoire des royaumes mossi* (Paris/Ouagadougou: CNRS/CVRS, 1970), 2 vols.
12 Savonnet-Guyot, roneo, 'Etat et sociétés au Burkina', p. 5.
13 We evoke here in just a few lines as long and complex an evolution as one could wish. For more details, cf. Savonnet-Guyot, *Etat et sociétés au Burkina*; A. S. Balima, *Genèse de la Haute-Volta* (Ouagadougou: Presses africaines, 1970); Ph. Lippens, *La Republique de Haute-Volta* (Paris: IIAP, Berger-Levrault, 1972); A. Nikiema, *Evolution du régime politique de la Haute-Volta depuis l'indépendance*, thèse pour le Doctorat d'Etat en Droit public, Université de Poitiers, Faculté de Droit et Sciences sociales, 1979; K. Sandwidi, *Les Partis politiques en Haute-Volta*, thèse pour le Doctorat en politique et droit du développement, Université de Poitiers, Institut de politique et droit du développement, 1981; M. Diawara, 'Syndicalisme et politique au Burkina Faso', mémoire pour la maîtrise en sociologie, Université de Bordeaux II, section de sociologie, 1985.
14 On this point, see the remarkable thesis of P. Labazée, 'Les Entrepreneurs du secteur industriel et commercial au Burkina Faso', thèse pour le Doctorat de IIIe Cycle en Anthropologie, Université de Paris VIII, Vincennes-Saint-Denis, January 1986, roneo. This thesis will be published shortly by Karthala (Paris) under the title *Enterprises et entrepreneurs du Burkina Faso.*
15 *Ibid.*, p. 508.
16 On this last point, see L. Filippi-Wilhelm, 'Traders and marketing boards in Upper-Volta: ten years of state intervention in agricultural marketing', in K. Arhin, P. Hesp, and H. Van Der Laan (eds.), *Marketing Boards in Tropical Africa* (London: Routledge and Kegan Paul, 1985), pp. 120–48; and M. Saul, 'Development of the grain market and merchants in Burkina Faso', *The Journal of Modern African Studies*, 24, 1 (1986), pp. 127–53.
17 Otayek, 'Avant-propos', p. 4. On the CMRPN, see C. Somé, *Haute-Volta: bilan de la politique de redressement national amorcée le 25 novembre 1980* (Bordeaux, CEAN, T and D, 1983).
18 On the army and politics in Burkina, see C. Somé, 'Sociologie du pouvoir militaire: le cas de la Haute-Volta', Thèse pour le Doctorat de IIIe Cycle d'Etudes africaines (Bordeaux, CEAN, 1979), roneo.
19 These diverse factions co-existed at the top levels of the state from November 1980 (CMRPN) to August 1983 (CNR); it is not superfluous to recall in this connection that Thomas Sankara was *Secrétaire d'Etat a l'Information* (secretary of state at the Ministry of Information) in the government of Colonel Zerbo, and prime minister in the first government of Commandant Ouedraogo.
20 For an analysis of the showdown that led from the CSP to the CNR, see L. Yarga, 'Les Prémices à l'avènement du Conseil national de la révolution en Haute-Volta, *Le Mois en*

Afrique, 213–14 (1983), pp. 24–41; and R. Otayek, 'The revolutionary process in Burkina Faso: breaks and continuities', in J. Markakis and M. Waller (eds.), *Military Marxist Regimes in Africa* (London: Frank Cass, 1986) pp. 82–100. *The Journal of Communist Studies* (special issue on military marxist regimes in Africa), vols. 1, 3 and 4 (September–December 1983).

21 For details, see Otayek, 'The revolutionary process in Burkina Faso'.

22 See P. Labazée, 'La Voie étroite de la révolution au Burkina', *Le Monde diplomatique* (February 1985), pp. 12–13.

23 See on these measures B. Tallet, 'L'Agriculture et les interventions de l'Etat', contribution to the day of study 'Changement politique et ordre social au Burkina Faso' (Bordeaux, CEAN, June 1986), roneo.

24 P. Labazée, 'Une nouvelle phase de la révolution au Burkina', *Politique africaine*, 24 (December 1986), p. 115. C. Savonnet-Guyot notes in this connection that, in its offensive against the Mossi chieftaincy, the CNR went much further than M. Yaméogo whose 'anti-chief' policy spared the Moogho Naaba and the five so-called 'superior' chiefs, in 'Le Prince et Le Naaba', *Politique africaine*, 20 (December 1985), p. 42.

25 Labazée, 'Une nouvelle phase', p. 115.

26 Thomas Sankara, interview published in *Sidwaya* (2 January 1987).

27 An English version of the DOP is published in *The Journal of Communist Studies*, vols. 1, 3, 4 (September–December 1983), pp. 143–66.

28 See on this subject G. Martin, 'Idéologie et praxis dans la révolution populaire du 4 août 1983 au Burkina Faso', *Genève-Afrique*, 26, 1 (1986), pp. 35–62, as well as the debate on this article in the same journal, pp. 155–9, and in 26, 2 (1986), pp. 134–77.

29 P. Labazée, 'La Société burkinabè vue par le pouvoir révolutionnaire: du discours à l'action', contribution to the day of study, 'Changement politique et ordre social au Burkina Faso', roneo, p. 1.

30 *Carrefour africain*, 885 (31 May 1985), pp. 16–17.

31 C. Dubuch, 'Langage du pouvoir, pouvoir du langage', *Politique africaine*, 20 (December 1985), p. 46.

32 J. P. Jacob, 'A Propos du Burkina Faso. Etat totalitaire et totalitarisme sans Etat', *Genève-Afrique*, 26, 1 (1986), p. 155.

33 M. P. Van Dijk, 'La Réussite des petits entrepreneurs dans le secteur informel de Ouagadougou', *Revue Tiers Monde*, 21, 82 (1980), p. 386.

34 For some precise and eloquent examples, see Dubuch, 'Langage du pouvoir'.

35 On this point, see the work of M. Duval on the Nuna, *Un totalitarisme sans Etat. Essai d'anthropologie politique à partir d'un village burkinabè* (Paris: L'Harmattan, 1985).

36 B. P. Bamouni, *Carrefour africain*, 888 (21 June 1985), p. 10.

37 On Burkina's Muslim community, cf. R. Otayek, 'La Crise de la communauté musulmane de Haute-Volta. L'islam voltaïque entre réformisme et tradition, autonomie et sub-ordination', *Cahiers d'études africaines*, 24, 3 (1984), pp. 299–320.

38 *Ibid.*

39 Bayart, 'Civil society in Africa'.

40 Moreover, one must underline in this connection that on the whole the Burkinabè administration is certainly less corrupt and more efficient than a good number of African states. This favoured the designs of the CNR.

41 *Carrefour africain* (23 October 1987).

3 Cameroon

1 This chapter is firstly based on documentation gathered during several field missions made at regular intervals from May 1984 to May 1987, and more particularly on a number of interviews with members of the Cameroonian political class. For a more chronological and

detailed analysis of the 1982–86 period, see my articles published in *Marchés tropicaux et méditerranéens*: 'Un printemps camerounais', 23 September 1983, pp. 2250–51; 'Une trop belle élection?', 20 January 1984, pp. 11–12; 'De la stupeur au soulagement', 23 March 1984, pp. 671–2; 'La Rentrée politique du président Biya', 11 January 1985, pp. 69–71; 'Les Premiers Pas du rassemblement démocratique du peuple camerounais', 21 June 1985, pp. 1543–4; 'Démocratisation du parti et réforme de l'état', 16 May 1986, pp. 1328–30; see also 'La Société politique camerounaise (1982–1986)', *Politique africaine*, 22 (1986), pp. 5–35.

H. Bandolo presents a well-informed account of the 1982–84 crisis, peppered with previously unpublished testimony but politically committed: *La Flamme et la fumée* (Yaoundé, SOPECAM, 1985). J. P. Biyiti bi Essam gives some information on the real-life experience of this period and, in particular, on the role of rumours: *Cameroun: complots et bruits de bottes* (Paris: L'Harmattan, 1984).

2 J.-F. Bayart, *L'Etat au Cameroun* (Paris: Presses de la Fondation Nationale des Sciences Politiques, 1979), p. 138.

3 *Ibid.*, p. 138. Subsequent interviews have not permitted me to validate this hypothesis.

4 Although unofficial, this hypothesis is not necessarily erroneous. Diverse interviews and opposing political sources authorise its confirmation.

5 *Le Monde*, 17 April 1984.

6 See in particular 'Open letter to all English-speaking parents of Cameroon from the English-speaking students of the North-West and South-West provinces' (Bamenda (?) 20 August 1985) and 'Memorandum presented to the Head of State and chairman of the Cameroon People's Democratic Movement by a joint committee of the elite of the North-West and South-West provinces resident in Littoral province' (Douala, 7 May 1985).

7 Mono Ndjana, 'De l'ethno-fascisme dans la littérature politique camerounaise' (Yaoundé, 11 March 1987).

8 Memorandum, 'Un éclairage nouveau', signed by 'some indigenous priests of the archdiocese of Douala' (Douala, Unesco Club, 16 March 1987).

9 C. Tardits (ed.), *Contribution de la recherche ethnologique à l'histoire des civilisations du Cameroun* (Paris: CNRS 1981); J. Boutrais, *et al.*, *Le Nord du Cameroun. Des hommes, une région* (Paris: ORSTOM, 1984).

10 Boutrais, *et al.*, *Le Nord du Cameroun*; V. Azarya, *Dominance and Change in North Cameroun: The Fulbe Aristocracy* (Beverly Hills: Sage, 1976).

11 F. Braudel, *L'Identité de la France. Espace et histoire* (Paris: Arthaud, 1986), ch. 1. On the number of constituent 'countries' within Cameroon, see *Atlas linguistique du Cameroun. Inventaire préliminaire* (Paris, 1983) and A. Beauvilain, J. L. Dongmo *et. al.*, *Atlas aérien du Cameroun. Campagnes et villes* (University of Yaoundé, 1983).

12 S. Diallo, 'Les Secrets du départ d'Ahidjo', *Jeune afrique*, 17 November 1982, pp. 37–38.

13 *Cameroon Tribune*, 30–1 January 1983.

14 P. F. Ngayap, *Qui gouverne au Cameroun?* (Paris: L'Harmattan, 1983). This work was made the object of a lengthy polemic in the *Cameroon Tribune* during July 1983.

15 Bayart, *L'Etat au Cameroun*, pp. 163–4.

16 Source: interviews.

17 *Le Messager*, 20 May 1984, p. 3.

18 *Cameroon Tribune*, January–June 1983.

19 See 'Paul Biya: l'appel du destin', *ESSTI* special, December 1983 and *Le Renouveau camerounais: certitudes et défis* (Yaoundé, ESSTI, 1983).

20 'Discours de clôture de S. E. Paul Biya', *L'Unité*, 661 (1983), pp. 34, 36.

21 *Cameroon Tribune*, 1 December 1983.

22 UPC, *Appel de l'UPC et du Manidem au peuple kamerunais, aux travailleurs des villes, aux jeunes et aux femmes du Kamerun* (Paris, UPC, 1983).

23 République du Cameroun, Ministère de l'Information et de la Culture, *Pour comprendre l'affaire Ahmadou Ahidjo* (Yaoundé, 1984).

24 G. Balandier, *Political Anthropology*, Smith trans. (Harmondsworth: Allen Lane, Penguin, 1970); R. L. Sklar, 'The nature of class domination in Africa', *Journal of Modern African Studies*, 17, 4 (1979), pp. 531–52, and *Nigerian Political Parties. Power in an Emergent African Nation* (Princeton: Princeton University Press, 1963).

25 *Cameroon Tribune*, 26 August 1983.

26 Sources: *La Gazette* and *Le Messager*, 1983–7.

27 J. L. Dongmo, *Le Dynamisme bamiléké (Cameroun)*, vol. 2. *La Maîtrise de l'espace urbain* (Yaoundé: Centre d'Edition et de Production pour l'Enseignment et la Recherche, 1981), pp. 173ff.

28 H. Manga, 'Dans le Wouri, le meilleur a gagné', *Le Messager*, 18 March 1986, p. 12.

29 J. S. Saul, *The State and Revolution in Eastern Africa* (London and New York: Monthly Review Press, 1979).

30 The expression is from the Minister George Ngango who was directing it to the Political Secretary of the party, Sengat-Kuoh (*La Gazette*, 23 August 1984; *Le Messager*, 27 September 1984).

31 *Le Messager*, 31 March 1986, p. 6.

32 Bayart, *L'Etat au Cameroun*.

33 J. F. Médard, 'L'Etat sous-développé au Cameroun', *Année africaine 1977* (1978), pp. 35–84.

34 I. Wilks, *Asante in the Nineteenth Century. The Structure and Evolution of a Political Order* (Cambridge: Cambridge University Press, 1975), pp. 195–6, 267ff, 699ff.

35 J. MacGaffey, *Entrepreneurs and Parasites. The Struggle for Indigenous Capitalism in Zaire* (Cambridge: Cambridge University Press, 1987); Republique française, Ministère des relations extérieures, coopération et développement, *Analyse 'ex post' de la promotion des PME et de l'artisanat en Côte-d'Ivoire* (Paris, 1986).

36 J. P. Warnier, *Echanges, développement et hiérarchies dans le Bamenda pré-colonial (Cameroun)* (Stuttgart: Frans Steiner Verlag, 1985).

37 J. Champaud, *Villes et campagnes du Cameroun de l'Ouest* (Paris: ORSTOM, 1983), p. 286.

38 M. P. Cowen, K. Kinyanjui, 'Some Problems of Capital and Classes in Kenya' (Nairobi: Institute of Development Studies, 1977, roneo); G. Kitching, *Class and Economic Change in Kenya. The Making of an African Petite-Bourgeoisie* (New Haven: Yale University Press, 1980).

39 J. Iliffe, *The Emergence of African Capitalism* (London: Macmillan, 1983), pp. 30–1 and 65ff.

40 Champaud, *Villes et campagnes*, p. 271.

41 D. B. Cruise O'Brien, *Saints and Politicians: Essays in the Organization of a Senegalese Peasant Society* (Cambridge: Cambridge University Press, 1975).

42 M. P. Cowen, 'The British state, state enterprise and an indigenous bourgeoisie in Kenya after 1945' (Dakar: Conference on The African bourgeoisie. The development of capitalism in Nigeria, Kenya, Ivory Coast, SSRC, 1980), p. 34; J.-F. Bayart, *L'Invention du politique en Afrique noire* (Paris: forthcoming), ch. 3; and *l'Etat en Afrique. La Politique du Ventre* (Paris: Fayard, forthcoming); Saul, *The State*.

43 R. A. Joseph, 'Theories of the African bourgeoisie: an exploration' (Dakar, Conference on The African bourgeoisie, 1980), pp. 17ff; M. G. Schatzberg, *Politics and Class in Zaire. Bureaucracy, Business, and Beer in Lisala* (New York: Africana Publishers, 1980).

44 G. Kitching, 'Politics, method and evidence in the "Kenya Debate"', in H. Bernstein and B. K. Campbell (eds.), *Contradictions of Accumulation in Africa. Studies in Economy and State* (Beverly Hills: Sage, 1985), p. 131.

45 S. Berry, *Fathers Work for their Sons. Accumulation, Mobility and Class Formation in an Extended Yoruba Community* (Berkeley and London: University of California Press, 1985).

46 P. Dessouane and P. Verre, 'Cameroun: du développement autocentré au national-libéralisme', *Politique africaine*, 22 (1986), pp. 111–19; J. C. Willame, 'Cameroun: les

avatars d'un libéralisme planifié', *ibid.*, 18 (1985), pp. 44–70; G. Courade, 'Des complexes qui coûtent cher', *ibid.*, 14 (1984), pp. 75–91.

47 M. Weber, *The Protestant Ethic and the Spirit of Capitalism*, trans. T. Parsons (London: Allen and Unwin, 1930), and R. Collins, 'Weber's last theory of capitalism: a systematization', *American Sociological Review*, 45, 6 (1980), pp. 931–2.

48 Sklar, *Nigerian Political Parties*; M. Kilson, *Political Change in a West African State. A Study of the Modernization Process in Sierra Leone* (New York: Atheneum, 1969), Y. A. Fauré, J. F. Médard (eds.), *Etat et bourgeoisie en Côte d'Ivoire* (Paris: Karthala, 1982); J. P. Olivier de Sardan, *Les Sociétés songhay-zarma (Niger, Mali). Chefs, guerriers, esclaves, paysans...* (Paris: Karthala, 1984); Cruise O'Brien, *Saints and Politicians*; C. Clapham, *Liberia and Sierra Leone. An Essay in Comparative Politics* (Cambridge: Cambridge University Press, 1976); T. P. Wrubel, 'Liberia: The dynamics of continuity', *Journal of Modern African Studies*, 9, 2 (August 1971), pp. 180–204; M. Lowenkopf, 'Political modernization in Liberia: a conservative model', *The Western Political Quarterly*, 25, 1 (March 1972), pp. 94–108.

49 Bayart, *L'Etat au Cameroun*, and *L'Etat en Afrique*.

50 Bayart, *L'Etat en Afrique*, ch. 7. On the concept of 'passive revolution', see, in addition to A. Gramsci's oeuvre, its commentary in J. A. Davis (ed.), *Gramsci and Italy's Passive Revolution* (London: Croom Helm, 1979); C. Mouffe (ed.), *Gramsci and Marxist Theory* (London: Routledge and Kegan Paul, 1979); C. Buci-Glucksmann, *Gramsci and the State* (London: Lawrence and Wishart, 1980).

4 Chad: the narrow escape of an African state, 1965–1987

1 J. Dunn (ed.), *West African States: Failure and Promise. A Study in Comparative Politics* (Cambridge: Cambridge University Press, 1978), p. 3.

2 The short space of this chapter does not allow me to dwell at any length upon the reasons that sparked off the peasant revolt, nor upon the earlier history of Frolinat. Interested readers are referred to R. Buijtenhuijs, *Le Frolinat et les révoltes populaires du Tchad, 1965–1976* (The Hague, Paris: Mouton, 1978). Very briefly it can be said that the northern revolts were first of all a rising of a Muslim population of peasants and herdsmen against alleged political oppression and economic neglect by the southern-dominated regime, although Frolinat professed to be a national and revolutionary anti-imperialist movement.

3 *Procès-verbal de rèunion de sous-commission No. 6*, Fort-Lamy, 24 February 1970, p. 9.

4 R. Buijtenhuijs, *Le Frolinat et les guerres civiles du Tchad, 1977–1984: la révolution introuvable* (Paris: Karthala, 1987).

5 B. Lanne, 'Le Sud du Tchad dans la guerre civile, 1979–1980', *Politique africaine* 3 (September 1981), p. 85.

6 *Marchés Tropicaux et Mediterranéens*, 27 March 1981.

7 'Bulletin Quotidien d'Afrique', *Agence France Presse*, 10 March 1981.

8 *Chemin (Le) de l'Unité*, Frolinat, Conseil national pour la révolution (N'jaména; 15 May 1981), p. 57.

9 M. Brandily, 'Le Tchad face nord, 1978 1979', *Politique africaine*, 16 (December 1984), p. 52.

10 M. P. Kelley, *A State in Disarray: Conditions of Chad's Survival* (Boulder and London: Westview Press, 1986).

11 'Bulletin Quotidien d'Afrique', *Agence France Presse*, 21 April 1984.

12 Buijtenhuijs, *Le Frolinat*.

13 A. le Rouvreur, *Sahéliens et Sahariens du Tchad* (Paris: Berger-Levrault, 1962), p. 24.

14 J.-P. Magnant, 'Peuple, ethnie et nation: le cas du Tchad', *Droit et Cultures*, 8 (1984), p. 43.

15 R. Lemarchand, 'The crisis in Chad', in G. J. Bender *et al.* (eds.), *African Crisis Areas and*

US Foreign Policy (Berkeley–Los Angeles–London: University of California Press, 1985), p. 243.

16 J.-L. Triaud, 'Le Refus de l'état: l'exemple tchadien', *Esprit*, 100 (April 1985).

17 Th. Michalon, 'Le Drame du Tchad et l'héritage colonial de l'Afrique: l'échec de la greffe jacobine', *Le Monde diplomatique*, April 1979.

18 Th. Michalon, 'L'Impuissance d'un état fictif', *Le Monde diplomatique*, September 1983.

19 S. Decalo, 'Regionalism, political decay, and civil strife in Chad', *Journal of Modern African Studies*, 18, 1 (1980), p. 25.

20 Kelley, *A State in Disarray*, p. 2.

5 Côte d'Ivoire: analysing the crisis

1 This impossibility has been officially presented as a 'refusal', and this latter conception has been obligingly taken up in the press: see for example, 'Houphouët refuse de payer', *Jeune Afrique*, 10 June 1987, pp. 28–33.

2 See for example, *Jeune Afrique* of 14 August 1985, p. 17 and *Fraternité-Matin* (government newspaper, Abidjan) of 27 January 1987, p. 1.

3 See for example: S. Calabre, *Prix et conjoncture sur les marchés à terme de produits* (Abidjan: CEDA, distributed by Karthala, Paris, 1985), p. 212. This is one way for the Ivorian government to refuse the 'laws' of a market in which it otherwise believes. The fall of the coffee and cocoa markets is a long way from being expressed in the prices at the time of consumption of the finished product. This phenomenon owes little to the 'rules' of the market, the circuits of processing and marketing being probably responsible.

4 This cry of relief, launched from the Ivorian presidency and embellishing the climate of the October 1985 congress of the PDCI-RDA (the Ivory Coast's only political party), had also been hastily passed on by the French media. See, for example, the issue of *Afrique-Industrie* of 1 March 1986, pp. 16–47: 'Côte-d'Ivoire: la crise est passée'.

5 N. B. Ridler, 'Comparative advantage as a development model: the Ivory Coast', *The Journal of Modern African Studies*, 23, 3 (1985), pp. 407–17. Another example of this type of analysis is furnished by J.-P. Foirry, 'L'Evolution conjoncturelle de la Côte-d'Ivoire de 1960 à 1985: quelques facteurs explicatifs de la crise actuelle', *Le Mois en Afrique* (April–May 1986), pp. 70–80.

6 See notably J.-P. Foirry, 'L'Evolution', who speaks of a 'counter-cyclic policy' for the refusal of Ivorian authorities to take measures checking economic activity during the 1978–80 period of sharp market downturns.

7 J.-P. Foirry, 'L'Evolution', for example, points out that the debt increase could have been mastered if the Ivorian government had decided upon a limitation of imports at the first signs of a perceptible downturn in the commodities market.

8 B. den Tuinder, *Ivory Coast. The Challenge of Success*, Report of a mission sent to the Ivory Coast by the World Bank (Baltimore and London: The Johns Hopkins University Press, 1978), p. 445.

9 *Ibid.* p. 188.

10 République française, Ministère de la coopération (G. Duruflé, coordinator of the study), *Déséquilibres structurels et programmes d'ajustement en Côte-d'Ivoire* (Paris: 1986) many graphs, multiple pagination. This voluminous report is the most detailed and best elaborated analysis of Ivorian economic developments.

11 On this last point, see L. Gouffern, 'Les Limites d'un modèle', *Politique africaine*, 6 (May 1982), pp. 19–34, for detailed reasons (corruption, over-protectionism in certain sectors, guaranteed incomes, etc.) for the non-competitiveness of Ivorian manufactured products.

12 For urban housing as a sector highly subsidised by the state to the benefit of the middle stratum of Ivorian society (it has been calculated that the standard financial liability assumed

by the state could reach close to 60 per cent of construction costs), see in particular: P. Haeringer, 'Vingt-cinq ans de politique urbaine à Abidjan ou la tentation de l'urbanisme intégral', *Politique africaine*, 17 (March 1985), pp. 20–40; and A. Manou Savina, P. Antoine, A. Dubresson and A. Yapi Diahou, 'Les En-haut des en-bas et les en-bas des en-haut. Classes moyennes et urbanisation à Abidjan', *Tiers monde*, 26, 101 (March 1985), pp. 55–67.

13 G. Duruflé, *Déséquilibres structurels*, p. 41.

14 *Ibid.*, p. 45.

15 S. Amin, *Le Développement du capitalisme en Côte d'Ivoire* (Paris: Les Editions de Minuit, 1967).

16 L. K. Mytilka, 'Foreign business and economic development', in I. W. Zartman and C. Delgado (eds.), *The Political Economy of Ivory Coast* (New York: Praeger, 1984), p. 255.

17 B. K. Campbell, 'The fiscal crisis of the state, the case of the Ivory Coast', in H. Bernstein and B. K. Campbell (eds.), *Contradictions of Accumulation in Africa* (Beverly Hills: Sage, 1985), pp. 267–310; and the same author's 'Crise fiscale et endettement. Le cas de la Côte-d'Ivoire', *Interventions économiques*, 16 (1986), pp. 95–110.

18 For the theoretical description of these mechanisms, see S. Amin, *Accumulation on a World Scale* (New York: Monthly Review Press, 1974), and for an application to the Ivory Coast, see Amin, *Le Développement*, pp. 269ff.

19 D. Bra Kanon, *Développement ou appauvrissement* (Paris: Economica, 1985), pp. 29ff., advances the argument of the general inflationary situation to justify the considerable investments decided upon in the Ivory Coast in the 1970s and 1980s. Apart from its obvious legitimising function (Bra Kanon is the Ivorian Minister of Agriculture), the reasoning is often sound.

20 Cf. in particular Duruflé, *Déséquilibres structurels*, pp. 24ff.

21 Cf., for example, W. F. Steel and J. W. Evans, 'Industrialisation in Africa south of the Sahara' (Washington: World Bank technical document, no. 25F, 1984), p. 103.

22 This analysis is the object of a work carried out in association with B. Contamin, an economist at the Université de Pau (France), being published.

23 This last stumbling block is made quite evident in the work of G. Duruflé and that of B. K. Campbell. But we see in this an obstacle that comes under the sub-Saharan model, not typically Ivorian.

24 And in particular J.-P. Foirry, 'L'Evolution', p. 75.

25 J.-P. Foirry, 'L'Evolution', p. 75, shows, for example, that while in 1973 91.7 per cent of the service sector's purchases took place in Ivory Coast, in 1978 those same purchases in the country represented no more than 38.1 per cent of sector purchases. The analysis of this phenomenon of increasing import content in the production process is meticulously undertaken by Duruflé, *Déséquilibres structurels*.

26 These figures are taken from G. Ancey, 'Analyse régionale des actions de l'Etat', *Revue économique et financière ivoirienne*, 16 (1981), pp. 10–15.

27 These are the rehabilitation and recovery plans implemented over the last few years in the Ivory Coast, adopted with (or under pressure from) international financial backers: recovery programme for the '*Fonds fiduciaire*' (1978/9); the enlarged credit term agreement with the IMF (1981/3); the structural adjustment loans (SAL) from the World Bank: SAL I (1981), SAL II (1983), SAL III (1986); confirmation agreement with the IMF (1984), to which one may add the loans concluded with the *Caisse centrale de coopération économique* (CCCE-Paris) in 1982, 1983, 1984, etc.

28 On clientelism and (neo) patrimonialism applied to a political analysis of Black Africa, see J.-F. Médard, 'The underdeveloped state in tropical Africa: political clientelism or neo-patrimonialism?' in C. Clapham (ed.), *Private Patronage and Public Power: Political Clientelism in the Modern State* (London: Frances Pinter, 1982) which refers to numerous works on the subject.

29 A. Zolberg, *One Party Government in the Ivory Coast* (Princeton: Princeton University Press, 1964); M. Cohen, *Urban Policy and Political Conflict* (Chicago and London: The University of Chicago Press, 1974); J.-F. Médard, 'La Régulation socio-politique', in Y.-A. Fauré and J.-F. Médard, *Etat et bourgeoisie en Côte-d'Ivoire* (Paris: Karthala, 1982), pp. 75ff.

30 L. Sylla, 'Genèse et fonctionnement de l'etat clientèliste en Côte-d'Ivoire', *Archives européènnes de sociologie*, 1 (1985) pp. 29–57, and especially E. Terray, 'Le Climatiseur et la véranda', in *Afrique plurielle, Afrique actuelle, Hommage à Georges Balandier* (Paris: Karthala, 1986), pp. 37–44, in which the author metaphorically (and quite nicely) denotes two coexisting 'systems of government': in the second, 'the State appears as a conglomerate of positions of power whose occupants are in a position at the same time to assure themselves of substantial revenues and to spread around situations, prebends, bonuses and services' (pp. 38–9). Instructive annotations follow that admirably describe the diverse patrimonial manners of decision and action at the summit of the state.

31 This was the most important governmental reshuffle since independence seeing that the holders of the principal portfolios (Economy and Finance, Plan, Agriculture, Foreign Affairs, etc.) were dismissed. Numerous less profound modifications have also taken place in the governmental teams.

32 For a more precise description of Ivorian political interplay since 1980 see the chronicles of J.-F. Médard, 'Jeunes et aînés en Côte-d'Ivoire', *Politique africaine*, 1 (January 1981), pp. 102–13; and Y.-A. Fauré, 'Nouvelle donne en Côte-d'Ivoire', *Politique africaine*, 20 (December 1985), pp. 96–109.

33 In such a system, these 'affairs' cannot but be orchestrated at the highest level. The disclosure of a scandal in a regime notably characterised by an official press is in itself a strictly political decision and necessarily controlled; the supervision of the denunciation, which signals the abandonment and disgrace of the agent, presupposes a centralised control such that the tightness and homogeneity of the ruling class not be threatened. Moreover, this is why certain procedures have been stopped before running their course.

34 Notably as regards recruiting, remuneration, allocations, material advantages, mode of management, etc. done on criteria and at levels extremely remote from those of administration strictly speaking.

35 The 'electoral opening up' of 1980, too commonly presented as an act of democratisation, has in reality been a true purge of the political personnel: consequently, renewal rate from the ballots in 1980 and 1985 has been successively 82 per cent and 65 per cent. The 'electoral body' has thus been an efficient instrument of presidential policy.

36 The IMF *Bulletin* of 3 December 1984, pp. 357–61, gives a very suggestive (but very partial) idea of this tension.

37 Between 1979 and 1984 total employment in the modern sector dropped 30 per cent and the decline has continued (Banque des données financières, Abidjan, *Centrale des bilans*, 1979 and 1984); as for revenues, we note that if the average annual growth of monetary revenue had been 3 per cent during the period between 1969–78, from 1978 to 1983 the decrease of this revenue calculated on the basis of 1965 has been of an average of 5.5 per cent by year (G. Duruflé and J.-L. Martin, *Evolution et répartition des revenus en Côte-d'Ivoire* (Paris: SEDES, 1984), pp. 41 and 42.

38 Cf. C. Vidal and M. Le Pape, *Pratiques de crise et conditions sociales à Abidjan* (Abidjan: ORSTOM and CNRS, 1986), many graphs, p. 102.

39 See, in particular, the analyses of Duruflé, *Déséquilibres structurels*, and Campbell, 'The fiscal crisis', to which we subscribe on these points.

40 See the J. Copans–R. Sandbrook debate (the latter accused by the former of an exclusively political analysis and an abandonment of class analysis) in *Politique africaine*, 26 (June 1987), pp. 2–14 and 38–40.

6 Ghana: the political economy of personal rule

1 Robert H. Bates, *Markets and States in Tropical Africa: the Political Basis of Agricultural Policies* (Berkeley: University of California Press, 1981).

2 Robert Jackson and Carl Rosberg, *Personal Rule in Black Africa* (Berkeley: University of California Press, 1982); Richard Sandbrook, *The Politics of Africa's Economic Stagnation* (Cambridge: Cambridge University Press, 1985).

3 Bates, *Markets and States*; Richard Rathbone, 'Ghana', in John Dunn (ed.), *West African States: Failure and Promise* (Cambridge: Cambridge University Press, 1978), pp. 22–35; Richard Jeffries, 'Rawlings and the political economy of underdevelopment in Ghana', *African Affairs*, 81, 324 (July 1982), pp. 307–17.

4 *West Africa*, 13 January 1986, pp. 67–85.

5 See, for example, Emil Rado, 'Notes towards a political economy of Ghana today', *African Affairs*, 85, 341 (October 1986), 563–72.

6 Martin Staniland, *What is Political Economy?* (Newhaven and London: Yale University Press, 1985).

7 The fullest academic account of the events of these years is that provided by Naomi Chazan, *An Anatomy of Ghanaian Politics: Managing Political Recession, 1969–1982* (Colorado: Westview Press, 1983).

8 Jeffries, 'Rawlings and the political economy of underdevelopment in Ghana'.

9 Elliot J. Berg, 'Structural transformation versus gradualism: recent economic development in Ghana and the Ivory Coast', in Philip Foster and Aristide R. Zolberg (eds.), *Ghana and the Ivory Coast* (Chicago: University of Chicago Press, 1971), pp. 187–230.

10 Emmanuel Hansen and Paul Collins, 'The army, the state and the Rawlings revolution', *African Affairs*, 79, 314 (January 1980), pp. 3–23.

11 Rathbone, 'Ghana', p. 30.

12 The term *Kalabule* probably derived from the Hausa expression *Kere kabure* (keep it quiet).

13 Mike Ocquaye, *Politics in Ghana, 1972–1979* (Accra: Tornado Publications, 1980), p. 17.

14 See especially Ayi Kwei Armah, *The Beautyful [sic] Ones Are Not Yet Born* (Nairobi: Heinemann, 1976).

15 Francis Teal, 'The foreign exchange regime and growth: a comparison of Ghana and the Ivory Coast', *African Affairs*, 85, 339 (April 1986), 267–82.

16 Charles Y. Mansfield, 'Tax-base erosion and inflation: the case of Ghana', *Finance and Development*, 17, 3 (September 1980), pp. 31–4.

17 Jeffries, 'Rawlings and the political economy of underdevelopment in Ghana'.

18 John Lonsdale, 'Political accountability in African history', in Patrick Chabal (ed.), *Political Domination in Africa* (Cambridge: Cambridge University Press, 1986), pp. 126–57.

19 Robert Price, 'Neo-colonialism and Ghana's economic decline: a critical assessment', *Canadian Journal of African Studies*, 18 (1984), pp. 163–93.

20 *West Africa*, 6 September 1982, p. 2319.

21 The works of Rodney, Leys, etc., provided the conceptual framework for much of the teaching in the Political Science, History and Law Departments of the University of Legon from the mid-1970s onwards. Regrettably, the growing foreign exchange shortage meant that hardly any copies of the most persuasive critiques of the 'dependency' perspective became locally available.

22 A vivid account of the events of this period is provided by Barbara E. Okeke, *4 June: A Revolution Betrayed* (Enugu: Ikenga Publishers, 1982); see also Ocquaye, *Politics in Ghana*.

23 Printed in Okeke, *4 June: A Revolution Betrayed*, p. 130.

24 *Ibid.*, p. 67.

25 *West Africa*, 9 July 1979, p. 1199.

26 For example, Hansen and Collins, 'The army, the state and the Rawlings revolution'.

27 Quoted in Bill Freund, *The Making of Contemporary Africa* (London: Macmillan, 1984), p. 234.
28 Richard Jeffries, 'The Ghanaian elections of 1979', *African Affairs*, 79, 316 (July 1980), pp. 397–414.
29 For an account, see Chazan, *An Anatomy of Ghanaian Politics*, pp. 306–27.
30 Donald I. Ray, *Ghana* (London: Frances Pinter, 1986), pp. 35–64.
31 Jeffries, 'Rawlings and the political economy of underdevelopment in Ghana'.
32 Zaya Yeebo, 'How the IMF tamed a leftist apostle', *African Events*, November 1984.
33 For my information here I am greatly indebted to two of my research students, Jeffrey Haynes and Paul Nugent. They are not of course responsible for my interpretation.
34 John Dunn, 'The politics of representation and good government in post-colonial Africa', in Chabal (ed.), *Political Domination in Africa*, p. 162.
35 Richard Dowden, *The Independent*, 7 March 1987, p. 6.

7 Liberia

1 I have discussed Liberian politics from a pre-coup viewpoint in C. Clapham, 'Liberia', in J. Dunn (ed.), *West African States: failure and promise* (Cambridge: Cambridge University Press, 1978), pp. 117–31. I have not, however, been able to visit Liberia since 1980, and this account therefore rests heavily on published sources, among which the magazine *West Africa* requires special mention. The outstanding account of Liberian politics up to early 1986 is J. Gus Liebenow, *Liberia: the Quest for Democracy* (Bloomington: Indiana University Press, 1987). A second essential source of materials on modern Liberia is the Liberia Working Group, based in Bremen, Federal Republic of Germany, which publishes the journal *Liberia-Forum* and the series of Liberia Working Group Papers, and also produced the useful collection of papers, R. Kappel, *et al.* (eds.), *Liberia: Underdevelopment and Political Rule in a Peripheral Society* (Hamburg: Institut fur Afrika-Kunde, 1986). Other important materials are published in *Liberian Studies Journal* by the Liberian Studies Association based in the United States.
2 See Amos Sawyer, *Effective Immediately: dictatorship in Liberia, 1980–1986: a personal perspective* (Liberian Working Group Papers No. 5, Bremen, 1987).
3 See Siapha Kamara, 'The role of the Putu Development Corporation in rural conscientization and mobilization in the 1970s', in Kappel *et al.*, *Liberia: Underdevelopment and Political Rule in a Peripheral Society*.
4 See Gunter Schroder and Werner Korte, 'Samuel K. Doe, the People's Redemption Council and power; preliminary remarks on the anatomy and social psychology of a *coup d'état*', *Liberia-Forum*, 2, 3 (1986).
5 Including the above cited works by both Liebenow and Sawyer.

8 Nigeria: power for profit – class, corporatism, and factionalism in the military

1 Federal Republic of Nigeria, *Objectives, Policies and Programmes of the Federal Military Government* (Lagos: May 1984), pp. 1–80. Except pp. 5–15 which contain some additions and amendments, this document is an almost verbatim version of the unpublished Presidential Committee Report commissioned and endorsed by President Shagari, and from which some portions were expunged. The Committee's Chairman was Adamu Ciroma, until then a minister in Shagari's Cabinet.
2 Sam C. Nolutshungu, 'Variations on a theme of order', Paper presented at the Conference on Nigeria held at Keele University, September 1980, p. 10.
3 R. Joseph, 'Class, state, and prebendal politics in Nigeria', *Journal of Commonwealth and Comparative Politics*, 21, 3 (November 1983), p. 22.

4 G. Williams, *State and Society in Nigeria* (Idanre, Nigeria: Afrografika, 1980), *passim*; and General Murtala Mohammed's inaugural speech to the Constitution Drafting Committee in *Report of the Constitution Drafting Committee*, 1 (Lagos, 1976), p. xii. Nolutshungu, above, doubtless shares this analysis but draws our attention to a large degree of order, consensus, and stability within the Nigerian social formation.

5 The explanations by both Finer and Huntington border on the unicausal, and the dispute between them is poorly formulated. Cf. S. G. Tyoden, 'The military and society in Nigeria', unpublished, n.d., Department of Political Science, University of Jos, Jos, Nigeria. Contrast the more balanced view of Forrest that 'prominent features of the Nigerian state and public policy are best analysed if the state is understood to be the site of class interaction. This approach has the advantage of relating state institutions, policies and personnel to civil society.' Tom Forrest, 'Notes on the political economy of state intervention in Nigeria', in R. Luckham (ed.), *Politics, Class and Development*, IDS Bulletin, 2, 1 (University of Sussex, July 1977), p. 42.

6 V. Droucopoulos and J. S. Henley, 'The pursuit of profit, the technocrats' role and the instability of the Nigerian state', *Review of African Political Economy* (*ROAPE*), 9 (May–August 1978), p. 61.

7 *The Times* (London), 2 January 1984, p. 4.

8 B. Beckman, 'Public enterprises and state capitalism', in Y. Ghai (ed.), *Law in the Political Economy of Public Enterprises* (Uppsala, 1977) p. 134. Cf. M. Martin, 'Corporate interests and military rule', in C. Allen and G. Williams (eds.), *Sub-Saharan Africa* (Macmillan, 1982), pp. 188–9.

9 D. Rimmer, 'Elements in the political economy', in K. Panter-Brick (ed.), *Soldiers and Oil* (London: Frank Cass, 1978), p. 147.

10 Williams, *State and Society*, p. 33.

11 *Ibid.*, pp. 34–6; Joseph, 'Class, state, and prebendal politics', p. 23.

12 C. C. Wrigley, 'The development of state capitalism in late colonial and post-colonial Nigeria', Paper presented to a Conference of the African Studies Association of the United Kingdom (Liverpool: 1974).

13 Williams, *State and Society*, p. 47.

14 Martin, 'Corporate interests', p. 189.

15 *West Africa* (London), 24 September 1973, p. 136.

16 Williams, *State and Society*, p. 49.

17 Paul Collins, 'The political economy of indigenization: the case of the Nigerian enterprises promotion decree', *The African Review*, 4, 4 (1974); B. Beckman, 'Whose state? state and capitalist development in Nigeria', *ROAPE*, 23 (January–April 1982); Claude Ake (ed.), *Political Economy of Nigeria* (London: Longman, 1985), pp. 173–200; and T. J. Biersteker, *Multinationals, the State, and Control of the Nigerian Economy* (Princeton: Princeton University Press, 1987).

18 Ayida was then Federal Permanent Secretary, Finance, and in 1975 became the Secretary to the Federal Nigerian Government. See his *The Nigerian Revolution, 1966–76* (Ibadan: University Press, 1973); and G. Williams (ed.), *Nigeria: Economy and Society* (London: Rex Collins, 1976), p. 186.

19 General O. Obasanjo, *Nzeogwu* (Ibadan: Spectrum Books, 1987), p. 2. As a young Nigerian officer confided to me, Nigerian officers are enjoined to develop greater friendship and trust with colleagues than even with their wives because it is the former who can be of assistance in the trenches.

20 R. Luckham, *The Nigerian Military* (Cambridge: Cambridge University Press, 1975), p. 144.

21 *Ibid.*, p. 193.

22 G. Williams and T. Turner, 'Nigeria', in John Dunn (ed.), *West African States: Failure and Promise* (Cambridge: Cambridge University Press, 1978), p. 134.

23 Mr Allison Ayida, interview, London, 9 February 1985. For a theoretical formulation, see A. H. M. Kirk-Greene, '*Angst* and the genesis of the Nigerian Civil War', Scandinavian Institute of African Studies Research Report No. 27, 1975.

24 Major-Gen. J. J. Oluleye, *Military Leadership in Nigeria* (Ibadan: University Press, 1985) pp. 45–9; and General O. Obasanjo, *My Command* (London: Heinemann, 1980), pp. 8–9.

25 Affecting only about half of the 120 or so officers investigated by a board of inquiry under Major-General R. A. Adebayo. A. Kirk-Greene and D. Rimmer, *Nigeria Since 1970* (London: Hodder & Stoughton, 1981), pp. 55–6.

26 Luckham, *The Nigerian Military*, pp. 180–2 shows that Northern officers in the 1960s could in fact be sub-divided into four broad categories, those from Moslem emirates, the Hausa-Fulani diaspora peoples (General Gowon for instance), the Middle Belt proper, and the Northern Yorubas (for example, Maj.-Gen. Tunde Idiagbon) from present Kwara State.

27 Tyoden, 'Military and society in Nigeria', p. 7.

28 The story is told of a Middle Belt officer close to Gowon who, because his village now came within two days' driving distance of a new state capital, spent a whole night tracing the new states' boundaries on an old map! Major-General J. Garba, '*Revolution*' *in Nigeria: Another View* (London: Africa Books Ltd., 1982), p. 92.

29 J. I. Elaigwu, *Gowon* (Ibadan: West Books, 1986), pp. 224–35.

30 Alhaji Ibrahim Damcida, interview, London, 5 January 1986. He was for many years Federal Permanent Secretary for Defence during Gowon's regime.

31 Major-General Garba, '*Revolution*' *in Nigeria*, pp. 77–9; Obasanjo, *My Command*, pp. 14, 57–8; *Africa Confidential*, 12, 16 (August 1971), p. 3; and A. Bolaji Akinyemi, 'Mohammed/Obasanjo foreign policy', in O. Oyediran (ed.), *Nigerian Government and Politics under Military Rule, 1966–79* (London: Macmillan, 1979), pp. 153–4.

32 Federal Republic of Nigeria, *Federal Military Government's Views on the Report of the Federal Assets Investigation Panel 1975* (Lagos, 1976).

33 Federal Republic of Nigeria, *Government Views on Second Report of the Federal Assets Investigation Panel* (Lagos, 1978), p. 3.

34 Oluleye, *Military Leadership*, p. 162.

35 See, for instance, the comments of Mr I. K. Ebong, then Federal Permanent Secretary, Economic Development and Reconstruction, who advised that defence spending be kept to the essentials 'if the nation's ability to deliver the goods in other important spheres is not to be impaired', *Daily Times* (Lagos), 17 July 1971. Ever since the war ended, the media has been replete with stories of officers being accused of, and arrested, court-martialed, or dismissed for, corruption. For a representative sample see *West Africa*, 26 December 1970, p. 1503; 2 January 1971, p. 21; 23 January 1971, p. 117; 14 May 1971, p. 553; 20 August 1971, p. 973; 12 February 1973, p. 218; 2 September 1974, p. 1088, 11 November 1974, p. 1390; 8 December 1975, p. 1502; and 1 November 1976, p. 1648.

36 Oluleye, *Military Leadership*, p. 160.

37 *Ibid.*, p. 161; and Elaigwu, *Gowan*, pp. 224 and 238.

38 T. Turner, 'Multinational corporations and the instability of the Nigerian state', *ROAPE*, 5 (January–April 1976), pp. 63–79. Cf. Droucopoulos and Henley, 'The pursuit of profit', pp. 60–3.

39 For recent accounts see B. Dudley, *An Introduction to Nigerian Government and Politics* (Macmillan Nigeria, 1982), pp. 97–100, 317n.; A. D. Yahaya, 'Nigerian public administration under military rule: the experience of the Northern states', in L. Adamolekun (ed.), *Nigerian Public Administration 1960–80* (London: Heinemann, forthcoming); Shehu Othman, 'Classes, crises and coup: the demise of Shagari's regime', *African Affairs*, 83, 333 (October 1984), pp. 441–61; and Herbert Ekwe-Ekwe, 'The Nigerian plight: Shagari to Buhari', *Third World Quarterly*, 7, 3 (July 1985), pp. 610–25.

40 Kaduna, originally a Gwari territory, was the capital of the defunct Northern region, established by Lord Lugard, and was thus a colonial town, belonging not to any ethnic

group but to the state itself. Hence it remains the focus for activities of those dependent on state patronage and on discrimination in favour of the North and lacking a powerful local political base.

41 Rufa'i Ibrahim, 'Of the Mafia, AWO and the race', *The Triumph* (Kano), 3 August 1983.

42 Also known as the Committee of Friends (COF), it was under the aegis of the late Chief Obafemi Awolowo who, together with his Yoruba devotees, have controlled an array of banks, firms, and businesses since the days of the Action Group. At the core of these businesses is the Odu'a Investment Company Limited which, like the New Nigerian Development Company in the Nigerian north, is mainly owned by the states in the defunct Western region. Its assets comfortably exceed N1 billion, with controlling interests of between 51–100 per cent in twenty-four subsidiaries; 8–49 per cent stakes in thirty-four associated companies; a few thousand shares to 7 per cent equity shareholding in such large firms and multinationals as the Niger Mills, Associated Electronics Products, Vitafoam, Nigerian Sugar Co., Boots Company, Food Specialities, UAC Nigeria, SCOA, John Holt Investments, Metal Box, United Bank for Africa, First Bank, and R. T. Briscoe; and it employs over 10,000 Nigerians. See *Sunday Times* (Lagos), 24 May 1987, p. 15. COF's political influence is captured by O. Oyediran (ed.), *The Nigerian 1979 Elections* (Macmillan Nigeria, 1981), p. 46.

43 An analysis of the ties of school, career experiences, and socio-political outlook of this 'generation of Nigerian nationalists, as well as northern nationalists' is in John N. Paden, *Ahmadu Bello* (London: Hodder & Stoughton, 1986), pp. 216–51, especially p. 245.

44 Obasanjo, *My Command*, p. 9.

45 See John Oyinbo, *Nigeria: Crisis and Beyond* (London: Charles Knight, 1971), *passim*, for a dispassionate account written under a pseudonym (Oyinbo meaning white person in Yoruba and Nigerian pidgin English) and certainly with the benefit of privileged information by an ex-British colonial officer who worked closely with Sir Ahmadu Bello and several northern bureaucrats for many years.

46 Confidential interviews.

47 Obasanjo, *My Command*, p. 15.

48 Interview, General Yakubu Gowon, London, 24 June 1985.

49 'The role of civil servants in a military regime', *Daily Times*, 11, 13 December 1973.

50 See, for instance, Ayida, 'The Nigerian Revolution, 1966–76'.

51 Dudley, *Nigerian Government and Politics*, pp. 97–8.

52 Brig. Mohammed's first broadcast to the nation on 29 July 1975. Text in G. Arnold, *Modern Nigeria* (London: Longman, 1977), pp. 173–6, and 1975 Independence Anniversary Broadcast, in O. Oyediran (ed.), *Survey of Nigerian Affairs 1975* (Ibadan: Oxford University Press for NIIA, 1978), pp. 220–23; Williams, *State and Society*, p. 99; and Nolutshungu, 'Variations', pp. 4–5.

53 Obasanjo, despite his wartime role, was a remarkable exception. General Obasanjo, interview, Ota, Nigeria, 10 October 1984.

54 Only some seven SMC and some four NCS members were probably unaffected by most of these varied influences.

55 M. Tukur and T. Olagunju (eds.), *Nigeria in Search of a Viable Polity* (Kaduna: Baraka Press, 1972).

56 Major-General Yar'adua, interview, London, 24 March 1985. Also see *West Africa*, 1 December 1975, p. 1462.

57 Kirk-Greene and Rimmer, *Nigeria Since 1970*, p. 12.

58 Yahaya, 'Nigerian public administration'.

59 Texts reproduced in Obasanjo, *A March of Progress: Collected Speeches* (Lagos: FMOI, n.d.), pp. 103–6, 185–90.

60 Oluleye, *Military Leadership in Nigeria*, p. 171.

61 Ayida, interview, London, 11 April 1985.
62 Particularly informative analyses of the Mohammed-Obasanjo period are to be found in I. Campbell, 'Army reorganisation and military withdrawal', in Panter-Brick (ed.), *Soldiers and Oil*, pp. 58–100; and M. J. Dent, 'Corrective government: military rule in perspective', in *ibid.* pp. 101–37.
63 Confidential interview, SMC Member, London. Also see Oluleye, *Military Leadership*, pp. 176–7, 194–5.
64 Oluleye, *Military Leadership*, pp. 178–82.
65 Campbell, 'Army reorganisation', p. 87.
66 Address to the Federal Permanent Secretaries and Departmental Heads at Dodan Barracks, 21 November 1975. Text in O. Oyediran (ed.), *Survey of Nigerian Affairs*, p. 251.
67 See, for instance, Obasanjo's address to the Federal Permanent Secretaries on 5 April 1977 in his *A March of Progress*, pp. 134–7.
68 Cabinet Office, 'Indiscipline', Ref. No. 39947/VI/141, 20 October 1977, pp. 1–4.
69 Federal Republic of Nigeria, Report of the Cabinet Committee on Nigerian Airways, unpublished, Lagos, 6 April 1978, p. 8.
70 *Ibid.*, p. 2.
71 *Ibid.*, p. 4.
72 *Ibid.*, p. 5.
73 *Ibid.*, p. 13.
74 Cf. Nolutshungu, 'Variations'.
75 Rufai Ibrahim, 'Letter To Balarabe Musa', *The Guardian* (Lagos), 18 November 1984.
76 *The Observer* (London), 12 February 1984, p. 1; and Major-Gen. Domkat Bali, Nigerian Defence Minister, *The Observer*, 20 May 1984, p. 3.
77 The sixteen generals comprised ten army, four airforce, and two naval officers. *New Nigerian* (Kaduna), 12 June 1987, pp. 1, 3.
78 A view oddly dismissed by Henry Bienen, *Political Conflict and Economic Change in Nigeria* (London: Frank Cass, 1985), pp. 53–4; and a theme which my own 'Classes, crises and coup' failed to address.
79 These were: the maintenance of strong defences; a proper balance in arms and men; constant high military preparedness; improved conditions of service, welfare, and benefits; greater capability and sophistication in local armament production; harmony between defence needs, foreign policy, and national development, and rationalization of defence expenditure with special emphasis on mobility and self-reliance. *Presidential Committee Report*, Appendix 1, p. xxxviii; and *Objectives, Policies and Programmes of the FMG*, p. 41.
80 Confidential briefing on defence to a selected audience in Jos, Nigeria, 22 February 1980. A related military ambition similarly found expression in Nigeria's nuclear dream, a theme explored by Folajinmi O. Adisa, 'The nuclear rationale in Nigeria', Centre D'Etude D'Afrique Noire, Université de Bordeaux, 1983, No. 3.
81 T. Forrest, 'The political economy of civil rule and the economic crisis in Nigeria (1979–84)', *ROAPE*, 35 (May 1986), pp. 4–26; Y. Bangura, 'The Nigerian economic crisis: contending explanations, official policies, and alternative solutions', Paper presented at the ROAPE Conference, Keele, England, 29–30 September 1984; Ekwe-Ekwe, 'The Nigerian plight'; and Othman, 'Classes, crises and coup'.
82 Cited in C. Legum (ed.), *Africa Contemporary Record 1981–82* (London, 1982), p. B521.
83 *The Guardian* (London), 11 January 1984.
84 Interview with *The Guardian* (Lagos), 25 March 1984, pp. 9–10.
85 Prior to the elections, Major-General Buhari, then GOC Third Armoured Division in Jos, suggested publicly that the army be given some security responsibilities in the course of the election in order to ensure a fair contest. He was ignored. *The Guardian* (London), 11 January 1984. For a formidable intervention on the Nigerian plight, see Lieutenant-General

T. Y. Danjuma, 'Corruption had existed, and flourished even during the 13 Years of corrective military rule', *The Guardian* (Lagos), 20 July 1986, pp. 8–10.

86 Ekwe-Ekwe, 'The Nigerian plight', Forrest, 'Civil rule and the economic crisis in Nigeria (1979–84)', and F. Iyayi, 'The primitive accumulation of capital in a neo-colony', *ROAPE*, 35 (May 1986), pp. 27–39.

87 An analysis of the manoeuvrings by the Kaduna Mafia prior to the 1983 elections is in Othman, 'Classes, crises and coup'.

88 For lists of the regime's three highest policy-making organs, see 'Nigeria after the coup', Special Survey, *Financial Times* (London), 23 January 1984, pp. 2, 5. Omitted from the SMC list is Mr G. Longe, then Secretary to the Federal Government.

89 *Objectives, Policies and Programmes of the FMG*, pp. 10–14, and *Presidential Committee Report, passim*.

90 Text of his maiden speech is reproduced in *National Concord* (Lagos), 2 January 1984, p. 9.

91 On the essentials of the crusade, see Brigadier Idiagbon's launching speech in *To Rescue the Nation* (Lagos, Federal Ministry of Information, n.d.), pp. 32–4; and *Daily Times* (Lagos), 21 March, and 10 April 1984.

92 Promulgated on 29 March 1984, the Public Officers (Protection Against False Accusation) Decrees 1984, pp. A53–68, provided for no appeal on conviction. Two journalists were jailed for one year each, while their paper was fined N50,000 for publishing investigative reports whose only error was that a military officer earmarked for a diplomatic post had been subsequently replaced by someone else.

93 *The Guardian* (London), 17 April 1984, p. 7.

94 Not surprisingly, pan-western revivalist meetings by western military governors, which all ceased after the dissolution of ICSA and ESIALA, also became perfectly respectable. Issues perceived as indications of northern concerns riding roughshod over southern interests and sensitivities are discussed in A. A. Akinola, *The Search for A Nigerian Political System* (London: Afroworld, 1986), pp. 19–22.

95 *Concord Weekly* (London), 8 August 1985, p. 30.

96 General O. Obasanjo, 'Nigeria: which way forward?', *Daily Times* (Lagos), 7 and 8 August 1985.

97 President Babangida, interview, *Newswatch* (Lagos), 9 December 1985, p. 17. 'Again, more rumblings', *Talking Drums* (London), 15 July 1985, p. 17, provides a perceptive and prophetic analysis of the crisis in, and collapse of, Buhari's SMC. Also see 'Imperfections in high places', *Talking Drums*, 3 June 1985, pp. 6–7, and 'Inside the Buhari SMC', 30 September 1985, pp. 8, 14.

98 After assuming power, Babangida alleged that his own telephone had been bugged, and he had 'retrieved most of the tapes'. *Newswatch* (Lagos), 9 December 1985, p. 17. He also exposed some of NSO's excesses, and appointed his aggrieved *protégé* to head a restored and more influential intelligence and security apparatus.

99 Major-General S. Abacha, Special Broadcast on the 27 August 1985 coup, BBC Monitor Transcript, ME/8042/B/9, London, 29 August 1985. Following findings by a special committee, Babangida's government later endorsed counter-trade as a short-term policy for economic revival, but said some persons associated with the roughly N2 billion deals signed with Austria, Brazil, France and Italy (halted for lack of agreement over oil shipments) would need to clarify their actions, and that all the deals were to be renegotiated to ensure that the 'interests of the nation are adequately protected'. *West Africa*, 16 December 1985, p. 2651.

100 *Africa Confidential* (London), 26 (13 March 1985), p. 7.

101 President Ibrahim Babangida, 'New Nigerian President's address to the nation', 27 August 1985, BBC Monitor Transcript, ME/8042/B/9-12, London, 29 August 1985.

102 Dr Junaid S. Muhammad, 'Unpopular essay: one man's observation of the goings on so far', Kano, n.d., pp. 1–18. The author's attempts to publish the text in the Press as an assessment of Babangida's fiftieth day in the office failed. The *New Nigerian* which published the first part inexplicably ceased further serialisation, but the whole article was widely circulated among members of the military and political elite.

103 R. Joseph, 'Ibrahim Babangida and the "unfinished state" of Nigeria', Paper presented at the Conference on West African States Since 1976, London, 25–27 June 1987, pp. 8–9.

104 *Daily Times*, 28 December 1985, pp. 1, 9; 'The coup plot verdicts', *West Africa*, 3 March 1986, pp. 444–6; and 'The final hour', *Newswatch*, 17 March 1986, pp. 13–17.

105 *The Guardian* (Lagos), 21 December 1985, p. 1.

106 A view also shared by Lieutenant-General T. Y. Danjuma, to whom the late Lieutenant-Colonel Iyorshe was an *aide-de-camp*. Personal conversation, Cambridge, England, 10 April 1987.

107 Address to officers of the First Mechanised Division, Kaduna. *West Africa*, 28 October 1985, p. 2282.

108 'Towards military disengagement from politics', address to graduands at the Command Staff College, Jaji, Kaduna. *New Nigerian* (Kaduna), 7 July 1987, pp. 2, 7.

109 'Two years of Babangida', *West Africa*, 24 August 1987, p. 1615, and Bola Olowd, 'The final shuffle', *West Africa*, 8 August 1988, p. 1433.

110 'Soyinka on proscription', *West Africa*, 1 August 1985, p. 1409.

111 Danjuma, 'Corruption had existed', p. 10.

112 *The Guardian* (Lagos), 21 December 1985, p. 2.

113 Luckham, *The Nigerian Military*, p. 279.

114 See I. D. Ayu, 'To adjust or to smash imperialism in Africa: militarism and the crisis', Paper presented to the International Conference on the Economic Crisis in Africa, Zaria, Nigeria, 11–17 March 1985; S. G. Tyoden, 'The military and the prospect for socialist construction in the Third World', Paper presented to the Seminar on Nigerian Economy and Society since the Berlin Conference, Zaria, 11–15 November 1985; T. Falola and J. Ihonvbere, *The Rise and Fall of Nigeria's Second Republic 1979–83* (London: Zed, 1985); D. Fatogun, 'The army in politics', *New Horizon* (Lagos), 6, 1–2 (1986); and E. Madunagu, 'The army as a political party', *The Guardian* (Lagos), 9, 16 January 1986. For an incisive critique see B. Beckman, 'The military as revolutionary vanguard: a critique', *ROAPE*, 37 (December 1986), pp. 50–62.

115 Nolutshungu, 'Variations', p. 7. But there is no good reason to share his view that such ideological opposition to the status quo will necessarily take a socialist form.

116 Beckman, 'The military as revolutionary vanguard', p. 5.

9 Senegal

1 D. B. Cruise O'Brien, 'Senegal', in J. Dunn (ed.), *West African States: Failure and Promise* (Cambridge: Cambridge University Press, 1978), p. 187.

2 *Ibid.*

3 See M. Weiss, E. Stetter, K. Voll (eds.), *Senegal: Mehrparteien System und Wahlen 1983. Dokumentation zur politischen Entwicklung* (Hamburg: Institute fur Afrika-kunde, 1983), pp. 115–16; *Le Soleil* (Dakar), 10 January 1983.

4 Cited in R. Fatton, *The Making of a Liberal Democracy. Senegal's Passive Revolution 1975–1985* (Boulder and London: Lynne Rienner, 1987), p. 77.

5 D. B. Cruise O'Brien, 'Les Elections sénégalaises du 27 février 1983', *Politique africaine* 11, September 1983.

6 Cited in Fatton, *Liberal Democracy*, p. 126.

7 Results in *West Africa*, 14 March 1988, p. 448.

8 Cruise O'Brien, 'Les Elections'.
9 *African International*, 'Les Dossiers de la rentrée', no. 87 (October 1986).
10 See F. Zuccarelli, *Un parti politique africain: L'union progressiste sénégalaise* (Paris: Librairie Générale de Droit et de Jurisprudence, 1970); also D. B. Cruise O'Brien, 'Clans, clienteles and communities', in *Saints and Politicians* (Cambridge: Cambridge University Press, 1975).
11 Fatton, *Liberal Democracy*, p. 116.
12 *Ibid.*
13 G. Greene, *Journey without Maps* (London: W. Heinemann and the Bodley Head, 1978; first published 1936), pp. 116, 283.
14 Fred Hayward, in conversation, London, June 1987.
15 Fatton, *Liberal Democracy*, p. 170.
16 Cf. notably: D. Cruise O'Brien, *Saints and Politicians. Essays in the Organization of a Senegalese Peasant Society* (Cambridge: Cambridge University Press, 1975); C. Coulon, 'Elections, factions et idéologies au Sénégal', in CERI/CEAN, *Aux Urnes l'Afrique* (Paris: Pedone, 1978), pp. 149–86; E. J. Schumacher, *Politics, Bureaucracy and Rural Development in Senegal* (Berkeley, Los Angeles, London: University of California Press, 1975); Zuccarelli, *Un parti politique africain*.
17 N. Caswell, 'Autopsie de l'ONCAD: la politique arachidière du Sénégal, 1966–1980', *Politique africaine*, 14 (1984), pp. 39–73.
18 J. S. Barker, 'The paradox of development: reflexions on a study of local–central relations in Senegal', in M. F. Lofchie (ed.), *The State of the Nations: Constraints of Development in Independent Africa* (Los Angeles: University of California Press, 1971).
19 On this evolution, one can refer to J. Copans, *Les Marabouts de l'arachide* (Paris: Le Sycomore, 1980), pp. 246ff.; and C. Coulon, *Le Marabout et le prince: Islam et pouvoir au Sénégal* (Paris: Pedone, 1981), pp. 289–95.
20 E. Le Roy, 'La Loi sur le domaine national a vingt ans: joyeux anniversaire', *Mondes en Développement*, 52 (1985), p. 676.
21 See C. Coulon, 'La Shar'ia dans tous ses états; droit étatique versus droit islamique (Kenya, Senegal)' (London, SOAS, 17/18 December 1987), to be published in C. Coulon and D. B. Cruise O'Brien (eds.), *L'Etat et les communautés Musulmanes en Afrique Noire* (Paris: Karthala, forthcoming).
22 See R. Collignon, 'La Lutte des pouvoirs publics contre les "encombrements humains" à Dakar', *Revue Canadienne des Etudes Africaines*, 18, 3 (1984), pp. 573–82.
23 Copans, *Les Marabouts*, p. 249.
24 On the initiatives in face of the action of SAED, see the recent article by C. Reboul, 'Les Associations de village de la vallée du fleuve Sénégal', *Revue Tiers Monde*, 27: 110 (1977), pp. 435–48; and especially the books of A. Adams, *Le Long voyage des gens du Fleuve* (Paris: Maspero, 1977) and *La Terre et les gens du Fleuve* (Paris: L'Harmattan, 1985).
25 J.-M. Gastellu, 'Le Paysan, l'état et les sécheresses, Ngohé Sénégal, 1972–1982', roneo, 1984. The remarks of J. M. Gastellu on the village of Ngohé, which he revisited in 1982 after a ten-year absence, are very significant here. He emphasises that the new legislation mentioned above, coupled with the effects of drought and the mechanisation of agriculture, have brought about a stronger state presence in the village.
26 J. Barker, 'Stability and stagnation: the state in Senegal', *Revue canadienne des études africaines*, 11:1 (1971), p. 24.
27 See G. Blanchet, 'Les Dirigeants sénégalais de l'indépendance à 1975', *Cahiers d'études africaines*, 18, pp. 48–78.
28 See Caswell, 'Autopsie de l'ONCAD', p. 171.
29 S. Gellar, *Senegal: An African Nation Between Islam and the West* (Boulder: Westview Press, 1986), p. 119.
30 See M. Fall, *Sénégal: l'état Abdou Diouf ou le temps des incertitudes* (Paris: L'Harmattan, 1986).

31 See in *Africa Confidential*, 28:1 (1987), the article entitled: 'Barons and modernists'.
32 World Bank, *World Development Report, 1986* (New York: Oxford University Press, 1986).
33 See J.-M. Bellot, 'Crise rurale au Sénégal', *Le Mois en Afrique*, 233–4 (1985), pp. 42–51.
34 See *Le Soleil*, 11 March 1985 and the article by M. Fall, 'Sénégal: cachuètes connection', *Politique africaine*, 19 (1985), pp. 85–6.
35 During the 1 May parade in Dakar (1986) numerous signs and slogans hostile to the *nouvelle politique industrielle* and the *nouvelle politique agricole* made their appearance, despite the relatively moderate but firm speech of the Secretary-General of the CNTS (see *Le Soleil*, 2 May 1986).
36 One should note however that in the Diourbel region, the Mouride region *par excellence*, the PDS obtained a percentage of votes superior to its national average; cf. D. B. Cruise O'Brien, 'Les Élections sénégalaises du 27 février 1983', *Politique africaine*, 11 (1983), pp. 11–12.
37 On the Islamic renewal, see M. Magassouba, *L'Islam au Sénégal. Demain les mollahs* (Paris: Karthala, 1985), chapters 9, 10, 11 and 12 in particular; C. Coulon, 'Sénégal', in Centre des hautes études d'Afrique et d'Asie modernes, *Contestations en pays islamiques* (Paris: CHEAM, 1984), pp. 63–88, and the same author 'L'Etat et l'Islam au Sénégal: divorce ou nouveau rapport de force', in *Année africaine 1984* (Paris: Pedone, 1986), pp. 47–59; Fall, *Sénégal, l'état Abdou Diouf*, chapter 2.
38 See C. Roche, *Histoire de la Casamance: conquête et résistance: 1850–1920* (Paris: Karthala, 1985; 1st edn, Dakar, Nouvelles éditions africaines, 1976).
39 Cf. *Africa Confidential*, 28, 3 (1987).
40 D. Darbon, 'Le Culturalisme bas-casamancais', *Politique africaine*, 14 (1984), pp. 125–8, and especially his work *L'Administration et le paysan en Casamance, Essai d'anthropologie administrative* (Paris: Pedone, 1988).
41 See M. P. Van Dijk, *Sénégal: le scrutin uniformel à Dakar* (Paris: L'Harmattan, 1986).
42 See M. Odeye, *Les Associations en villes africaines: Dakar-Brazzaville* (Paris: L'Harmattan, 1985).
43 The implantation of the Mourides in Dakar has been studied by M. C. Diop in 'La Confrérie mouride: organisation politique et mode d'implantation urbaine', Thèse de IIIe cycle, Université de Lyon II, 1980.
44 B. Badie, *Les Deux états: pouvoir et société en Occident et en terre d'Islam* (Paris: Fayard, 1986).
45 To repeat the expression of J.-F. Bayart in 'Civil society in Africa', in P. Chabal (ed.), *Political Domination in Africa* (Cambridge: Cambridge University Press, 1986).
46 Economist Intelligence Unit, *Country Report, Senegal, the Gambia, Guinea Bissau, Cape Verde*, 1 (1987), p. 9.

10 Sierra Leone: state consolidation, fragmentation and decay

1 Research for this study was made possible by a Fulbright grant and generous research support from the Graduate School Research Committee of the University of Wisconsin-Madison. I want to acknowledge the generosity and kindness of scholars and officials in Sierra Leone, to thank Murray Edelman, Crawford Young, Richard Rathbone, Jimmy Kandeh, and Richard Stryker for their comments and suggestions on an earlier draft of this chapter, and to express my appreciation for the outstanding contributions of my research assistants Erica Julseth and Joshua Forrest.
2 See, for example, Major-General J. S. Momoh (1986), *The Making of a President: The New Order*, and his 'What is constructive nationalism' (State House, *mimeo*, 23 May 1986).
3 In order to facilitate analysis of the state, I have employed Crawford Young's useful typology of major imperatives of the state. These include: hegemony over the territory of the

nation; security to preserve the state; autonomy both externally (sovereignty) and internally (national interests as distinct from those of any part); legitimacy to facilitate non-coercive exercise of its authority; and the revenue essential to its operation as an effective functioning institution. See C. Young and T. Turner, *The Rise and Decline of the Zairian State* (Madison: University of Wisconsin Press, 1985).

4 Chabal (1986), building on Sklar (1983), provides an excellent discussion of the relationship between democracy and accountability, during his discussion of democracy which he defines as 'a political system in which mechanisms and institutions exist to promote and enforce the accountability of rulers to those over whom they rule'. P. Chabal, *Political Domination in Africa* (Cambridge: Cambridge University Press, 1986), p. 5. See also R. Sklar, 'Democracy in Africa', *African Studies Review*, 26, 3/4 (September–December 1983), pp. 11–24.

5 The Sierra Leone civil service had a long history of being free of extensive patronage. After a series of disputes over 'political' appointments with A. J. Momoh who headed the civil service, Albert Margai removed Momoh and asserted political control, ensuring opportunities for patronage.

6 Stevens often talked about the wisdom of the common people. He was fond of noting that his father did not know how to read but 'he had sense' and adding that many people who could read did not have sense. In his rhetoric, at least, he expressed a strong desire to include the people more actively in the political process. In an interview with the author in 1975 he noted: 'We are trying to get the illiterates into the process. If we leave government up to the five or ten per cent literate, they will mess it up... We need a lot of activity on the level of the illiterates.'

7 On chiefs in politics, see J. Cartwright, *Politics in Sierra Leone: 1947–67* (Toronto: Toronto Press, 1970); W. Barrows, *Grassroots Politics in an African State: Integration and Development in Sierra Leone* (New York: Africana Publishing Corp., 1976); R. Tangri, 'Conflict and violence in contemporary Sierra Leone chiefdoms', *Journal of Modern African Studies*, 14, 2 (June 1976), pp. 311–21; C. Allen, 'Sierra Leone', in J. Dunn (ed.), West African States. Failure and Promise (Cambridge: Cambridge University Press, 1978).

8 Interview with President Siaka Stevens, by the author, August 1970.

9 For an excellent discussion of the APC's actions against chiefs who had been particularly zealous in support of the SLPP and of APC efforts to assert control over chiefs, see Tangri, 'Conflict and violence in contemporary Sierra Leone chiefdoms', *Journal of Modern African Studies*, 14, 2 (June 1976), pp. 311–21.

10 J.-F. Bayart, 'La Société politique camerounaise (1982–1986)', *Politique Africaine*, 22 (June 1986), pp. 5–35.

11 Interview with the author, August 1970.

12 For example, he had helped young men set up a business in Kambia; assisted a farmer near Boa; provided rice for a woman and her children in Freetown; and given aid to a Limba woman, down on her luck, who had once donated money to pay the rent for the APC headquarters when it was a struggling opposition party. Stevens was prepared to help many of those who came to seek his assistance and kept a stockpile of rice in State House for this purpose. Interviews with Siaka Stevens, by the author.

13 Bayart notes that civil society is not a 'discrete entity' but plural in nature including those in institutions like parties and trade unions who represent civil society as well as subject populations. J.-F. Bayart, 'Civil society in Africa', in Chabal, *Political Domination in Africa*, pp. 111–12.

14 In an interview with the author in August 1970, Siaka Stevens noted that one of his primary difficulties had been to regain control of the military after the enlisted men's coup. Control had been complicated by the fact that the enlisted men had imprisoned all but three of the officers in the army and police. He noted that restoration of control over the military and

police had taken time away from what should have been a major focus on economic and political policies.

15 For example, there were reports of attempted coups in October 1970, March 1971, and July 1974. See T. S. Cox, *Civil-Military Relations in Sierra Leone* (Cambridge, Mass.: Harvard University Press, 1976).

16 Interview of Ibrahim Taqi, by the author, August 1970.

17 Interview with Governor-General Banja Tejan-Sie by the author in August 1970. He noted that the NDP had the support of a large number of university students who were leaving the APC, Temnes who were disillusioned with the APC, and Mendes who were tired of both the conflicts within the SLPP and the failures of the APC. The ministers were Mohammed Forna (Finance) and Mohammed Bash-Taqui (Development), plus Taqi and John Karefa-Smart.

18 For an excellent discussion of this process in both the colonial and post-colonial era see Jimmy Kandeh, 'Domination of state, class and political ethnicity: a comparative study of state-society relations in colonial and post-colonial Sierra Leone (1896–1986)', Ph.D. thesis, University of Wisconsin, 1987.

19 Jackson and Rosberg provide an excellent discussion of personal rule. See R. H. Jackson and C. Rosberg, *Personal Rule in Black Africa* (Berkeley: University of California Press, 1982).

20 C. Young, 'The colonial state and its connection to current political crises in Africa', unpublished paper presented at the Woodrow Wilson International Center for Scholars, Washington DC, 19 May 1984, p. 60.

21 Among the worst of the ethnic conflicts was that in Koinadugu between Fula and Yalunka communities mobilised for the 1982 election, and factional violence in Pujehun. Both cases involved national elite intervention which was the major factor creating levels of violence previously unknown in Sierra Leone, including loss of life, property, and dislocation of the population.

22 In this case APC leaders made concerted efforts to remove the incumbent chief and replace him with a candidate close to high government officials. The efforts so incensed people in the chiefdom that even detractors of the chief joined the chorus of protest. Finally, a group of local notables and important political figures met with President Stevens to 'beg' that this state intrusion be ended. Stevens ordered the effort stopped. Yet even in this victory for traditional processes, the power of the ruler was clear. There were many other cases in which popular resistance to state intervention in chieftaincy affairs was effective, including the unsuccessful effort to unseat Paramount Chief Kapuwa Matoe III in Kenema District in 1984–5.

23 Barrows, *Grassroots Politics*, provides an excellent chronicle of the futile efforts of prime minister Albert Margai to undermine Salia Jusu-Sheriff by taking sides in a chieftaincy dispute in the Kenema South Constituency in 1967.

24 There were instances of manipulation, but in general, where complaints were made and substantiated, violators were disqualified. There were efforts by some SLPP officials to affect the outcome of the 1967 elections, but these were generally thwarted or countered by the opposition parties and were not, in any case, decisive.

25 There were widespread reports of irregularities during the referendum although support for the one-party state was extensive in some areas of the country.

26 For more detailed discussion see F. Hayward and A. R. Dumbuya, 'Changing electoral patterns in Sierra Leone: the 1982 single-party elections', *African Studies Review*, 28, 4 (1985), pp. 62–86; also F. Hayward and J. D. Kandeh, 'Perspectives on twenty-five years of elections in Sierra Leone', in Hayward (ed.), *Elections in Independent Africa*.

27 It should also be noted that many of the problems in 1986 were due to the failures of an incompetent and often corrupt electoral commission which was neither prepared for nor accustomed to the idea of free and open electoral competition.

28 The turnout fell from 65 per cent in 1982 to 59 per cent in 1986. The registration totals were about the same as those in 1982, since a new register of voters had not been compiled and the opportunity for voters to make changes in the register, by adding their name or changing their place of residence, had been brief and poorly publicised.

29 Interviews with President Momoh by the author, Freetown, May–June 1986.

30 See, for example, the piece 'MPs debate regime's "wrong fiscal policies"', *West Africa*, 30 March 1987, p. 633.

31 Unless otherwise noted, economic data are compiled from material supplied by the World Bank, the Bank of Sierra Leone, and the IMF Yearbook, *International Financial Statistics*. For a useful economic analysis, see also C. Allen, 'Sierra Leone', in J. Dunn, *West African States: Failure and Promise* (Cambridge: Cambridge University Press, 1978).

32 According to the *Annual Report* of the National Diamond Mining Company for the 1980/1 year.

33 While it is difficult to know exactly how much was spent on preparations to host the OAU, development expenditure (which in 1979–80 was almost exclusively related to the OAU meeting) jumped more than 300 per cent from an average of about Le 32 million a year to Le 100 million in 1979–80. Most of this expenditure involved foreign borrowing. (Ministry of Development and Economic Planning, Freetown, Sierra Leone.)

34 Rural tax revenue exceeded government expenditure on agriculture, in spite of chronic shortages of rice and other food products which could be grown in the fertile conditions prevailing in Sierra Leone, as well as the shortage of foreign exchange which could have been used for non-substitutable needs.

35 Bayart in 'Civil society in Africa' makes this point for Africa as a whole and suggests that in Sierra Leone under Stevens the structures of accumulation absorbed the state. In Chabal (ed.), *Political Domination in Africa*, p. 115.

36 Interview with Siaka Stevens, August 1981.

37 Both were major corruption scandals during the Stevens government. While a great deal of publicity was given to these diversions of public funds, such actions seemed to be endemic during the 1970s and 1980s. Major new scandals were uncovered in August 1987 indicating that the pattern continued. In contrast to earlier cases, however, efforts were being made to get restitution of the funds. On 17 August, however, President Momoh ordered the former minister of agriculture to repay Le 6.4 million to the treasury within fourteen days. See *West Africa*, 31 August 1987, p. 1683.

38 J. Lonsdale, 'States and social processes in Africa; a historiographical survey', *African Studies Review*, 24, 2/3 (June–September 1981). See also Chabal (ed.), *Political Domination in Africa*, p. 129.

39 One could see the effectiveness of this approach in public acclaim for Stevens wherever he travelled during this period, whether it was on the way to his office in Freetown, or to meet the people in upcountry villages and towns. People flocked to see him, his speeches captured their hearts and their enthusiasm, and his personal touch did much to create a sense of national identity.

40 SLPP attacks on the opposition press and free speech in general gained support for the APC from among the professionals, intellectuals, students, and urban masses. Because of the growing pattern of intimidation, there developed a very effective protective network of mass support demonstrated in 1965 when the SLPP was planning to arrest Stevens for criticism of SLPP corruption. When word got out that this was about to take place, taxi drivers spread the word throughout Freetown and in minutes his house was surrounded by thousands of citizens who were committed to preventing the police from making an arrest.

41 As shown in his rebuff of Stevens' complaints about the way in which the Code of Conduct was enforced during the 1986 election.

42 Former President Siaka Stevens complained, in an interview with the author in 1986, that he was no longer being consulted by President Momoh.
43 For one view of the interest of the state, see R. Miliband, 'State power and class interests', *New Left Review*, 38 (March–April 1983), pp. 57–68.
44 J.-F. Bayart, 'Civil society in Africa', in Chabal (ed.), *Political Domination in Africa*, p. 115.
45 See Cartwright, *Politics in Sierra Leone*, ch. 4.
46 See F. Hayward, ed., *Elections in Independent Africa* (Boulder: Westview Press, 1987), chs. 1–2.
47 For a fascinating account of this pattern of two-party competition in Ghana see Chazan, 'The anomalies of continuity: perspectives on Ghanaian elections since independence', in Hayward (ed.), *Elections*, ch. 3.
48 The Back-Benchers' Association became increasingly active after the 1973 election in which the SLPP felt forced to withdraw. A number of APC back-benchers, led by S. G. M. Fania, saw their role as one of 'watch dog' or 'shadow cabinet' within the party. In 1975, the Back-Benchers' Association became increasingly critical, especially of APC efforts to establish a one-party state. It was largely for those reasons that the party leadership denied Fania the party symbol to contest the general elections in 1977. Interviews with Fania by the author, June and July 1981.
49 See, for example, the discussion of the Back-Benchers' Association as a powerful force in politics and the 'unofficial opposition' in 'Momoh's musical chairs', *West Africa*, 13 April 1987, pp. 700–1.
50 During 1985 Stevens was sometimes 'booed' when he travelled. Even as he was stepping down from office, officials felt it wise to keep the public away from a ceremony to unveil a bust of Stevens in front of the new ministerial buildings lest there be protests and violence.
51 This effort was made somewhat more difficult by the fact that the APC officials had encouraged the electoral commission to remove many of their names from the electoral list because of their opposition to APC policies in the late 1970s and 1980s. Many insisted on voting even if their names had been purged.
52 In 1986, the Bank of Sierra Leone held up the processing of paperwork for the import of badly needed oil (in the middle of shortages which resulted in electricity blackouts and severely curtailed transportation throughout the country) because State House had worked through a new supplier not favoured by those in the Bank. It took the personal intervention of the president to get even grudging progress.
53 One of the major difficulties for President Momoh and his supporters is to bring corruption under control in the ruling elite, the bureaucracy, party, military and police. A whole series of recent revelations about corruption at all levels makes clear both how commonplace it has become and how very much money is being siphoned from the treasury, and ultimately, the people.

11 Conclusion

1 See especially Niccoló Machiavelli's *Prince* and *Discourses* and the classic gloss in J. G. A. Pocock, *The Machiavellian Moment* (Princeton: Princeton University Press, 1975).
2 Alasdair MacIntyre, *Against the Self-Images of the Age* (London: Duckworth, 1971), pp. 260–79.
3 For the importance of this point see, for example, John Dunn (ed.), *The Economic Limits to Modern Politics* (Cambridge: Cambridge University Press, 1989), along with Dunn, *The Politics of Socialism* (Cambridge: Cambridge University Press, 1984) and *Rethinking Modern Political Theory* (Cambridge: Cambridge University Press, 1985).
4 See Bayart, ch. 3 (in this volume).

5 For a local instance see John Dunn and A. F. Robertson, *Dependence and Opportunity: Political Change in Ahafo* (Cambridge: Cambridge University Press, 1973), esp. ch. 8 and Dunn, *Political Obligation in its Historical Context* (Cambridge: Cambridge University Press, 1980), pp. 112–56; and for a national instance see Naomi Chazan, 'The anomalies of continuity: perspectives on Ghanaian elections since independence', in Fred M. Hayward (ed.), *Elections in Independent Africa* (Boulder and London: Westview Press, 1987), pp. 61–86. For particularly sharp discontinuities see the chapter by Hayward above (ch. 10).

6 Samuel P. Huntington, *Political Order in Changing Societies* (New Haven: Yale University Press, 1965). See D. B. Cruise O'Brien, 'Modernization, order and the erosion of a democratic ideal', *Journal of Development Studies*, 8, 4 (1972), pp. 351–78.

7 See especially D. B. Cruise O'Brien, *Saints and Politicians* (Cambridge: Cambridge University Press, 1975). Compare the less sanguine assessment of Coulon above.

8 See Jeffries, *above*.

9 For a more encouraging intersection see Jeffries, *above*.

10 For the overwhelming significance of this point see Dunn (ed.), *Economic Limits*.

11 See, for example, Tony Killick's exemplary *Development Economics in Action: A Study of Economic Policies in Ghana* (London: Heinemann Educational Books, 1978), and the increasingly sophisticated interpretations of the development of the Kenyan and Tanzanian economies and of the role played by state policy and action in shaping these.

12 See Istvan Hont and Michael Ignatieff (eds.), *Wealth and Virtue: The Shaping of Political Economy in the Scottish Enlightenment* (Cambridge: Cambridge University Press, 1983), esp. ch. 1.

13 See especially Gavin Kitching, *Class and Economic Change in Kenya: The Making of an African Petite Bourgeoisie* (New Haven: Yale University Press, 1980).

14 See Dunn (ed.), *Economic Limits*.

15 See especially Jean-François Bayart, *L'Etat au Cameroun* (Paris: Presse de la Fondation Nationale des Sciences Politiques, 1979) and 'Civil society in Africa', in Patrick Chabal (ed.), *Political Domination in Africa* (Cambridge: Cambridge University Press, 1986), pp. 109–25, along with Bayart above (chapter 3 in this volume).

16 For Sen's defence of envisaging the standard of living in terms of human functionings and capabilities see Amartya Sen, *The Standard of Living: The Tanner Lectures, Clare Hall, Cambridge 1985* (Cambridge: Cambridge University Press, 1987).

17 Even here the performance is far from being despicable: see John Sender and Sheila Smith, *The Development of Capitalism in Africa* (London: Methuen, 1986); Kitching, *Class and Economic Change in Kenya* (Newhaven and London: Yale University Press, 1980); Bill Warren, *Imperialism: Pioneer of Capitalism* (London: Verso Books, 1980); John Iliffe, *The Emergence of African Capitalism* (London: Macmillan, 1983).

18 For a helpful account see Deborah Baumgold, *Hobbes's Political Theory* (Cambridge: Cambridge University Press, 1988).

19 Cf. Carl Schmitt, *The Concept of the Political*, trans. George Schwab (New Brunswick: Schmitt Rutgers, 1976).

20 See John Dunn, 'Trust and political agency', in Diego Gambetta (ed.), *Trust: Making and Breaking Cooperative Relations* (Oxford: Basil Blackwell, 1988), pp. 73–93.

21 See note 1 and Michael Oakeshott, *Rationalism in Politics* (London: Methuen, 1962), esp. pp. 1–36, 111–36; Alasdair MacIntyre, 'Ideology, social science and revolution', *Comparative Politics*, 5, 3 (1973), pp. 321–42.

22 See especially Kitching, *Class and Economic Change in Kenya*.

OTHER BOOKS IN THE SERIES

217

218

Index